OXFORD READINGS IN PHILOSOPHY

THEORIES OF RIGHTS

Also published in this series

The Concept of Evidence, edited by Peter Achinstein
The Philosophy of Law, edited by Ronald M. Dworkin
Moral Concepts, edited by Joel Feinberg
Theories of Ethics, edited by Philippa Foot
The Philosophy of History, edited by Patrick Gardiner
The Philosophy of Mind, edited by Jonathan Glover
Knowledge and Belief, edited by A. Phillips Griffiths
Scientific Revolutions, edited by Ian Hacking
Philosophy and Economic Theory, edited by Frank Hahn and Martin Hollis
Divine Commands and Morality, edited by Paul Helm
Reference and Modality, edited by Leonard Linsky
The Philosophy of Religion, edited by Basil Mitchell
Aesthetics, edited by Harold Osborne
The Theory of Meaning, edited by G. H. R. Parkinson
The Philosophy of Education, edited by R. S. Peters
Political Philosophy, edited by Anthony Quinton
Practical Reasoning, edited by Joseph Raz
The Philosophy of Social Explanation, edited by Alan Ryan
The Philosophy of Language, edited by J. R. Searle
Semantic Syntax, edited by Pieter A. M. Seuren
Causation and Conditionals, edited by Ernest Sosa
Philosophical Logic, edited by P. F. Strawson
The Justification of Induction, edited by Richard Swinburne
Locke on Human Understanding, edited by I. C. Tipton
Kant on Pure Reason, edited by Ralph C. S. Walker
The Philosophy of Perception, edited by G. J. Warnock
Free Will, edited by Gary Watson
The Philosophy of Action, edited by Alan R. White
Leibniz: Metaphysics and Philosophy of Science, edited by R. S. Woodhouse

Other volumes are in preparation

THEORIES OF RIGHTS

EDITED BY

JEREMY WALDRON

OXFORD UNIVERSITY PRESS
1984

Oxford University Press, Walton Street, Oxford OX2 6DP

London New York Toronto
Delhi Bombay Calcutta Madras Karachi
Kuala Lumpur Singapore Hong Kong Tokyo
Nairobi Dar es Salaam Cape Town
Melbourne Auckland

and associated companies in
Beirut Berlin Ibadan Mexico City Nicosia

Oxford is a trade mark of Oxford University Press

Published in the United States
by Oxford University Press, New York

British Library Cataloguing in Publication Data
Theories of rights.—(Oxford readings in philosophy)
1. Rights (Philosophy)
I. Waldron, Jeremy
323.4'01 B105.R5
ISBN 0-19-875063-3

Library of Congress Cataloging in Publication Data
Main entry under title:
Theories of rights.
(Oxford readings in philosophy)
Bibliography: p.
Includes index.
1. Civil rights—Addresses, essays, lectures.
I. Waldron, Jeremy. II. Series.
JC571.T44 1984 323.4 84-9648
ISBN 0-19-875063-3 (pbk.)

Typeset by Joshua Associates, Oxford
Printed in Hong Kong

CONTENTS

INTRODUCTION

I

THE IDEA that political morality and social choice are to be based wholly or partly on some account of the rights of the human individual is a familiar theme in Western politics. We find it explicitly in the liberal theories of John Locke and Thomas Paine, implicitly in the moral and political philosophy of Immanuel Kant, and at least problematically in the work of Jean-Jacques Rousseau and John Stuart Mill. At the level of practice, we see the idea not only in the rhetoric but in the constitutional innovations of the American and French Revolutions. If 'the end in view of every political association is the preservation of the natural and imprescriptable rights of man',[1] then governments must be set up and constitutions structured in such a way that it becomes impossible for individual rights to be pushed aside for the sake of the private interests of those in power or even in pursuit of other social goals and aspirations.

But this idea has never gone unchallenged. Even in the liberal tradition, some philosophers insisted that rights could be taken seriously only if they were understood to be based on a prior theory of social and political morality such as the theory of utilitarianism. The idea that the rights of man could be a *starting-point* for political morality (in the way that a theory of human nature was usually taken to be a starting-point) was regarded by Jeremy Bentham and other utilitarians as wild and pernicious nonsense.[2] Outside the liberal tradition, the critique was much more radical. Both conservative and socialist thinkers were appalled by what they took to be a celebration of the claims that the individual might make on his own behalf, asserting his own exclusive

[1] Declaration of the Rights of Man and the Citizen (French National Assembly, 27 August 1789), Article II.

[2] Jeremy Bentham, 'Anarchical Fallacies' (1824), in *The Works of Jeremy Bentham*, ed. John Bowring (Edinburgh, 1843), Vol, II, pp. 491 ff; also 'Supply Without Burthern', in *Jeremy Bentham's Economic Writings*, ed. W. Stark (London, 1952), Vol, I, pp. 332 ff.

interests against those of the communities that had nurtured him and against the wider human community of which he was inevitably a part and in which alone his true fulfilment was to be found. As Karl Marx put it in an important early discussion, 'none of the so-called rights of man goes beyond egoistic man, . . . an individual withdrawn behind his private interests and whims and separated from the community'.[3]

The same idea and the same controversies have dominated the political practice and the philosophy of the twentieth century too. But the modern discussion of rights has a couple of distinctive features.

First, there has been an attempt by philosophers and jurists to be much more precise in their use of the concept of a right. Their predecessors had known of course that *right* was related logically to *duty* and *obligation* and also to the concept of law-like rules and principles. But (with rare exceptions) there was no systematic attempt to draw out the details of these relationships. Rights-theorists, for their part, had good reason not to do so: such an analysis would reveal the compromises they were making and the issues they were fudging behind the stark absolutism of their declarations as they took over the difficulties and uncertainties of the traditional ideas of *ius* and *dominium* and turned them to the purposes of modern liberal ideology.[4] The radical critics had no interest in analysis of the idea either: they were more interested in exploring other political concepts such as *community* and *civic virtue* which the rights-theorists in their view had so rudely pushed aside. The outstanding exception was Bentham. He was determined to *show*, not merely to assert, that rights-talk could be made intelligible if and only if it was reduced systematically to the language of positive law and its utilitarian underpinnings. No doubt the analytical project in the twentieth century has been assisted by an atmosphere in philosophy congenial to analysis in general and preoccupied to the point of obsession with analytical rigour and precision. But in the philosophy of rights, the more direct inspiration has come from the work of Bentham and the utilitarian theorists of positive law who followed in his wake.[5]

The second distinctive feature of the modern debate has been a pre-

[3] Karl Marx, 'On the Jewish Question', in *Karl Marx: Selected Writings*, ed. David McLellan (Oxford, 1977), p. 54.

[4] For a helpful discussion, see Richard Tuck, *Natural Rights Theories: Their Origin and Development* (Cambridge, 1979).

[5] Besides Bentham, see John Austin, *Lectures on Jurisprudence* (4th edn.), ed. R. Campbell (London, 1873), Lectures XII ff.; *Salmond on Jurisprudence* (12th edn.), ed. P. Fitzgerald (London, 1966), pp. 217 ff.; Hans Kelsen, *Pure Theory of Law* (Berkeley, 1970), pp. 125 ff.

occupation with foundations. Rights have not been immune from emotivist or relativist doubts about moral truth and objectivity in general. Indeed, sometimes the doctrine of the natural rights of man has seemed peculiarly vulnerable to ethical scepticism. The idea of *natural* rights is seen as a particularly glaring example of the 'Naturalistic Fallacy', purporting to derive certain norms or evaluations from descriptive premisses about human nature. And the idea that there might be such things as *human* rights, valid for all peoples in all times and places, has often seemed implausible in the face of the wide variety of what we would call 'oppressive' and 'inhumane' practices that are taken for granted—even expected —in different parts of the world.[6]

But it would be wrong to suggest that the discussion of human rights has been seriously impeded by these difficulties. Many rights-theorists simply repudiate ethical scepticism and moral relativism.[7] Others persevere in the (quite plausible) belief that theories in meta-ethics do not by themselves entail any view about what can or should be said at the level of first-order moral judgement.[8] Even if it is true, for example, that moral judgements are nothing but expressions of attitudes, it does not follow that it is mistaken or fallacious to express the attitudes we have, nor does it follow that it is wrong to give vent to an attitude which is categorical and implicitly universal in the scope of its application. To say that a statement like 'All men have the right to equal liberty' is just an expression of emotion is not to make any recommendation about the desirability or otherwise of expressing emotions of this sort.[9] Nevertheless, awareness of these epistemological difficulties has made a difference to the way people have written and thought about rights. If meta-ethical realism is untenable, then rationally resolvable disputes in ethics become possible only between those who share certain fundamental values or principles in common. So it becomes important, in the area of rights as elsewhere, for philosophers to identify clearly the deep assumptions on which their theories depend. If, for example, two different theories of rights rest on a common commitment to the importance of individual liberty, there is in principle no

[6] These difficulties are discussed by Margaret MacDonald in 'Natural Rights' (reprinted here).

[7] See, e.g. Carl Friedrich, 'Rights, Liberties, Freedoms: A Reappraisal', *American Political Science Review*, 57 (1963), p. 844; H. J. McCloskey, 'Moral Rights and Animals', *Inquiry*, 22 (1979), pp. 43–4, 48–9.

[8] See, e.g., W. T. Blackstone, 'Equality and Human Rights', *The Monist*, 52 (1968), pp. 626–7.

[9] For a useful general discussion of this point, see Simon Blackburn, 'Rule-Following and Moral Realism', in *Wittgenstein: To Follow a Rule*, eds. S. Holtzman and C. Leich (London, 1981), pp. 174 ff.

reason why any detailed disagreements between them should not be rationally resolvable. But if the theories are based on different fundamental values—if, for example, one is based on liberty and the other on a commitment to equality—then, to the extent that there is incompatibility between these deep commitments, there may be no way of resolving their surface disagreements. The meta-ethical problem has thus driven modern proponents of individual rights to take a much greater interest in the deep values and principles that underlie the detail of the particular rights that they proclaim.

Those are the distinctive features of the modern debate. The papers reprinted in this volume represent the second feature more than the first. Almost all of them are concerned in different ways with the question of the fundamental assumptions and commitments that a plausible theory of rights might involve.[10] But the first issue—the analysis of rights-claims—is also important and it may be worth saying something about it here.

II

It is widely believed that talk about individual rights is most at home in the context of positive law, and that theories of natural, moral, or human rights which go beyond the rights secured by particular legal systems are at best parasitic on this. As Bentham put it, 'right is with me the child of law: . . . a natural right is a son that never had a father'.[11] I want to argue that this preoccupation with the connection between rights and positive law is a mistake.

Certainly, there is something reassuring about a law which creates a right explicitly. When a statute says that from the beginning of next year everyone shall have the right to some benefit, nobody can be in any doubt about the existence of the right. It is there written down in a form that everyone can appeal to.[12] But even within the framework of positive law other cases are less straightfoward. There is a rule in most legal systems making homicide an offence: does this confer on every person a legal right to life? In England, there is a legal duty to refrain from inflammatory racial abuse: does this mean that members of racial groups have a legal right not to be insulted? How we answer these questions will depend on what logical relations we recognize between the concepts of right, duty, offence, and rule. Exactly the

[10] See especially the papers by Vlastos, Hart, and Dworkin.

[11] Bentham, 'Supply Without Burthern', p. 334.

[12] For a disagreement about whether rights *are* created explicitly in the law, see H. L. A. Hart, 'Definition and Theory in Jurisprudence', *Law Quarterly Review*, 70 (1954), pp. 49 f.; and D. M. MacCormick, 'Rights in Legislation', in *Law, Morality and Society: Essays in Honour of H. L. A. Hart* (Oxford, 1977), pp. 189–91.

same issues arise when we move from positive law to the critical standards of morality. Someone who is committed to a principle which he formulates as 'Everyone has a right to basic subsistence' and who is prepared to deploy that principle in evaluating social and economic arrangements is committed obviously and explicitly to the recognition of a moral right to subsistence. As in the case of the explicit statute, the right is there in the normative standard which he articulates, and it exists in the fairly straightforward sense that talk about it is made intelligible by referring to the terms in which his normative commitments are couched. But other moral principles may be less explicit. We have, it may be said, a duty of charity; does this amount to the recognition of a moral right in those who may be recipients of charitable assistance? Once again that will depend on how we propose to relate the concepts of duty, rule, and right. Of course, in the realm of moral standards, the situation is complicated by the fact that people even in the same society may deploy different principles and disagree among themselves without the sense which we find in legal disputes that there is one final set of standards to which everyone can, and in the last analysis must, appeal. But that is a point about moral evaluation in general: it is not particularly a point about moral rights. The existence and irresolvability of diversity and disagreement in ethics pose exactly the same difficulties for talk about moral rights—no more and no less—as they pose for talk about moral duties, rules, principles, and values. Unless it is proposed that we should give up critical moral evaluation altogether, it is difficult to see the case for confining talk of rights in particular to the context of positive law. Certainly, Bentham and those who follow him in this are right to point out the importance of establishing systematic relations between rights and other elements of the normative systems in which rights occur. But they have made a mistake (and, I think, an elementary one) in suggesting that this cannot be done except in relation to the normative system embodied in the law of the land. Other normative systems, which are put about in a critical rather than a positive or a descriptive spirit, may be vaguer or more contestable than systems of law, but by itself that is insufficient to show that they are therefore required to abandon one of their most fruitful and important critical concepts.

Having said all that, it has to be acknowledged that most of the pioneering work in the analysis of the concept of a right has been done in relation to legal rights. The first step to a rigorous understanding of the concept was to notice the ambiguities in the use of phrases like 'P has a right to X'. The account of these ambiguities given by

Wesley N. Hohfeld in 1919 is justly famous.[13] Hohfeld noted that the phrase may be used to convey any (combination) of the following ideas.

(1) It may mean 'P has no duty (to a particular person Q or to people in general) not to do X'. This relation is sometimes spoken of as a *bare liberty*, though Hohfeld used the term 'privilege' (presumably to indicate that the idea is often used to convey P's special position in relation to an otherwise generally applicable duty, e.g. 'A policeman has the right to be out after curfew').[14] It is sometimes said that Thomas Hobbes's right of nature ('every man has a right to every thing') is a Hohfeldian privilege, but I think Hobbes was getting at a slightly different and somewhat stronger idea: the idea that it is perfectly rational for P to do X and that he cannot be criticized in that regard.[15]

(2) Talk of P's right to do X may be meant to indicate that Q (or everyone) has a duty to let P do X. The existence of such a duty gives P some sort of claim against Q, and this second relation is often referred to as a *claim-right*. Of course, 'to let P do X' is a loose phrase, and a claim-right may involve anything from a purely negative duty not to impede P's action to a positive requirement to do what one can to make it possible for P to do X. The class of claim-rights therefore includes rights to active assistance as well as rights to negative freedom. In addition, legal philosophers have thought it necessary to distinguish between claim-rights *in personam* and claim-rights *in rem*. A right *in personam* is correlative to a duty peculiarly incumbent on an assignable person: the most familiar example of this sort of correlativity is the relation between the rights and duties arising out of a contract. Claim-rights *in rem*, on the other hand, are correlative to duties in principle incumbent on everyone. Some of the property rights I have in this typewriter are of this sort: everyone has a duty to refrain from using it unless he has my permission. This example illustrates the further point that some rights *in rem* may arise out of particular contingent transactions (e.g. my purchase of the typewriter) while others may be conceived to be rights held, as it were, *ab initio* (e.g. the claim-right not to be imprisoned without due process).[16]

[13] Wesley N. Hohfeld, *Fundamental Legal Conceptions as Applied in Judicial Reasoning* (Yale, 1919). There is a useful summary of Hohfeld's account in J. Feinberg, *Social Philosophy* (Englewood Cliffs, NJ, 1973), ch. 4.

[14] For a helpful discussion of the way in which privileges interact with claim-rights, see H. L. A. Hart, 'Bentham on Legal Rights', in *Oxford Essays in Jurisprudence*, Second series, ed. A. W. B. Simpson (Oxford, 1973), pp. 175–6.

[15] Thomas Hobbes, *Leviathan* (1651), ch. 14; see also Hobbes, *De Cive or The Citizen*, ed. Sterling Lamprecht (New York, 1949), ch. 1, sect. 7, pp. 26–7. (Cf. Tuck, *Natural Rights Theories*, ch. 6.)

[16] The distinction between rights *in rem* and rights *in personam* is

(3) The third sense of 'right' which Hohfeld distinguished involves the ability or *power* of an individual to alter existing legal arrangements. I have a right to sell this typewriter or leave it to someone in my will. These rights are concerned not so much with the immediate acts that I perform (e.g. handing you the typewriter) as with the effect of those actions. By selling the typewriter, I bring about a change in legal relations: someone else now acquires all the rights (the privileges, the claim-rights, and indeed the powers) that ownership involves while I now acquire the duties and so on correlative to those rights. Powers themselves are not correlative to duties but to liabilities: if I have a legal power, someone (or everyone) is liable to have his legal position changed by an exercise of my will. (We should note too that powers may exist independently of other sorts of rights: for example, there are circumstances in which a trustee may have a duty not to transfer trust property to another, and so no privilege or claim-right to transfer it, but in which nevertheless he has the power to effect such a transfer if the purchaser acts without notice and in good faith).[17]

(4) Oddly, we sometimes use the term 'right' to describe not only a power but also the correlate of the lack of a power—an *immunity* from legal change. If P has an immunity with regard to X, then Q (or maybe everyone) lacks the power to alter his legal position in regard to X. Constitutionally guaranteed privileges and claim-rights often also involve an immunity: not only do I have no duty not to do X or not only do others have a duty to let me do X, but also no one—not even the legislature—has a power to alter that situation. The duties and the rights with which they are correlated are immune from legal change.

These distinctions were developed in the analysis of legal rights, but they have obvious applicability in the moral sphere. In particular, the distinction between moral privileges and moral claim-rights has proved important in developing theories of human rights and relating them to the rest of morality.[18] But there are problematic aspects in the analysis of rights which Hohfeld's account leaves unresolved, and these have become more significant as rights-theorists have attempted to extend the analysis into new fields of political concern.

unfortunately conflated with the distinction between rights that do and rights that do not arise out of contingent transactions in sect. II of Hart's paper 'Are There Any Natural Rights?' Hart uses the terms 'special right' and 'general right' to capture both distinctions.

[17] I am indebted for this example to G. W. Paton, *A Textbook of Jurisprudence*, 4th edn. (Oxford, 1972), p. 293.

[18] See, e.g., J. Waldron, 'A Right to do Wrong', *Ethics*, 92 (1981), pp. 21–39, and the exchange between Waldron and W. Galston in *Ethics*, 93 (1983), pp. 320–7.

First, Hohfeld's account leaves unanalysed the concept of a duty. But even in positive law this is far from a straightforward concept. We think naturally of an explicit requirement or prohibition backed up with a direct sanction—the idea of duty involved in the criminal law. But what about the less simple case of a regulation imposing a tariff on an action which may or may not be calculated to discourage it? Or what about the familiar array of cases in civil law where the invocation of a sanction or the effective implementation of a requirement depend on the initiation of a certain procedure? In these cases, the concept of duty already seems to involve those of power and liability. The situation is of course even less clear in the case of moral duties. The idea of a moral duty may be something as stern and specific as the Ten Commandments or it may refer more broadly to any reasonable expectation that an action should or should not be done. Attempts have been made to pin the concept down more precisely than this, but they are bound to be frustrated by actual usage.[19] We need to recognize that when we apply the Hohfeldian analysis in the moral sphere, we must expect claims about moral rights to reflect the vagueness and indeterminacy afflicting claims about moral duty and obligation in general. Once again, this need not be taken as a criticism of the idea of moral rights, but it gives us fair warning of the degree of precision we are entitled to expect with this subject-matter.

Hohfeld's *claim-right* is generally regarded as coming closest to capturing the concept of individual rights used in political morality. To say that P has a natural right to free speech, for example, is usually to say (maybe among other things) that people owe a duty to him not to interfere with the free expression of his opinions. But this raises the question of what it is for a duty to be *owed to* someone in particular, the question of how the idea of *a duty to P* differs from the simple idea of *a duty*. When a person's rights are violated, we say not only that something wrong has been done but that the right-bearer himself has been wronged. He is conceived to have a unique relation to the duty and to cases of its violation: he can validly demand its performance and he, above all others, is entitled to complain when it is violated.[20] Until we understand the nature of this special relation, we are not in a position to move definitionally from statements about duties to statements about the rights of individuals.

[19] Cf. J. Raz, 'Promises and Obligations', in *Law, Morality, and Society*, pp. 223 ff.

[20] For this point, see, e.g. Joel Feinberg, *Rights, Justice, and the Bounds of Liberty* (Princeton, 1980), chs. 6–7; A. I. Melden, *Rights and Persons* (Oxford, 1977), pp. 22 ff.; V. Haksar, 'The Nature of Rights', *Archiv für Rechts- und Sozialphilosophie*, 64 (1978), pp. 183 ff.

Two broadly different accounts of the special relation between duties and right-bearers have been proposed: the 'Choice Theory' of rights, defended in a number of papers (one of which is reprinted here) by H. L. A. Hart, and the 'Benefit' or 'Interest Theory', associated originally with Bentham's analysis but defended in various forms by modern writers such as David Lyons, Joseph Raz, and Neil MacCormick.

The Choice Theory singles out the right-bearer in virtue of the power that he has over the duty in question. When an individual Q has a duty to do something, maybe there is some other individual P who is in a position to control that duty in the sense that his say-so would be sufficient to discharge Q from the requirement. This degree of control makes P a right-bearer on Hart's account. For example, when Q makes a promise to P he acquires a duty to perform the promise, but it is a duty from which P may release him at any time and P, the promisee, has the corresponding right. One way of looking at this, I suppose, is to say that Q has a duty and P has a Hohfeldian power in relation to that duty. But it would be a mistake to say that Hart believes that rights are nothing but *conjunctions* of powers and claims. Rather, the point of his analysis is that P can be said to have a right whenever the reasons for holding Q to be under a duty are also in themselves reasons for holding that P's say-so would be sufficient to release Q from the duty. This is evident in the case of promises, since the underlying reason for holding people to their promises—usually the promisee's reliance on the expectation induced by the promise—is itself a reason for giving the promisee this power of waiver. Hart has conceded, however, that this analysis does not offer an adequate account of all legal rights, let alone the rights recognized in social and political morality.[21] Most of us believe, for example, that we have duties not to kill, maim, and torture other humans, but few of us believe that there are good reasons for allowing the potential victims of these actions (or anyone else) to set aside our duty not to perform them. If nevertheless we think, as most of us do, that these duties are related to fundamental human rights, then some account other than Hart's must be offered of the relation between rights and duties.

The alternative analysis is based on Bentham's account of legal rights. An individual P can be said to have a right, Bentham said, if someone else Q has a duty to perform some act (or omission) which is in P's interest.[22] Now, of course, in a utilitarian system, all duties are conceived to promote some individual benefit; but we can say

[21] H. L. A. Hart, 'Bentham on Legal Rights', pp. 196–8.

[22] See Hart, 'Bentham on Legal Rights', pp. 171–9, and the notes thereto, for a presentation of Bentham's theory.

that a given duty is correlated with a right only if it is possible to say in advance which individual in particular stands to benefit from the performance of that duty. For example, if I perform my duty to return the £100 I borrowed from you, all sorts of people may benefit in fact: your family when you take them out to dinner to celebrate; someone bidding against me in an auction next week; the grocer down the street who benefits from the general climate of credit worthiness in the community; and so on. But neither Bentham nor the modern proponents of the Benefit Theory would say that those benefits give rise to claims of right. A benefit giving rise to a right must be so intimately related to the duty that it is possible to say in advance that unless this benefit is conferred, the duty has not been carried out. The interest of the person being benefited must lie at or near the immediate ground of the duty.[23] So, in the case of my duty to pay back the £100, only the benefit to you of receiving the money (and not any consequential benefit to you or anyone else) can be regarded as forming the basis of a right that I should pay back the money.

Some philosophers have taken this analysis a step further. Instead of saying that P has a right whenever he stands to benefit from the performance of a duty or whenever a duty is imposed for his benefit, they suggest that P can be said to have a right (in a moral theory or a legal system) whenever the protection or advancement of some interest of his is recognized (by the theory or the system) as a reason for imposing duties or obligations on others (whether duties and obligations are actually imposed or not).[24] This view has a number of advantages. It makes it possible to talk about rights in advance of determining who exactly is under the relevant duty. I can say, for example, that a child in Somalia has a right to be fed, meaning not that some determinate individual or agency has a duty to feed him, but simply that I recognize his interest in being fed as an appropriate ground for the assignment and allocation of duties.[25] Secondly, it provides a more satisfactory basis for the individuation of rights than a strictly Hohfeldian approach. It has often been noted that the traditional human rights (e.g. free speech, religious freedom, and the right to work, etc.) are not single or atomic claim-rights but tangled clusters of Hohfeldian elements, each of them involving all sorts of privileges, powers, claim-rights, immunities, and so on. There was a period when it was fashionable

[23] Cf. David Lyons, 'Rights, Claimants and Beneficiaries', *American Philosophical Quarterly*, 6 (1969), esp. pp. 175–80.

[24] See MacCormick, 'Rights in Legislation', pp. 192 ff., and J. Raz, 'Right-Based Moralities' (reprinted here).

[25] Cf. Joel Feinberg, *Rights, Justice and the Bounds of Liberty*, pp. 139–40; MacCormick, 'Rights in Legislation', pp. 200–4.

to try and split these clusters into their constituent elements, and to insist that each element must be justified separately in making a claim for the overall right or freedom in question. The present approach, however, restores the integrity of the clusters by concentrating on the single interest which underlies and generates all the detailed Hohfeldian elements. Thus the right of free speech, for example, is understood in terms of recognition that an individual's interest in self-expression is a sufficient ground for holding other individuals and agencies to be under duties of various sorts rather than in terms of the detail of the duties themselves.[26]

The debate between Choice and Interest Theories of rights is obliquely related to another debate which is probably of more substantial importance. Some people have attempted to relate the idea of rights to a particular aspect of moral personality: the active, practical, and assertive side of human life, as opposed to the passive, affective, or even pathological side. Rights have been seen as a basis of protection not for all human interests but for those specifically related to choice, self-determination, agency, and independence. On this view, the duties correlative to rights are mainly negative in character: they are duties to refrain from obstructing action or interfering with choice, rather than duties to provide positive assistance. This understanding is related in turn to more general considerations of political morality—in particular to principles of *laissez-faire* and minimalist theories of the state. That whole approach has been under steady attack throughout the twentieth century, to the extent that few now take seriously the suggestion, quite common a few decades ago, that recognition of the so-called socio-economic rights (rights to positive assistance such as free medical care, elementary education, or a decent standard of living) is a category mistake or a debasement of the language of rights. People still disagree about the detail of the socio-economic rights, but it is not now seriously suggested that rights to liberties are the only sort of rights there can be.[27]

Clearly, the Choice Theory of rights connotes a conception of the right-bearer as agent and chooser rather than merely potential victim or potential recipient of assistance. It is no accident that Hart's

[26] This is, I think, a more satisfactory way of preserving the unity or integrity of the cluster than picking out one of the Hohfeldian elements in particular as the '*core*' of the overall right-claim: cf. Carl Wellman, 'A New Conception of Human Rights', in *Human Rights*, edd. E. Kamenka and A. E.-S. Tay (London, 1978), pp. 53 ff.

[27] See the discussion between M. Cranston and D. D. Raphael in *Political Theory and the Rights of Man* (London, 1967). See also T. D. Campbell, *The Left and Rights* (London, 1983), chs. 6 and 9.

presentation of the Choice Theory was associated with a more general thesis that the right to liberty was both fundamental to and presupposed by all other claims about individual rights. It is significant also that Hart's analysis is in principle incompatible with the attribution of rights to beings incapable of exercising powers of waivers, such as babies and ducks. (Hart regards this as an advantage of this theory while his opponents see it as further evidence of its inadequacy). But we should note that, although Benefit and Interest Theories are more accommodating to the socio-economic rights (and to the rights of children and animals too),[28] still, in any such theory, not *every* interest is going to be regarded as the basis of a right but only those whose protection or advancement is taken to be a matter of special concern. A given Interest Theory may concentrate on a very small class of human interests, and if the principle of that demarcation is a special concern for interests related to liberty, then the dispute between libertarian and socio-economic conceptions of rights will be reproduced *within* the overall framework of the Interest or Benefit Theory.

III

I referred earlier to the idea that political morality or even morality in general might be thought to be *based* on individual rights. The distinction between *right-based*, *duty-based*, and *goal-based* theories was introduced by Ronald Dworkin and has been taken up by John Mackie and a number of other writers.[29] But this distinction is bound to seem mysterious if we simply postulate a *logical* relationship between rights and duties. If P's having a right is *defined* in terms of Q's having a duty, how can some theories be right-based while others are duty-based?[30] Our account of rights in terms of requirements generated by individual interests provides a better basis for the distinction. Let me explain.

Theories of political morality recognize requirements of various sorts, to perform or refrain from certain acts in certain circumstances.

[28] But for doubts about animal *interests*, see R. G. Frey, *Interests and Rights: The Case Against Animals* (Oxford, 1980). It should always be borne in mind that the Interest Theorists do not define rights in terms of a concept which is itself lucid and uncontestable; rather what they have done is to indicate how controversies about rights lock into the wider framework of controversies about interests. This is, if anything, an advantage rather than a criticism of their analysis.

[29] Ronald Dworkin, *Taking Rights Seriously*, rev. edn. (London, 1978), pp. 169–73; J. L. Mackie, 'Can There Be a Right-Based Moral Theory', and J. Raz, 'Right-Based Moralities'. (Both reprinted here.)

[30] Cf. Neil MacCormick, *Legal Right and Social Democracy* (Oxford, 1982), p. 142.

The *basis* of a political theory has to do with the way in which those requirements are generated and justified. Consider as a paradigm the requirement that policemen and others should refrain from torturing people. Most of us think that the reason for this requirement has to do with the profound and traumatic suffering that torture necessarily involves. If so, that is, if our recognition of this requirement is generated by a concern for the interests of those who might be tortured, we may say that the requirement is *right*-based. But some people think there are other grounds for concern in this case: it may be thought that the deliberate infliction of suffering debases and degrades the torturer, derogating from his humanity and undermining his rational integrity. If this is what we think, then to that extent our concern about torture may be described as *duty*-based.[31] Now, of course, most people feel both sorts of concern. But if it is possible to identify one sort of concern as more basic than another in a theory, to that extent the *theory* may be called right-based or duty-based. (The most notable example of a duty-based theory is the moral theory of Kant: even his concern that agents should be treated as ends not merely as means, which many philosophers have used as the basis for theories of rights, derives in the last resort from a deeper concern for the rational integrity of those who are disposed to treat distinctively human characteristics in a purely instrumental way[32].)

The distinction between right-based and goal-based theories is less easy to state. The intuitive idea is that a requirement is right-based if it is generated by a concern for some individual interest, goal-based if it is generated by a concern for something taken to be an interest of society as a whole. This is straightforward if the social interest is something like national glory, but it is less so when more familiar goals like general utility or prosperity are appealed to since these cannot be defined independently of the interests of individuals. Nevertheless it is possible to distinguish between a concern that focuses on a particular individual interest and a concern for interests generally. A prohibition on torture is right-based only if the implications of torture for a single individual are taken to be sufficient to generate the requirement; but if it is argued that no single interest can generate a requirement until the impact of the action in question on other interests has been considered, then we are dealing with a utilitarian goal-based approach.

[31] Another useful way of describing moral requirements justified in this way is to say that they are '*agent-relative*': see T. Nagel, 'The Limits of Objectivity', in *The Tanner Lectures on Human Values*, Vol. I, ed. S. McMurrin (Cambridge, 1980), pp. 103 ff.

[32] Immanuel Kant, *Groundwork to the Metaphysics of Morals*, translated by H. J. Paton *sub nom.* 'The Moral Law' (London, 1961), pp. 95–8.

Of course, the single interest that grounds a right-based approach need not be the peculiar interest of an assignable individual. It may be an interest which each individual shares with every other. (This will be so in the case of *human* rights.) Nevertheless a right-based theory would take the interest of each individual considered one at a time (no matter how common the interest is) to be sufficient to generate the requirement.[33]

This account of what is distinctive about right-based theories explains also why they are controversial. They presuppose that the fundamental concerns of political morality must be concerns which can be focused on individuals one at a time. Even within the confines of liberal philosophy, this is disputable. Joseph Raz argues in the paper reprinted in this volume, that this approach radically under-estimates the importance of indivisible and non-excludable public goods (such as a tolerant society or the existence of certain forms of life) in constituting even individualist ideals such as autonomy.[34]

IV

Rights, we have seen, are individualistic considerations, but they have also often been characterized in terms of their strength, their urgency, their peremptory character, even their conclusiveness in political argument. Many rights-theorists concede that utilitarian or other social ideals are important in political morality, and they may even concede that *every* interest *qua* interest has some sort of claim to satisfaction; but they reserve the language of rights for interests and considerations that they take to have *special* importance, an importance which would warrant overriding other values and ideals whenever they conflict with the protection of rights.

In a pure right-based theory, this is quite straightforward: it is simply a case of fundamental considerations dominating subordinate and derivative ones. But there are more complex cases which have made the detailed exploration of the special weight accorded to rights one of the main themes of modern discussion. We need to consider the place of rights in pluralistic theories and also in theories which are not fundamentally right-based at all: if rights are derivative from or co-ordinate with other moral considerations, can they still retain their

[33] This account builds on the discussions of Dworkin, *Taking Rights Seriously*, pp. 90–2 and 172, and MacCormick, 'Rights in Legislation', p. 205, and also on many helpful conversations with Dworkin and Raz.

[34] For more radical misgivings, see Robert Young, 'Dispensing with Moral Rights', *Political Theory*, 6 (1978); John Charvet, 'A Critique of Human Rights', in *Human Rights: Nomos XXIII*, edd. J. R. Pennock and J. W. Chapman (New York, 1981), and Campbell, *The Left and Rights*, pp. 92–102.

characteristic urgency and conclusiveness? Also, as theories of rights become more complex, we need to consider cases where rights conflict *inter se*: to resolve such conflicts it is imperative to know exactly how the special importance of each right-claim is to be understood. These issues are addressed in many of the papers reprinted here, particularly those by Dworkin, Gewirth, Scanlon, Lyons, and Vlastos.

We should perhaps distinguish three ways in which the special force of rights may be understood. On the most straightforward model, a right is nothing but a particularly important interest: it is assigned a greater weight than ordinary interests and therefore counts for more in utilitarian or other welfarist calculations. Still, in principle, it can be outweighed: a similar interest matched against it, or a sufficient quantity of the more mundane interests will ensure that it is not conclusive in generating a final requirement. On the second model, the interests protected by rights are given lexical priority over other interests.[35] They are to be protected and promoted to the greatest extent possible before other interests are even taken into consideration. This makes rights absolute against considerations of mere utility, but leaves open the possibility of what Robert Nozick has called 'a utilitarianism of rights' (maximizing fulfilment, minimizing violations) when they conflict *inter se*.[36]

The third model is most controversial. On this account, rights are understood not as specially or lexically weighted interests, but as the basis of strict constraining requirements on action. The function of a right is to exclude certain forms of behaviour involving other people from intentional consideration. Rights, in other words, define the boundaries of practical deliberation: your having the right not to be tortured makes it wrong even to contemplate torturing you. (This conception of rights is perhaps best known from Robert Nozick's *Anarchy, State, and Utopia*, but it is represented here in Alan Gewirth's paper 'Are There Any Absolute Rights?'[37]) There are two things to note about this view. It depends crucially on a distinction between practical deliberation and consequential foresight (the sort of distinction

[35] For lexical priority, see John Rawls, *A Theory of Justice* (Oxford, 1971), pp. 42–5.

[36] Robert Nozick, *Anarchy, State and Utopia* (Oxford, 1974), p. 28.

[37] Ibid. pp. 28–51; for a similar idea in deontological theories of ethics, see G. E. M. Anscombe, 'Modern Moral Philosophy', in her collection *Ethics, Religion and Politics* (Collected Philosophical Papers, Vol. III, Oxford, 1981), p. 40; and Nicholas Denyer, 'Chess and Life: The Structure of a Moral Code', *Proceedings of the Aristotelian Society*, NS 82 (1981–2), p. 59. There is a useful discussion of this approach to rights in Amartya Sen, 'Rights and Agency', *Philosophy and Public Affairs*, 11 (1981).

invoked by the Doctrine of Double Effect[38]). If others are wrongdoers or the world is of a certain sort, we may have no choice but to contemplate the avoidable occurrence of the very actions and events whose consideration at an intentional level is absolutely ruled out by this approach. Some philosophers are therefore sceptical about such a distinction: to contemplate the occurrence of an event which we could prevent is *already* to take up a practical attitude to it, they will say.[39] Secondly—and more intriguingly—given this distinction between intention and foresight, the Nozickian approach to rights is arguably incompatible with the idea of a right-based theory as I have characterized it. Consider the case where the only way to stop a terrorist torturing five people is to accede to his demand that we torture a sixth. Someone whose moral theory is ultimately right-based may well have qualms about torturing the sixth man and he may even think it finally wrong to do so, but he will not exclude it absolutely from consideration. The reason is simple: the interest which for him generates the requirement not to torture the sixth man is exactly the same as the interest which each of the other five has at stake in the matter. If a recognition of the importance of protecting this interest lies at the basis of the moral requirement as he sees it, then he must admit to being torn practically in both directions in this case. A requirement that the possibility of torturing the sixth man should be excluded absolutely from consideration cannot therefore be based on a concern for that man's interest in not being tortured; it must be based on some sort of *agent-relative* concern about the action or intention that would be involved in torturing.[40] A strict deontology of side-constraints, then, even when it is located in what purports to be a theory of rights, indicates the dominance of a duty-based approach to political morality.[41]

Most rights-theorists stop short of this sort of absolutism. The strength of rights for them is characterized by one of the other two

[38] For the Doctrine of Double Effect, see, e.g. Philippa Foot, 'The Problem of Abortion and the Doctrine of Double Effect', in her collection *Virtues and Vices* (Oxford, 1978).

[39] See H. L. A. Hart, *Punishment and Responsibility* (Oxford, 1968), pp. 122 ff., and Jonathan Glover, *Causing Death and Saving Lives* (Harmondsworth, 1977), chs. 6–8.

[40] For an extraordinarily helpful exploration of such an approach, see Nagel, 'The Limits of Objectivity', pp. 131 ff.

[41] That Nozick's theory of rights should be regarded as a duty-based theory sounds paradoxical; but the claim is consistent with the underlying Kantianism of his view, and the paradox is consistent with his well-known failure ever to articulate fully his theory.

models. Ronald Dworkin's formulation is perhaps best known. Dworkin attempted to capture the special force of rights in his famous image of the trump card: if considerations of the general interest are the normal determinant of the way in which political decisions ('tricks') are taken, then rights can be conceived as 'political trumps held by individuals'.[42] An individual has a right when there is a reason for assigning some resource, liberty, or opportunity to him even despite the fact that normally decisive considerations of the general interest (or other collective goals) would argue against that assignment. But this does not mean that rights can withstand the force of extraordinary or overwhelming considerations of utility. How things stand in those cases is a matter of how the right in question is justified. Like T. M. Scanlon and Gregory Vlastos, Dworkin insists that in cases of conflict we should look, not to the terms of the formulation of the right, but to the values and deep considerations that back it up.[43] In addition to this formal account, Dworkin has also attempted to provide a substantial explanation of the values underlying certain rights. On Dworkin's view, rights are taken to be safeguards introduced into legal and political morality to prevent the corruption of the egalitarian character of welfarist calculations by the introduction of what he calls 'external preferences'.[44] But Dworkin has conceded that this is a somewhat limited explanation. It does not explain the trumping force of rights against non-welfarist social goals. And even within a utilitarian framework, the explanation, if it works at all, works only on the assumption of a fundamental right to equality underlying both the utilitarian considerations and the particular claims of right that trump them. The force of this underlying right, and of other rights which are derived from it directly, is not captured either by the trumping image nor explained by the external preferences argument.[45] Rather, the force derives simply from the fact that the first premiss of Dworkin's theory is the right to equality rather than anything else.

There have been attempts to provide a more general account of the

[42] Dworkin, *Taking Rights Seriously*, p. ix.

[43] Ibid., pp. 191 f.; cf. Scanlon, 'Rights, Goals and Fairness', and Vlastos 'Justice and Equality' (both reprinted here).

[44] This argument was presented in Dworkin, *Taking Rights Seriously*, pp. 232–8, 272–8, and 357–8. Dworkin's paper 'Rights as Trumps' (reprinted here) restates and elaborates the argument, and attempts to answer the criticism of H. L. A. Hart put forward in his paper, 'Between Utility and Rights', in *The Idea of Freedom: Essays in Honour of Isaiah Berlin*, ed. Alan Ryan (Oxford, 1979), pp. 86–97. For somewhat different criticisms of Dworkin's line, see J. Raz, 'Professor Dworkin's Theory of Rights', *Political Studies*, 26 (1978).

[45] Cf. Dworkin, *Taking Rights Seriously*, pp. 355–7 and 367–8.

special force of rights which might be integrated into the framework of an overall utilitarian or welfarist approach. The interest in 'rule-utilitarian' theories and various forms of 'indirect' or 'two-level' utilitarianism reflects a hope that some of the more oppressive or 'counter-intuitive' implications of direct consequentialist reasoning can be avoided and that robust protection for certain key interests of the individual can be accommodated in a mature theory of social utility.[46] But in 'Utility and Rights' (reprinted here), David Lyons suggests that this might prove in the end impossible: that is, it may be impossible for a utilitarian to account for our conviction that rights and the interests they protect have moral force in relation to the determination of individual and government action which is not exhausted by the impact of that action (or actions of that sort) on the general welfare. It has to be said, however, that this suggestion remains controversial, and Lyons may well have underestimated the resources of the utilitarian tradition.[47]

It is one thing to suggest that a utilitarian theory can generate moral considerations that have the special force of rights, quite another to show that these utilitarian 'rights' would have the same *content* as the rights that are cherished in the liberal tradition. Attempts have been made to produce utilitarian arguments for free speech, civil liberty, economic equality, toleration, and so on, but the arguments are always at best marginal and contingent and, in any case, much more heavily qualified than the corresponding liberal principles. There is, as Ronald Dworkin has pointed out, always a temptation to argue 'backwards' in these cases, to assume that there *must* be a utilitarian justification for our firmly held 'intuitions' about right and justice.[48] That this is a mistake is shown by the fact that in one politically contentious area at least—the question of law and order and the legal rights of criminal suspects—considerations of social utility seem to pull in quite a different direction from the liberal arguments culminating in the right to silence, habeas corpus, and the presumption of innocence, and so on. We must not let the *formal* sophistication of modern utilitarianism blind us to the fact that, at the level of content, utilitarians remain perfectly happy about (indeed are necessarily and profoundly committed to) the possibility of trading off the interests in life or liberty

[46] See, e.g., R. M. Hare, *Moral Thinking: Its Levels, Method and Point* (Oxford, 1981), chs. 2–3 and 8–9.

[47] For an immediate response to Lyon's argument, see Kent Greenawalt, 'Utilitarian Justifications for Observance of Legal Rights', and R. M. Hare, 'Utility and Rights', both in *Ethics, Economics and the Law: Nomos XXIV*, edd. J. R. Pennock and J. W. Chapman (New York, 1982).

[48] Cf. Dworkin, 'Is There a Right to Pornography?', p. 193.

of a small number of people against a greater sum of the lesser interests of others.

Non-utilitarian theories, on the other hand, tend to be technically less sophisticated; often they contain little more than a bare assertion that certain rights are intuitively evident or are at any rate to be taken as first principles.[49] One or two philosophers have tried to go beyond this and produce what amount almost to *transcendental* arguments for rights. These arguments attempt to show that the denial of rights or the overriding of them in certain cases is rationally self-defeating, because the denial or the overriding themselves involve an implicit recognition of the force of human rights. In the long and important article 'Justice and Equality' reprinted here, Gregory Vlastos argues that rights have to do with the value or worth we ascribe to human agents as such, in virtue of the fact that they are beings capable of valuing. On this account, rights have priority over considerations like utility or desert because they reflect the conditions under which it becomes possible for an agent to recognize and act on considerations like utility and desert. It is plausible to suppose that freedom of thought and self-expression and the satisfaction of elementary needs are conditions of this sort. More recently, Alan Gewirth has pursued an even more radical project along these lines.[50] Gewirth wants to show, not merely that a recognition of P's rights is implicit in any attempt to justify one's actions to P, but that a claim about P's rights (and therefore, in consistency, a recognition of the rights of other agents) is implicit in every one of P's actions. Gewirth therefore hopes to deal with the meta-ethical problem of the justification of rights to those who purport to reject all talk of morality, as well as the ethical problem of locating the importance of rights in relation to other normative considerations.

It is too early to judge the success of Gewirth's programme.[51] But the kind of argument discussed in the previous paragraph does seem to indicate a most promising approach to the idea of rights. Questions about rights generally arise when it is proposed that the interests of one or more individuals should be traded off for the sake of others' or in the name of some allegedly more important moral or political ideal. If we make such a proposal, it seems plausible to insist that we ought at least to produce reasons for our action which are in principle capable

[49] See, e.g., Nozick, *Anarchy, State and Utopia*, p. ix.

[50] Alan Gewirth, *Reason and Morality* (Chicago, 1978), and *Human Rights: Essays on Justification and Applications* (Chicago, 1982), (The paper by Gewirth reprinted here contains only a passing reference to his overall programme.)

[51] But see the discussion by R. B. Friedman, A. A. Morris, and M. P. Golding in *Human Rights: Nomos XXIII*, pp. 148–74.

of being accepted by the people whose interests are at stake. But this requirement seems to imply that we must leave intact at least those interests that are central to each person's capacity to recognize and understand moral reason and moral argument (again, his freedom of thought and expression and maybe certain basic interests in material well-being). Otherwise, we are indicating that we do not take seriously the task of justifying our action *to him*. This line of argument has obvious Kantian roots, and reaches back through Kant to some of the more interesting ideas involved in the 'Social Contract' tradition, in particular the idea that social and political arrangements should not be such as to rule out the hypothesis that they were set up by universal consent.[52] With these roots, the argument also has connections with John Rawls's conception of justice and political morality. If the role of a theory of justice is to enable all the members of a society to justify to one another their shared institutions and the basic arrangements for the distribution of benefits and burdens in their society, then maybe we can find the first principles of such a theory in the conditions and presuppositions of the activity of justification itself.[53] These ideas have yet to be elaborated in a fully convincing theory. But it is, I think, in this area rather than in pious lip-service to slogans about human dignity or autonomy that the real importance of theories of rights is to be found.

[52] See *Kant's Political Writings*, ed. Hans Reiss (Cambridge, 1970), pp. 79 ff.; John Locke, *Two Treatises of Civil Government*, ed. Peter Laslett (Cambridge, 1960), II, chs. 9 and 11; Thomas Hobbes, *Leviathan*, ed. C. B. MacPherson (Harmondsworth, 1968), pp. 268–71.

[53] John Rawls, *A Theory of Justice* (Oxford, 1971). For a most useful recent statement of Rawls's conception, see 'Kantian Constructivism in Moral Theory' (The John Dewey Lectures), *Journal of Philosophy*, 77 (1980), esp. pp. 517 ff.

I

NATURAL RIGHTS

MARGARET MACDONALD

DOCTRINES of natural law and natural rights have a long and impressive history from the Stoics and Roman jurists to the Atlantic Charter and Roosevelt's Four Freedoms.[1] That men are entitled to make certain claims by virtue simply of their common humanity has been equally passionately defended and vehemently denied. Punctured by the cool scepticism of Hume; routed by the contempt of Bentham for 'nonsense upon stilts'; submerged by idealist and Marxist philosophers in the destiny of the totalitarian state; the claim to 'natural rights' has never been quite defeated. It tends in some form to be renewed in every crisis in human affairs, when the plain citizen tries to make, or expects his leaders to make, articulate his obscure, but firmly held conviction that he is not a mere pawn in any political game, nor the property of any government or ruler, but the living and protesting individual for whose sake all political games are played and all governments instituted. As one of Cromwell's soldiers expressed it to that dictator: 'Really, sir, I think that the poorest he that is in England hath a life to live as the greatest he.'[2]

It could, perhaps, be proved hedonistically that life for most ordinary citizens is more *comfortable* in a democratic than a totalitarian state. But would an appeal for effort, on this ground, have been sanctioned between 1939 and 1945? However true, it would have been rejected as inefficient because *uninspired*. Who could be moved to endure 'blood and toil, tears and sweat' for the sake of a little extra comfort? What, then, supplied the required inspiration? An appeal to the instinct of national self-preservation? But societies have been known to collapse inexplicably almost without waiting to be physically defeated. No

Reprinted by permission of the Editor of the Aristotelian Society from *Proceedings of the Aristotelian Society 1947–48*, copyright 1949 The Aristotelian Society, pp. 35–55.

[1] Freedom of Speech and Worship; Freedom from Want and Fear of all persons everywhere.

[2] *Clarke Papers*, Vol. I, p. 301.

doubt there are several answers, but at least one, I suggest, was an appeal to the values of freedom and equality among men. An appeal to safeguard and restore, where necessary, the Rights of Man, those ultimate points at which authority and social differences vanish, leaving the solitary individual with his essential human nature, according to one political theory, or a mere social fiction, according to another.

All this sounds very obscure. And the doctrine of natural law and of the natural rights of man is very obscure—which justifies the impatience of its opponents. It seems a strange law which is unwritten, has never been enacted, and may be unobserved without penalty, and peculiar rights which are possessed antecedently to all specific claims within an organized society. Surely, it will be said, the whole story now has only historical interest as an example of social mythology? Nothing is so dead as dead ideology. All this may be true,[3] but nevertheless the doctrine is puzzling. For if it is sheer nonsense why did it have psychological, political, and legal effects? Men do not reflect and act upon collections of meaningless symbols or nonsense rhymes.

There seems no doubt that the assertions of certain Greek philosophers about the 'natural' equality of men and their consequent right to freedom caused intelligent contemporaries to become uneasy about the institution of slavery;[4] that doctrines of the primal Rights of Man were significantly connected with the French and American Revolutions. It even seems probable that the Communist Manifesto owed much of its success not to its 'scientific' analysis of capitalist society, but to its denouncement of a wage slavery degrading to human nature and its appeal to all workers to assert their equal brotherhood. A major crime of capitalist society for Marx and Engels was that it had destroyed all ties between men other than naked self-interest and had 'resolved personal worth into exchange value'. Only after the proletarian revolution would *human* history begin and men treat each other as equal human beings, not as exploiter and exploited. The object of the transfer of class power is to end class power and to reveal or restore some essential human nature at present disguised by distorting social relationships.

So even if the theory were dead, the puzzle of its effects would remain, and suggest that it had been introduced to solve a genuine problem of political and social philosophy. And it is interesting, therefore to inquire what the problem was; whether it has found an alternative solution, or is bogus and insoluble.

[3] It is not quite true, for the doctrines of natural law and consequent natural rights flourish in Catholic social philosophy. See e.g., Jacques Maritain, *The Rights of Man and Natural Law* (1944).

[4] Cf. *The Open Society*, by K. Popper; Vol. I, esp. pp. 58–9.

Why should people have supposed, and, as I believe, continue to suppose, in obscure fashion, that they have 'natural' rights, or rights as human beings, independently of the laws and governments of any existing society? It is, surely, partly at least, because no existing social compulsion or relationship is self-justifying. Men may always ask why they should or should not endure it and expect a convincing answer. And, ultimately, it would seem, they may challenge the dictates of all existing governments and the pressures of every society if they find them equally oppressive, i.e. if they deny what the individual considers his fundamental 'right'. But since, *ex hypothesi*, this 'right' is denied by every existing law and authority, it must be a right possessed independently of them and derived from another source. If, for example, the laws of every existing society condemn a human being to be a slave, he, or another on his behalf, may yet hold that he has a 'right' to be free. What sort of proposition is this and how is such a claim to be justified? This seems to be one most important problem which the doctrine of natural rights tried to solve.

I. NATURAL LAW, NATURAL LAWS, AND NATURAL RIGHTS

There are an indefinite number of different types of propositions and other forms of human utterance. I will, for my present purpose, notice three. (1) Tautological or analytical propositions which state rules for the uses of symbols or which follow from such rules within a linguistic or logical system. (2) Empirical or contingent propositions which state matter of fact and existence. Propositions which describe what does or may occur in the world and not the symbolic techniques employed in such description. (3) Assertions or expressions of value. With the help of this classification it may be possible to show that some of the difficulties of the doctrine of natural rights have been due to an attempt to interpret propositions about natural rights as a curious hybrid of types (1) and (2) of the above classification.

For in the theory which conceived of natural rights as guaranteed by a 'natural' law, the position seems to have been considered in the following terms. The 'rights' of a slave, for example, derive from the laws in any society which govern his artificial status as a slave. Yet he has a right to be free. But in virtue of what status and law? Only it seems by his status of being a man like other men. This, however, is a natural status as opposed to one determined by social convention. Every man is human 'by nature'; no human being is 'by nature' a slave of another human being. There must then be an essential human nature which determines this status and a law governing the relations of human beings as such, independently of the laws of all particular societies concerning their artificial relationships. But essential human nature or human 'essence' is constituted by those properties expressed in the definition of 'human being'. And what is expressed or entailed by a definition is a necessary or analytic proposition. Thus by a logical fusion of the characteristics of two different types of proposition, statements about natural rights tended in this theory to be represented as statements of a necessary natural fact.

But not even statements of actual fact, necessary or contingent. For another element intervened. Though the slave had an actual 'right' to be free, he was not free, because no existing law admitted his right. Because laws were imperfect, he was not free though he 'ought' to be. And this introduces into the situation a further complication. By nature a man must be that which yet he is not. Or, it follows from the definition of 'human being' that every human being is, or must be, free—or possess any other 'natural' right though his freedom is ideal and not real. But the ideal as well as the actual is natural fact.

Thus the Roman lawyers, who gave the earliest authoritative statements of the doctrine of natural law, conceived of natural law as an ideal or standard, not yet completely exemplified in any existing legal code, but also as a standard fixed by nature to be discovered and gradually applied by men. And the good lawyer kept his eye on this standard as the good gardener keeps his eye fixed on the prize rose which he is hoping to reproduce among his own blooms next summer. For the lawyer, said Ulpian, is not merely the interpreter of existing laws but also the priest or guardian of justice, which is the 'fixed and abiding disposition to give every man his right'.[5] This standard was not determined by men, but by nature, or, sometimes, by God. It was fact and not fancy.

The institution of slavery showed that no existing code was perfectly just. Thus natural *law* is only imperfectly realized in positive *laws*. And it is significant that the lawyers and later political theorists who adopted this distinction talked only of natural *law* and the Law of Nature, never of natural laws and laws of nature. But what is most characteristic of legal codes and systems is that they consist of many laws, regulating the different relations of men as debtor and creditor, property owner and thief, employer and employee, husband and wife, etc. But natural law was not conceived of as consisting of ideal regulations corresponding to all positive laws. Indeed, if completely realized, some positive laws would be abolished, e.g. those relating to slave owner

[5] Sabine, *History of Political Theory*, p. 170.

and slave. Natural law was not formulated in natural *laws*. It was neither written nor customary and might even be unknown. But it applies, nevertheless, to all men everywhere whether they are debtors or creditors, masters or servants, bond or free. But how is it discovered?

It seems probable that the concept of natural law influenced the later conception of natural or scientific laws obtained by the observation of natural events. For natural law applies impartially to all men in all circumstances, as the law of gravitation applies to all bodies. But the law of gravitation is obtained by deduction from the observation of bodies in sense perception. Are the Law of Nature and the Rights which it implies known by similar observation of the nature of man? The law of gravitation, like all other laws of nature, states a uniformity exemplified in the actual movements of natural bodies. But no existing society may observe the Law of Nature or guarantee natural rights. These cannot, therefore, have been learned from observation of the actual practice of existing societies.

'Man is born free', said Rousseau, 'and everywhere he is in chains'. What sort of proposition is this? Did Rousseau observe ten or ten million babies immediately after birth and record when the infant limbs were manacled? The law of nature applies to all men equally, said Cicero. For if we had not been corrupted by bad habits and customs 'no one would be so like his own self as all men would be like others'.[6] But since everyone everywhere has been subjected to customs and laws of varying degrees of imperfection, where and when did Cicero observe our uncorrupted nature? How can facts about nature be discovered which have never been observed or confirmed by observation?

The answer lies in the peculiar status given to reason in the theory. Propositions about natural law and natural rights are not generalizations from experience nor deductions from observed facts subsequently confirmed by experience. Yet they are not totally disconnected from natural fact. For they are known as entailed by the intrinsic or essential nature of man. Thus they are known by reason. But they are entailed by the proposition that an essential property of men is that they have reason. The standard of natural law is set by reason and is known because men have reason. But that men have reason, i.e. are able to deduce the ideal from the actual, is a natural fact. And it is by having this specific, and natural, characteristic of being rational that men resemble each other and differ from the brutes. Reason is the great leveller or elevator. According to Sir Frederick Pollock, 'Natural law was conceived to be an ultimate principle of fitness with regard to the

[6] *Laws*, Bk. 1, 10, 28–9 (trans. C. W. Keyes).

the nature of man as a rational and social being which is, or ought to be, the justification of every form of positive law.'[7] 'There is, in fact', said Cicero, 'a true law—namely right reason—which is in accordance with nature, applies to all men and is unchangeable and eternal.'[8] And for Grotius, too, 'The law of nature is dictate of right reason.'[9]

Let it be admitted that all or most human beings are intelligent or rational. And that what is known by reason is certainly true. But, also, what can be known by unaided reason is what *must* be true, and perhaps what *ought* to be but never what *is* true of matter of fact. And statements which are logically certain are tautological or analytic and are neither verified nor falsified by what exists. Statements about what ought to be are of a peculiar type which will be discussed later, but it is certain that they say nothing about what *is*. Because it is confused on these distinctions, the theory of natural law and natural rights constantly confounds reason with right and both with matter of fact and existence. The fact that men do reason is thought to be somehow a natural or empirical confirmation of what is logically deduced by reason as a standard by which to judge the imperfections of what exists.

II. THE SOCIAL CONTRACT

Though the Roman lawyers conceded that man might be entitled by natural law to that which he was denied by every positive law, they do not seem to have related this to any particular doctrine of legal and political authority. But in the seventeenth century the doctrines of natural law and natural rights were directly connected with the contract theory of the State. Because he is rational, Locke emphasized, man is subject to the law of nature even before the establishment of civil society. And he never ceases to be so subject. By right of the law of nature men lived in a state of freedom, equality, and the possession of property 'that with which a man hath mixed his labour'. True, this picture differs from that of Hobbes whose 'natural man' is constantly at war, possesses only the right to preserve his life, if he can, but usually finds it short and nasty. Nevertheless, even Hobbes's unpleasant savages have sufficient sense, or reason, to enable them to escape their 'natural' predicament. Locke's natural individualists are peaceful property-owners who nevertheless sometimes dispute and want an impartial arbitrator. Civil society is formed by compact that natural rights may be better preserved. Man did not enter society, said Paine, to become

[7] The History of the Law of Nature, *Essays in the Law* (1922).
[8] *Republic*, Bk. 3, p. 22 (trans. Sabine and Smith).
[9] Bk. 1, ch. 1, sect. x, 1.

worse than he was before by surrendering his natural rights but only to have them better secured. His natural rights are the foundation of all his civil rights. It was essential for the social contract theorists to deny that all rights are the gift of civil society, since existing societies denied certain rights which they affirmed. In order to claim them, therefore, it was supposed that they had been enjoyed or were such as would be enjoyed by rational creatures in a 'natural' as opposed to an established society. The Declaration of the French Revolutionary Assembly enunciated the Rights of Man and of citizens; the two being distinct.

His 'natural' rights attach, by virtue of his reason, to every man much as do his arms and legs. He carries them about with him from one society to another. He cannot lose them without losing himself. 'Men are born free and equal', said the French Assembly, 'in respect of their *natural* and *imprescriptible* rights of liberty, property, security, and resistance of oppression.' The framers of the American Declaration of Independence declare as self-evident truths that all men are created equal, that they are endowed by their creator with certain inalienable rights, among which are Life, Liberty, and the Pursuit of Happiness, and that governments are instituted to secure these rights.' The free people of Virginia proclaimed that the rights with which men enter society they cannot by any concept deprive themselves or their posterity of.

These were self-evident truths about a state which men might have left or not yet attained but which was 'natural' to them as opposed to accidental or conventional. A person is accidentally a native of England, France, America; a Red Indian, negro, or Jew. His social environment is determined by accident of birth. He may change his family by adoption and his citizenship by naturalization. And he is accidentally, or conventionally, a doctor, soldier, employer, etc. These conventionalities determine his civic and legal rights in a particularly society. But he is not accidentally human. Humanity is his essence or nature. There is no essence of 'being Greek' or 'being English'; of 'being a creditor' or 'being an old-age pensioner', all of which properties, however, might be the basis of civil rights. The nature of man determines his 'natural' rights. And since, though not accidental, it also seemed to be a matter of fact that men exist and are rational, rights claimed on account of this fact seemed also to be natural and to follow from the essence of man, even though they might be denied. But the essence of man is expressed in the definition of the word 'man'. So that the statement 'Men have natural rights' is equivalent to the prepositional function '*x* is human entails *x* has natural rights', which is tautology. Again, the ambiguity inherent in the theory between what is necessary and what is natural is revealed. It is hard to believe that a barren tautology generated the ardours of that time in which it was good to be alive and to be young was 'very heaven'.[10] But what is meant by the nature or essence of man by 'being rational' or 'having reason'?

III. RIGHTS AND REASON

' "Man" equals "rational animal" Df.' is the fossil preserved in logic textbooks since Aristotle. It was never accompanied by any adequate account of the meaning of 'rational', which was, however, generally assumed to include the capacity to abstract and generalize by the use of symbols in speech and writing; to formulate and understand general propositions and laws and to perceive necessary or logical connections between propositions. It is true that Aristotle himself used the term 'reason' more widely to include the practical intelligence manifested in various skills and the appropriate behaviour of the well-trained character in various moral situations. But usually reason is conceived to be the capacity by which men understand abstractions. This was certainly Kant's view. To be rational is to be able to think abstractly. And the most characteristic activities of men, including living in societies, are due to this capacity to use reason. It is peculiar to men and shared by no other animal. Hence the basis of the equality of men for the exponents of natural law, and of their intrinsic worth for Kant is the fact that they all have reason. Men share all other characteristics with the brutes and might themselves have them in varying degrees, but reason was alike in all men, it was man's defining characteristic. Hence it is the foundation, too, of his natural rights, as a human being.

It is probable that other animals do not abstract and generalize for they do not use symbols. But neither is it true that all men do this with equal skill. Reason, in this sense, is no less or no more invariable among human beings than sense perception, and the rights of man might as well depend upon eyesight as upon rationality. But if the term reason is to be used more widely to include non-verbal manifestations of intelligence, knowing-how as well as knowing-that,[11] then intelligence does not set an unbridgeable gulf between men and other living creatures. For in many activities, those, i.e. of hunting, building, fighting, and even social organization, other creatures display skill, adaptability of means to ends, and other characteristics which are evidence of intelligence in men. And as for social life, ants use tools, domesticate other insects, and live a highly organized social life. Bees and wasps manage

[10] Wordsworth in *The French Revolution*.

[11] See Presidential Address to the Aristotelian Society by Professor G. Ryle, 1945, and *The Concept of Mind* (1948), ch. 11.

their affairs by a complicated system of government. Moreover, many of the characteristic human activities depend very little on abstract thought or use of symbols, e.g. cooking, sewing, knitting, carpentry. And at a higher level the excellence of pictures, sculptures, symphonies, is not due to their expression of abstract thought. But where in this variety are we to find the constant factor by which to determine human rights? What passport will admit to the Kingdom of Ends?

What may be agreed is that only at a certain level of intellectual development do men claim natural rights. Savages do not dream of life, liberty, and the pursuit of happiness. For they do not question what is customary. Neither do the very depressed and downtrodden. It was not the slaves who acclaimed their right to be free but the philosophers and lawyers. Marx and Engels were not themselves wage slaves of the industrial system. It is generally agreed that the doctrines of natural rights, natural law, and the social contract, are individualistic. To claim rights as an individual independently of society, a man must have reached a level of self-consciousness which enables him to isolate himself in thought from his social environment. This presupposes a considerable capacity for abstraction. To this extent natural rights, or the ability to claim natural rights, depends on reason. But it does not follow from this that reason alone constitutes the specific nature of man or that the worth of human beings is determined solely by their IQs. Reason is only one human excellence.

But the Aristotelian dream of fixed natures pursuing common ends dies hard. It reappears in M. Maritain's account of the Rights of Man cited earlier. He says, for example,

> . . . there is a human nature and this human nature is the same in all men . . . and possessed of a nature, constituted in a given determinate fashion, man obviously possesses ends which correspond to his natural constitution and which are the same for all—as all pianos, for instance, whatever their particular type and in whatever spot they may be, have as their end the production of certain attuned sounds. If they do not produce these sounds, they must be attuned or discarded as worthless . . . since man has intelligence and can determine his ends, it is up to him to put himself in tune with the ends necessarily demanded by his nature.[12]

And men's rights depend upon this common nature and end by which they are subject to the natural or 'unwritten' law. But this seems to me a complete mistake. Human beings are not like exactly similar bottles of whisky each marked 'for export only' or some device

[12] loc. cit., p. 35.

indicating a common destination or end. Men do not share a fixed nature, nor, therefore, are there any ends which they must necessarily pursue in fulfilment of such nature. There is no definition of 'man'. There is a more or less vague set of properties which characterize in varying degrees and proportions those creatures which are called 'human'. These determine for each individual human being what he *can* do but not what he *must* do. If he has an IQ of 85 his intellectual activities will be limited; if he is physically weak he cannot become a heavyweight boxer. If a woman has neither good looks nor acting ability she is unlikely to succeed as a film star. But what people may do with their capacities is extremely varied, and there is no one thing which they must do in order to be human. It would be nonsense to say: 'I am not going to be an actress, a school teacher, a postman, a soldier, a taxpayer, but simply a human being.' For what is the alternative? A man may choose whether he will become a civil servant or a schoolmaster, a conservative or a socialist, but he cannot choose whether he will be a man or a dog. There is certainly a sense in which it is often said that in the air-raid shelter or in the battle people forgot that they were officers or privates, assistant secretaries or typists, rich or poor, and remembered only that they were all human beings, i.e. all liable to die without regard to status. But that is always true. They did not remember that they were something *in addition* to being the particular human being they each were and which they might be without being any particular individual. And, as individuals, when the 'All Clear' sounded, each returned to pursue his or her own ends, not the purpose of the human race. Certainly, many human beings may co-operate in a joint enterprise to achieve a particular end which each chooses. But that cannot be generalized into the spectacle of all human beings pursuing one end. There is no end set for the human race by an abstraction called 'human nature'. There are only ends which individuals choose, or are forced by circumstances to accept. There are none which they *must* accept. Men are not created for a purpose as a piano is built to produce certain sounds. Or if they are, we have no idea of the purpose.

It is the emphasis on the individual sufferer from bad social conditions which constitutes the appeal of the social contract theory and the 'natural' origin of human rights. But it does not follow that the theory is true as a statement of verifiable fact about the actual constitution of the world. The statements of the Law of Nature are not statements of the laws of nature, not even of the laws of an 'ideal' nature. For nature provides no standards or ideals. All that exists, exists at the same level, or is of the same logical type. There are not, by nature, prize roses, works of art, oppressed or unoppressed citizens. Standards are determined by human choice, not set by nature independently of men. Natural events cannot tell us what we ought to do until we have made certain decisions, when knowledge of natural fact will enable the most efficient means to be chosen to carry out those decisions. Natural events themselves have no value, and human beings as natural existents have no value either, whether on account of possessing intelligence or having two feet.

One of the major criticisms of the doctrine of natural rights is that the list of natural rights varies with each exponent. For Hobbes, man's only natural right is self-preservation. More 'liberal' theorists add to life and security, liberty, the pursuit of happiness, and sometimes property. Modern socialists would probably include the right to 'work or adequate maintenance'. M. Maritain enumerates a list of nine natural rights which include besides the rights to life, liberty, and property of the older formulations, the right to pursue a religions vocation, the right to marry and raise a family, and, finally, the right of every human being to be treated as a person and not as a thing.[13] It is evident that these 'rights' are of very different types which would need to be distinguished in a complete discussion of the problem. My aim in this paper, however, is only to try to understand what can be meant by the assertion that there are some rights to which human beings are entitled independently of their varying social relationships. And it seems difficult to account for the wide variations in the lists of these 'rights' if they have all been deduced from a fixed human nature or essence, subject to an absolutely uniform 'natural law'. Nor is the disagreement one which can be settled by more careful empirical observation of human beings and their legal systems. The doctrine seems to try to operate by an analogy which it is logically impossible to apply.

The word 'right' has a variety of uses in ordinary language, which include the distinction between 'legal right' and 'moral right'. 'A has a legal right against B' entails B has a duty to A which will be enforced by the courts. A has a claim against B recognized by an existing law. No person has a legal right which he cannot claim from some other (legal) person and which the law will not enforce. That A has a moral right against B likewise entails that B has a duty to A. But it is not necessarily a duty which can be legally enforced. A has a right to be told the truth by B and B has a corresponding duty to tell A the truth. But no one, except in special circumstances recognized by law, can force B to tell the truth, or penalize him, except by censure, if he does

[13] loc. cit., p. 60.

not. No one can, in general, claim to be told the truth, by right, under penalty. But a creditor can claim repayment of a debt or sue his debtor.

When the lawyers said that a slave had a right in natural law to be free, they thought of a legal right not provided for by any existing statute, enactment, or custom and to whose universal infringement no penalties attached. But this, surely, is the vanishing point of law and of legal right by which a slave might demand his freedom. But perhaps there was a moral right and a moral obligation. The slave ought to be free and maybe it was the duty of every slaveholder to free his slaves and of legislators to enact laws forbidding slavery. But until this happened there was no law which forbade a man to keep slaves. Consequently, there is no point in saying there was 'really' a natural law which forbade this. For the natural law was impotent. Statements about natural law were neither statements of natural fact nor legal practice.

So, does it follow that a 'natural' right is just a 'moral' right? Kant said, in effect, that to treat another human being as a person, of intrinsic worth, an end in himself, is just to treat him in accordance with the moral law applicable to all rational beings on account of their having reason. But this is not quite the sense in which the term 'natural rights' has been historically used. Declarations of the Rights of Man did not include his right to be told the truth, to have promises kept which had been made to him, to receive gratitude from those he had benefited, etc. The common thread among the variety of natural rights is their *political* character. Despite their rugged individualism, no exponent of the Rights of Man desired to enjoy them, in solitude, on a desert island. They were among the articles of the original Social Contract; clauses in Constitutions, the inspiration of social and governmental reforms. But 'Keep promises', 'Tell the truth', 'Be grateful' are not inscribed on banners carried by aggrieved demonstrators or circulated among the members of an oppressed party. Whether or not morality can exist without society, it is certain that politics cannot. Why then were 'natural rights' conceived to exist independently of organized society and hence of political controversies? I suggest that they were so considered in order to emphasize their basic or fundamental character. For words like freedom, equality, security, represented for the defenders of natural rights what they considered to be the fundamental moral and social values which should be or should continue to be realized in any society fit for intelligent and responsible citizens.

When the contract-theorists talked of the rights of human beings which men had enjoyed in the state of nature, they seemed to be asserting unverifiable and nonsensical propositions since there is no evidence of a state of nature in which men lived before the establishment of civil societies. But they were not simply talking nonsense. They were, in effect, saying 'In any society and under every form of government men ought to be able to think and express their thoughts freely; to live their lives without arbitrary molestation with their persons and goods. They ought to be treated as equal in value, though not necessarily of equal capacity or merit. They ought to be assured of the exclusive use of at least some material objects other than their own bodies; they ought not to be governed without some form of consent. And that the application of these rights to the particular conditions of a society, or their suspension, if necessary, should be agreed with them.' The exponents of the natural Rights of Man were trying to express what they deemed to be the fundamental conditions of *human* social life and government. And it is by the observance of some such conditions, I suggest, that human societies are distinguished from ant-hills and beehives.

This, however, has frequently been denied by utilitarian, idealist, and marxist philosophers who, though differing in other respects, agree in holding that the rights of an individual must be determined only by the needs and conveniences of society as a whole. Surely, they say, there can be no 'natural' right to life in any society when a man may be executed as a criminal or killed as a conscripted soldier. And very little right to liberty exists when external danger threatens the state. 'The person with rights and duties', says the evolutionist utilitarian Ritchie, 'is the product of society and the rights of the individual must, therefore, be judged from the point of view of society as a whole and not the society from the point of view of the individual.'[14] It is the duty of the individual to preserve society for his descendants. For individuals perish but England remains. But the plain man may well ask why he must preserve a society for his descendants if it neither is, nor shows any prospect of being, worth living in? Will his descendants thank him for this consideration? All that seems to follow from Ritchie's view is that at any time the members of a society may agree to sacrifice some goods in order to achieve a certain result. And the result will include the restoration of basic rights. Does the ordinary citizen consider that he has no right to life and liberty because he agrees to (or does not protest against) the suspension of those rights in an emergency? He would be very unlikely to approve of such suspension if he thought the result would be the massacre or enslavement of himself, his contemporaries, and possibly his children and descendants

[14] Ritchie, *Natural Rights*, p. 101.

at the arbitrary will of a ruler or government. To suspend, or even to forfeit rights, as a criminal does, also temporarily, is not to deny rights. Nor is it to deny that such practices must be justified to the individuals required to submit to them. Though it may be much more useful to society that a man should remain a slave and even that he may be happier in that condition, it is not possible to prove to him that he has no right to be free, however much society wants his slavery. In short, 'natural rights' are the conditions of a good society. But what those conditions are is not given by nature or mystically bound up with the essence of man and his inevitable goal, but is determined by human decisions.

IV. PROPOSITIONS AND DECISIONS

Assertions about natural rights, then, are assertions of what ought to be as the result of human choice. They fall within class 3 of the division stated on page 23 as being ethical assertions or expressions of value. And these assertions or expressions include all those which result from human choice and preference, for example in art and personal relations, as well as in morals and politics. Such utterances in which human beings express choices determined by evaluation of better and worse have been variously interpreted, and it is, indeed, difficult to introduce a discussion of the topic without assuming an interpretation. I have tried, for example, to avoid the use of the words 'proposition' and 'statement' in referring to these utterances since these words emphasize a relation between what is asserted and a fact by which it is verified or falsified. And this leads either to the attempts of the natural law and natural rights theories to find a 'natural' fact which justifies these assertions or to search for non-sensible entities called 'Values' as the reference of ethical terms. Yet, of course, it is, in some sense, true that 'No one ought to be ill-treated because he is a Jew, a negro or not able to count above ten.' Alternatively, to talk of 'expressions of value' sounds as though such utterances are sophisticated ways of cheering and cursing. Just as the blow becomes sublimated into the sarcastic retort so our smiles of delight at unselfish action and howls of woe at parricide become intellectualized into apparent judgements about good and evil, right and wrong, without, however, losing their fundamentally emotive character.[15] On this view, value judgements do not state what is true or false but are expressions of feeling, sometimes combined with commands to do or forbear. But whatever its emotional causes and effects, an articulate utterance does not seem to be simply a substitute for

[15] Cf. A. J. Ayer, *Language, Truth and Logic*, ch. 6.

a smile or a tear. It says something. But I cannot hope in a necessarily brief discussion to do justice to the enormous variety of value utterances. So I will plunge, and say that value utterances are more like records of *decisions* than propositions.[16] To assert that 'Freedom is better than slavery' or 'All men are of equal worth' is not to state a fact but to *choose* a side. It announces *This is where I stand*.

I mentioned earlier that in the late war, propaganda appeals to defend our comforts and privileges would have been rejected as uninspiring but that appeals to defend the rights of all men to freedom and equality obtained the required response, at least in all but the depraved and cynical. I now suggest that they did so because they accorded with our decisions about these ultimate social values. For whether or not we were more or less comfortable as a result, we should not choose to act only upon orders about which we had not in some way been consulted, to suppress the truth, to imprison without trial, or to permit human individuals or classes of individuals to be treated as of no human value.

Two questions suggest themselves on this view. Firstly, if ethical judgements, and particularly the ethical judgements which concern the fundamental structure of society are value decisions, who makes these decisions and when? Is this not, as much as the natural law theory, the use of an analogy without application? I did safeguard myself to some extent by saying that these assertions are 'more like' decisions than they are like propositions. They are unlike propositions because they are neither tautologies nor statements of verifiable fact. But it is also true that if asked when we decided in favour of free speech or democratic government or many of our social values we could not give a date. It is, therefore, suggested that we no more record a decision by a value assertion than we signed a Social Contract. Nevertheless, I think the analogy does emphasize important differences between value and other assertions. For, if intelligent, we do choose our politics as we choose our friends or our favoured poems, novels, pictures, symphonies, and as we do not choose to accept Pythagoras' theorem of the law of gravitation. And when challenged we affirm our decision or stand by our choice. We say, 'I did not realize how much I valued free speech until I went to Germany in 1936', indicating that a choice had been made, but so easily that it had seemed scarcely necessary to record its occurrence.

For, indeed, the fundamental values of a society are not always

[16] Karl Popper makes a similar distinction in an interesting discussion of value judgements in *The Open Society*, Vol. I, ch. 5.

recorded in explicit decisions by its members, even its rulers, but are expressed in the life of the society and constitute its quality. They are conveyed by its 'tone' and atmosphere as well as its laws and Statutory Rules and Orders. The members of a society whose values are freedom and equality behave differently, walk, speak, fight differently from the members of a slave society. Plato expressed this nastily in the Republic[17] when he said that in a democracy even the horses and asses behaved with a gait expressive of remarkable freedom and dignity, and like everyone else became 'gorged with freedom'. Suspicion, fear, and servility are absent, or, at least, inconspicuous in such a society. And no one who visited Germany after 1933 needs to reminded of the change of atmosphere.

Decisions concerning the worth of societies and social institutions are not made by an *élite*, by rulers, or a governing class but, explicitly or by acceptance, by those who live and work in a society and operate its institutions. But these decisions may be changed by the effective propaganda of a minority who have reached other decisions of whose value they desire to convince the majority. Perhaps, ultimately, men get the societies and governments which they choose, even if not those which they deserve, for they may deserve better than passion, indolence, or ignorance permits them to choose.

This leads to a second question. Upon what grounds or for what reasons are decisions reached? Consider the expression of the doctrine of equality; that all human beings are of equal worth, intrinsic value, or are ends in themselves. Is there an answer to the question, Why? On what *evidence* is this assertion based? How can such a decision be maintained despite the obvious differences between human beings? The answer of the natural law theorists and of Kant was that the 'natural' fact that all men have reason proves that they are of intrinsic worth, and are thus entitled to the Rights of Man. It is not clear, however, whether imbeciles and lunatics forfeit human rights. No one can deny that they are human beings. A person who becomes insane does not thereby become a mere animal. But if statements about the possession by anything of a natural characteristic is related to a decision of worth as evidence for a conclusion, then it would be illogical to retain the decision when the characteristics were absent or had changed. It is irrational to continue to believe a proposition when evidence shows that it is false. I affirm that no natural characteristic constitutes a *reason* for the assertion that all human beings are of equal worth. Or, alternatively, that *all* the characteristics of *any* human being are equally

[17] Bk. 8, 563.

reasons for this assertion. But this amounts to saying that the decision of equal worth is affirmed of all human beings *whatever their particular characteristics*. It does not follow that they are of equal *merit* and that their treatment should not vary accordingly, in ways compatible with their intrinsic value. But even a criminal, though he has lost merit and may deserve punishment, does not become worthless. He cannot be cast out of humanity.

I am aware that this view needs much more elaboration, and especially illustration, than can be given in a very limited space. I can, therefore, indicate only in a general way the type of value assertions and the manner in which they are related to each other and to other assertions. They are not related as evidence strengthening a conclusion. For decisions are not true or false and are not deduced from premisses. Do we, then, decide without reason? Are decisions determined by chance or whim? Surely, it will be said, the facts have some relevance to what is decided? To say that decisions are made without reason looks like saying that we choose by tossing a coin; opening the Works of Shakespeare or the Bible at random and reading the first sentence; or shutting our eyes and sticking a pin into the list of starters to pick the Derby winner. These seem very irrational methods of choice. Nevertheless, we do sometimes choose by a not very dissimilar procedure. If two candidates for a post are of exactly equal merit, the selectors may well end by plumping for one or the other. This, it may be said, was justified because there was 'nothing to choose between them', not that the decision bore no relation to their merits. But there are some choices into which merit hardly enters. Those involving personal relations, for instance. It would seem absurd to try to prove that our affections were not misplaced by listing the characteristics of our friends. To one who asked for such 'proof' we should reply, with Montaigne:[18]

> If a man urge me to tell him wherefore I loved him, I feel it cannot be expressed but by answering, because it was he, because it was myself. . . . It is not one especial consideration, nor two, nor three, nor four, nor a thousand. It is I wot not what kind of quintessence of all this commixture which seized my will.

Yet it is also correct to say that our decisions about worth are not merely arbitrary, and intelligent choices are not random. They cannot be proved correct by evidence. Nor, I suggest, do we try to prove them. What we do is to support and defend our decisions. The relation of the

[18] 'Of Friendship', Essays (trans. John Florio).

record of a decision to the considerations which support it is not that of proof to conclusion. It is much more like the defence of his client by a good counsel.

Consider an analogous situation in art. Suppose one were trying to defend a view that Keats is a greater poet than Crabbe. One would compare passages from each writer, showing the richness and complexity of the imagery and movement of Keats's verse and the monotonous rhythm, moral platitudes, and poverty-stricken images of Crabbe. One would aid the effect by reading passages aloud for their comparable musical effects; would dwell on single lines and passages which show the differences between the evocative language of Keats and the conventional 'poetic diction' of Crabbe. The 'Season of mists and mellow fruitfulness' of the one and the 'finny tribes', etc., of the other. One might eventually resort to the remarks of the best critics on both writers. In short, one would employ every device to 'present' Keats, to build up a convincing advocacy of his poetry. And the resistance of Crabbe's defender might collapse, and he would declare the case won with the verdict 'Keats is the better poet'. But nothing would have been *proved*. Crabbe's supporter might still disagree. He would dwell on Crabbe's 'sincerity'; his genuine sympathy with the poor and excuse his poetic limitations as due to a bad tradition for which he was not responsible. He might add that Crabbe was one of Jane Austen's favourite poets. And if he so persisted he would not be *wrong*, i.e. he would not be believing falsely that Crabbe was a better poet than Keats but much more persuasion would be needed to induce him to alter his decision.

Compare with this the correct attitude to the proof of a scientific law. If the empirical evidence is conclusive then a person who rejects the conclusion is either stupid or biased. He is certainly believing a false proposition. We do not 'defend' the law of gravitation but all instructed persons accept the proof of the law.

On the other hand, we do not refer to Mill's proof but to his 'magnificent defence' of civil liberty. For a successful defence involves much more than statement of facts. The facts of the case are known to both the prosecuting and defending counsel. The question is, should the accused be condemned or acquitted? The skilful lawyer uses these facts, but he uses them differently from the scientist. He marshals them so as to emphasize those which favour his client. He interprets those which appear unfavourable in terms of legal decisions in similar cases which would benefit the accused. He chooses language which does not merely state, but impress; he uses voice, gesture, facial expression, all the devices of eloquence and style in order to influence the decision of the jury in favour of his client. His client may still lose, but he would admit that he has a better chance of winning if he briefs a good counsel.

But, it may be asked, is this a recommendation to take fraudulent advocacy as our model for defending the rights of man? Not at all. Lawyers and art critics are not frauds, but neither are they scientists. They are more like artists who use material with results which impress and convince but do not *prove*. There is no conceivable method of *proving* that Keats is a better poet than Crabbe or that freedom is better than slavery. For assertions of value cannot be subjected to demonstrative or inductive methods. It is for this reason that such assertions have been regarded as simple expressions of feeling or emotion like cries of pain and anger. But we do not defend or support a cry of pain or shout of joy though it may be related to a cause. If our value choices are defensible their defence requires other methods.

The lawyer says: 'I agree that my client was on the premises; I deny that his being there in those circumstances constitutes a *trespass*. This may be confirmed from *Gower v. Flint* where this ruling was given in similar circumstances.' The critic says: 'You agree that Keats's imagery is *rich* and *complex*; his language *original* and *powerful*: that Crabbe, on the contrary, is *frigid* and *conventional* in language; *meagre* in imagery, etc. etc.' The lawyer supports his plea from previous decisions. The critic likewise appeals not to physical or psychological facts about the occurrences of marks on paper, internal pictures, etc., but to previous decisions *evaluating* these and other occurrences. Rich and powerful poetry is good; frigid and meagre versifying is bad. If we stand by our previous decisions it does not follow that we *must* on account of them make a further decision now, but they are certainly relevant. Incorporated into a system of skilful advocacy they may win a favourable verdict. But, on the other hand, we may reject our former decisions. Elaborate imagery, lyrical quality, are dismissed as *barbarous* or *sentimental*; our choice is now for the *plain* and *elegant* statement. Such a complete change in systems of evaluation seems to occur in different ages. The eighteenth century listened to Shakespeare, but gave the palm to Pope. The Victorians saw Georgian houses but chose sham Gothic. So we may present the authoritarian with an attractive picture of a free and democratic society, and if he already values independence, experimentation, mutual trust, he may agree that these values are realized in such a society. But he may call independence, insolence; experimentation, rash meddling; and the picture will fail in its effect.

There are no certainties in the field of values. For there are no true or false beliefs about values, but only better or worse decisions and choices. And to encourage the better decisions we need to employ devices which are artistic rather than scientific. For our aim is not intellectual assent, but practical effects. These are not, of course, absolutely separate, for intellectual assent to a proposition or theory is followed by using it. But values, I think, concern only behaviour. They are not known, but accepted and acted upon.

Intellectuals often complain that political propaganda, for example, is not conducted as if it were scientific argument. But if moral values are not capable of scientific proof it would be irrational to treat them as if they were. The result of a confusion of logical types is to leave the field of non-scientific persuasion and conviction to propagandists of the type of the late Dr Goebbels.

II

JUSTICE AND EQUALITY

GREGORY VLASTOS

I

THE CLOSE connection between justice and equality is manifest in both history and language. The great historic struggles for social justice have centred about some demand for equal rights: the struggle against slavery, political absolutism, economic exploitation, the disfranchisement of the lower and middle classes and the disfranchisement of women, colonialism, racial oppression. On the linguistic side let me mention a curiosity that will lead us into the thick of our problem. When Aristotle in Book V of the *Nicomachean Ethics* comes to grips with distributive justice, almost the first remark he has to make is that 'justice is equality, as all men believe it to be, quite apart from any argument.'[1] And well they might if they are Greeks, for their ordinary word for equality, *to ison* or *isotes* comes closer to being the right word for 'justice' than does the word *dikaiosyne*, which we usually translate as 'justice'.[2] Thus, when a man speaks Greek he will be likely to say 'equality' and *mean* 'justice'. But it so happens that Aristotle, like Plato and others before him, believed firmly that a just distribution is in general an unequal one.[3] And to say this, if 'equal' is your word

Reprinted by permission of Prentice-Hall, Inc., from *Social Justice*, ed. Richard B. Brandt, copyright © 1962 by Prentice-Hall, Inc., pp. 31–72.

[1] 1131a 13.

[2] 'Righteousness', the quality of acting rightly, would be closer to the sense of *dikaiosyne*: at *Nicomachean Ethics* 1129b 27 ff. Aristotle finds it necessary to explain that, though his theme is *dikaoisyne*, he will not be discussing 'virtue entire' or 'complete virtue in its fullest sense'. No one writing an essay on *justice* would find any need to offer this kind of explanation; nor would he be tempted regardless of his theory of justice, to offer (as Plato does at *Rep*. 433ab) 'performing the function(s) for which one's nature is best fitted' as a *definition* of 'justice'.

[3] Plato, *Gorgias* 508a (and E. R. Dodds ad loc., in Plato, *Gorgias* (Oxford, 1959); *Rep*. 558c; *Laws* 744bc, 757a ff. Isocrates, *Areopagiticus* 21–22; To *Nicocles* 14. Aristotle, *Nic. Eth*. 1131a 15 ff., and the commentary by F. Dirlmeier, *Aristoteles, Nikomachische Ethik* (Berlin, 1956), pp. 404–7.

for 'just', you would have to say that an 'equal' distribution is an *unequal* one. A way had been found to hold this acrobatic linguistic posture by saying that in this connection *isotes* meant 'geometrical equality', i.e. proportionality; hence the 'equal' (just, fair) distribution to persons of unequal merit would have to be unequal. This *tour de force* must have provoked many an honest man at the time as much as it has enraged Professor Popper[4] in ours. We may view it more dispassionately as classical testimony to the strength of the tie between equality and justice: even those who meant to break the conceptual link could not, or would not, break the verbal one. The meritarian view of justice paid reluctant homage to the equalitarian one by using the vocabulary of equality to assert the justice of inequality.

But when the equalitarian has drawn from this what comfort he may he still has to face the fact that the expropriation of his word 'equality' could be carried through so reputably and so successfully that its remote inheritance has made it possible for us to speak now in a perfectly matter of fact way of 'equitable inequalities' or 'inequitable equalities'. This kind of success cannot be wholly due to the tactical skill of those who carried out the original manœuvre though one may envy the virtuosity with which Plato disposes of the whole notion of democratic equality in a single sentence (or rather less, a participial clause) when he speaks of democracy as 'distributing an odd sort of equality to equals and unequals'.[5] The democrats themselves would have been intellectually defenceless against that quip. Their faith in democracy had no deep roots in any concept of human equality; the *isonomia* (equality of law) on which they prided themselves was the club-privilege of those who had had the good judgement to pick their ancestors from free Athenian stock of the required purity of blood. But even if we could imagine a precocious humanitarian in or before Plato's time, founding the rights of the citizen on the rights of man, it is not clear that even he would be proof against Plato's criticism. For what Plato would like to know is whether his equalitarian opponent really means to universalize equality: would he, would anyone, wish to say that there are no just inequalities? That there are no rights in respect of which men are unequal?

[4] K. R. Popper, *The Open Society and its Enemies* (London, 1949), pp. 79–80. 'Why did Plato claim that justice meant inequality if, in general usage, it meant equality? To me the only likely reply seems to be that he wanted to make propaganda for his totalitarian state by persuading the people that it was the "just" state'. He adds shortly after: 'His attack on equalitarianism was not an honest attack', p. 80.

[5] *Rep.* 588c; and cf. *Laws* 757a: 'For when equality is given to unequals the result is inequality, unless due measure is applied.'

One would think that this would be among the first questions that would occur to equalitarians, and would have had long since a clear and firm answer. Strange as it may seem, this had not happened. The question has been largely evaded. Let me give an example: Article I of the Declaration of Rights of Man and Citizen (enacted by the Constituent Assembly of the First French Republic in 1791) reads: 'Men are born and remain free and equal in rights. Social distinctions can be based only upon public utility.' Bentham takes the first sentence to mean that men are equal in *all* rights.[6] One would like to think that this was a wilful misunderstanding. For it would be only too obvious to the drafters of the Declaration that those 'social distinctions' of which they go on to speak would entail many inequalities of right. Thus the holder of a unique political office (say, the president of a republic) would not be equal in all rights to all other men or even to one other man: no other man would have equal right to this office, or to as high an office; and many would not have equal right to any political office, even if they had, as they would according to the republican constitution, equal right of eligibility to all offices. But if this is in the writers' minds, why don't they come out and say that men are born and remain equal in some rights, but are either not born or do not remain equal in a great many others? They act as though they were afraid to say the latter on this excessively public occasion, lest their public construe the admission of some unequal rights as out of harmony with the ringing commitment to human rights which is the keynote of the Declaration. What is this? Squeamishness? Confusion? Something of both? Or has it perhaps a sound foundation and, if so, in what? Plato's question is not answered. It is allowed to go by default.

There is here, as so often in the tradition of natural rights, a lack of definiteness which is exasperating to those who look for plain and consecutive thinking in moral philosophy. Coming back to this tradition fresh from the systems of Plato or Hobbes or Hume, with their clean, functional lines, one feels that whether or not the case for inequality has ever been proved, it has at least been made clear from both the aristocratic and the utilitarian side; while the case for equality, housed in the rambling and somewhat run-down mansion of natural rights, has fared so poorly that when one puts a question like the one I just raised, one can't be sure of what the answer is, or even that there

[6] He assumes it entails that, e.g., 'the rights of the heir of the most indigent family (are) equal to the rights of the heir of the most wealthy', the rights of the apprentice equal to those of his master, those of the madman and the idiot equal to those of the sane, and so forth. 'A Critical Examination of the Declaration of Rights', in *Anarchical Fallacies*. In *Works* (London, 1843), ed. John Bowring, Vol. II, pp. 489 ff., at p. 498.

is supposed to be one. And much the same is true of several other questions that remain after one has completely cut out one earlier source of confusion: the mythological prehistory of a supposed state of nature. Taking 'natural rights' to mean simply *human* rights—that is to say, rights which are human not in the trivial sense that those who have them are men, but in the challenging sense that in order to have them they need only be men—one would still like to know:

(1) What is the range of these rights? The French Declaration states: 'these rights are liberty, property, security, and resistance to oppression.' The imprudent beginning—'these rights are' instead of Jefferson's more cautious, 'among these rights are'—makes it look as though the four natural rights named here are meant to be all the rights there are. If so, what happened to the pursuit of happiness? Is that the same as liberty? As for property, this was not a natural right before Locke,[7] and not always after him, for example, not for Jefferson.[8] And what of welfare rights? They are not mentioned in the French document, nor are they implied by 'security'.

(2) Can the doctrine of natural rights find a place for each of the following well-known maxims of distributive justice:

1. To each according to his *need*.
2. To each according to his *worth*.
3. To each according to his *merit*.
4. To each according to his *work*.[9]

And we might add a fifth which does not seem to have worked its way to the same level of adage-like respectability, but has as good a claim as some of the others:

5. To each according to the *agreement* he has made.

By making judicious selections from this list one can 'justicize'[10] extreme inequalities of distribution. It is thus that Plato concludes that the man

[7] Locke's argument that property is a natural right is a momentous innovation, 'a landmark in the history of thought'. O. Giercke, *Natural Law and the Theory of Society 1500 to 1800* (Cambridge, 1950), p. 103. But this is not to say that, if one looks hard enough, one will not find anticipation of Locke's theory. See E. S. Corwin, *The "Higher Law" Background of American Constitutional Law*, Great Seal Books ed. (Ithaca, 1955), p. 61, n. 60; J. W. Gough, *Locke's Political Philosophy* (New York, 1950, p. 80). (For some of these references, and for other useful suggestions, I am indebted to Dr Hugo Bedau).

[8] See, e.g. Ursula M. von Eckardt, *The Pursuit of Happiness in the Democratic Creed* (New York, 1959), p. 103–8.

[9] For a similar enumeration see Charles Perelman, *De la Justice* (Brussels, 1945).

[10] Cf. W. Frankena, 'The Concept of Social Justice' in *Social Justice*, ed. R. Brandt (Englewood Cliffs, NJ, 1962), p. 5.

who can no longer work has lost his right to live,[11] and Bentham that no just limits can be set to the terms on which labour can be bought, used, and used up.[12] Hobbes, most frugal of moral philosophers, operates with just the last of these maxims;[13] making the keeping of covenants the defining element of justice, he decimates civil liberties *more geometrico*.[14] These premisses were not, of course, the only ones from which such morally dismal results were reached by these clear-headed and upright men; but they were the controlling ones. If merit or work or agreement, or any combination of the three, are made the final principles of distributive justice, it will not be hard to find plausible collateral premisses from which to get such results. What then should a natural-rights philosopher do with these maxims? Must he regard them as fifth-columnists? Or can he keep them as members of his working team, useful, if subordinate, principles of his equalitarian justice? Can this be done without making concessions to inequality which will divide his allegiance to equality?

(3) Finally, are natural rights 'absolute', i.e. are their claims unexceptionable? If I have a natural right to a given benefit does it follow that I ought to be granted that benefit in all possible circumstances no matter how my other rights or those of others might be affected? Is this the meaning of the well-known statements that natural rights are 'inalienable' and 'imprescriptible'?

I believe that all these questions admit of reasonable answers which, when worked out fully, would amount to a revised theory of natural rights or, what is the same thing, a theory of human rights: I shall use the two expressions interchangeably. Progress has been made in this direction in recent years in a number of important essays.[15] I shall

[11] *Rep.* 406e–407a.

[12] 'When the question of slavery is not considered there is little to say respecting the conditions of master and its correlative conditions, constituted by the different kinds of servants. All these conditions are the effects of contract; these contracts the parties interested may arrange to suit themselves.' *Principles of the Civil Code*. In *Works*, ed. Bowring, Vol. 1, p. 341.

[13] The fifth: 'the definition of *Injustice* is no other than *the not performance of covenant*. And whatsoever is not unjust is just.' *Leviathan*, Pt. I, ch. 15.

[14] That 'nothing the sovereign representative can do to a subject, on what pretense soever, can properly be called injustice or injury' (op. cit., Pt. II, ch. 21) is presented as a logical consequence of (a) every subject is the 'author' of each act of his sovereign and (b) no man can be the author of injustice or injury to himself. (a) follows from the definitions of 'sovereign' and 'subject', Pt. I, ch. 18.

[15] The ones to which I am most indebted are: R. B. Perry, *Puritanism and Democracy* (New York, 1944), pp. 446 ff.; Margaret Macdonald, 'Natural Rights', *Proc. Aristotelian Society*, 1947–48 (reprinted here); A. I. Melden and W. K. Frankena, 'Human Rights', in *Science, Language and Human Rights* (Philadelphia,

borrow freely results reached by various contributors to this work, though without taking time to make explicit acknowledgements or register specific disagreements.

Let me begin with the answer to the third of the questions I raised. Are human rights absolute? All of these writers would say, 'No.' I am convinced that in this they are right,[16] and am even prepared to add that neither is there anything explicitly contrary to this in that branch of the classical theory which is of greatest interest to us today: in Locke, for example.[17] Locke has indeed been understood to mean that natural rights are absolute.[18] But nowhere does Locke *say* this. Contrariwise he believes many things which imply the opposite. For example, he would certainly approve of imprisonment as a punishment for crime; and we hear him recommending that beggars be detained in houses of correction or impressed in the navy.[19] Such constraints he would have to reckon justified exceptions to that freedom of movement which all persons claim in virtue of their natural right to liberty. So too he would have to think of the death penalty for convicted criminals, or of a military order which would bring death to many of those obeying it, as justified exceptions to some men's natural right to life. Even the right to property—indeed, that special form of it which is upheld more zealously than any other right in the *Second Treatise*, one's right not to be deprived of property without consent[20]—could not be unconditional; Locke would have to concede that it should be overruled, e.g. in a famine when stores of hoarded food are requisitioned by public authority. We would, therefore, improve the consistency of Locke's

1952); the symposium on 'Are There Natural Rights?' by H. L. A. Hart, S. M. Brown, and Frankena in *Philosophical Review*, 64 (1955); R. Wollheim, 'Equality and Equal Rights', *Proc. Aristotelian Society*, 1955–56 (reprinted in F. A. Olafson, *Justice and Social Policy* (Englewood Cliffs, NJ; 1961)); R. Brandt, *Ethical Theory* (Englewood Cliffs, NJ; 1959) ch. 17; A. I. Melden, *Rights and Right Conduct* (Oxford, 1959); and cf. H. L. A. Hart, *The Concept of Law* (New York and Oxford, 1961), ch. IX,'Laws and Morals'.

[16] For this I am especially indebted to discussion with Richard Brandt.

[17] Nor in the Thomist version as interpreted by J. Maritain. See his distinction between the 'possession' and the 'exercise' of a natural right (unexceptionable and exceptionable, respectively), *Man and the State* (Chicago, 1951), pp. 101–3.

[18] e.g., E. F. Carritt, *Ethical and Political Thinking* (Oxford, 1947), pp. 154 ff. Brandt, op. cit., p. 442. No text is cited from Locke to support this very widespread interpretation. Such statements as 'the obligations of the law of nature cease not in society', *Second Treatise of Government*, 135, are too general to determine the point at issue here.

[19] See his proposals for the reform of the Poor Law submitted to the Board of Trade in 1697; H. R. Fox-Bourne, *Life of Locke* (London, 1876), Vol. 2, pp. 379–81.

[20] 138, 139. Cf. other references in J. W. Gough, op. cit., p. 85, n.1.

theory if we understood him to mean that natural rights are subject to justified exceptions.[21] In any case, I shall adhere to his view here and, borrowing from current usage, shall speak of human rights as 'prima-facie' rights[22] to mean that the claims of any of them may be overruled in special circumstances.[23] Can one say this without giving away the radical difference with the traditional doctrine fixed between natural rights and all others? To this the answer would be that, though in this respect all rights are alike, the vital difference remains untouched: one need only be a man to have prima-facie rights to life, liberty, welfare, and the like; but to be a man is not all one needs to have a prima-facie right to the house he happens to own or the job he happens to hold. As for the 'inalienability' and the 'imprescriptibility' of natural rights, we may understand them with this proviso to mean exactly what they say: that no man can alienate (i.e. sign away, transfer by contract)[24] a prima-facie natural right, his own or anyone else's; and that no people can lose prima-facie natural rights by prescription, e.g. in virtue of the time-hallowed possession of despotic power over them by a royal dynasty.[25]

Does this entirely allay our misgivings? It does not, and it should

[21] Admitting that to do this is to add something of substance to his own explicit doctrine. He himself never refers to cases such as those I have mentioned as exceptions to natural rights.

[22] See Frankena, 'Human Rights' (n. 15 above), p. 127, and 'Are There Natural Rights?' pp. 228 ff.; Brandt, op. cit., pp. 41 ff. For some objections to this usage see Sir David Ross, *The Right and the Good* (Oxford, 1939), p. 20; for strong opposition, A. I. Melden, *Rights and Right Conduct*, pp. 18 ff. I am not entirely happy with this usage, but neither can I propose a better. Part of the objection is met by the clarification in the following note.

[23] Given 'right' = 'justified claim' (*Oxford English Dictionary*), prima facie qualifies "justified." A prima-facie right is one whose claim has *prima-facie* justification, i.e. is justified, unless there are stronger counter-claims in the particular situation in which it is made, the burden of proof resting always on the counter-claims. 'Claim' here has a much broader sense than 'asserted claim'; it is related to 'claiming' in much the same way as 'proposition' to 'propounding'; it is something which may be claimed, as a proposition is something which may be propounded. To say that a right is a justified claim is to say that it is something which could be claimed with justification, i.e. a claim which others have the obligation to grant if (but not, only if) it is asserted.

[24] The normal sense of 'alienate' when applied to rights in legal, or quasi-legal, contexts. To defend the inalienability (though without using this word) of one's right to be free from subjection to the arbitrary will of another, Locke thinks it sufficient to argue that one cannot forfeit this right 'by compact or his own consent', *Second Treatise*, 23, and cannot 'transfer to another' (135) this right by a voluntary act.

[25] For the relevant sense of 'prescription', see the *Shorter Oxford English Dictionary*, s.v., II (b): 'uninterrupted use or possession from time immemorial, or for a period fixed by law as giving a title or right; hence title or right acquired by such use or possession'. On prescription as the foundation of rights of

not. To say that a natural right is a prima-facie right is to say that there are cases in which it is perfectly just to disallow its claim; and unless we have definite assurance as to the limits within which this may occur, we have no way of telling whether we are better off with this prima-facie right than we would be without it. If *anything* may count as an allowable exception, then what does the right give us that we would otherwise lack? If only some things are to count, we need to know what sort of things these are to be, in order to know what, if anything, our right is worth. Richard Brandt does give us some such information. He implies that only for *moral* reasons will the exceptions be allowed.[26] This tells us something, but not enough. How can we know what moral reasons will not be forthcoming to nullify the efficacy of the natural right? From William Frankena's remarks we get something stronger: to 'justicize' an exception we may adduce only considerations of justice ('just-making' ones).[27] This is better, but still not enough. What we ought to know is whether the considerations of justice which allow us to make exceptions to a natural right in special circumstances are the same considerations which require us to uphold it in general. For if we are to have two sets of 'just-making' reasons, one set requiring us to uphold these rights, the other permitting us to overrule them, we shall be in a state of moral uncertainty and anxiety about our natural rights, and our condition will not be improved if we label it with Professor Gallie 'moral polyarchy'.[28] We must find *reasons for our natural rights which will be the only moral reasons for just exceptions* to them in special circumstances.

This may look like a predictably unfulfillable demand, for it seems self-contradictory. But it is certainly not the latter. There is nothing self-contradictory about saying that reasons requiring a general pattern of action may permit, or even require, a departure from it in special circumstances. Thus my reasons for eating three meals a day are say, pleasure and physical need; for these same reasons I might eat on special occasions four or five meals in a single day, or two or one. The

government and property see, e.g. Edmund Burke: 'Our constitution is a prescriptive constitution; it is a constitution whose sole authority is that it has existed time out of mind. . . . Prescription is the most solid of all titles, not only to property, but, which is to secure that property, to government.' 'Reform of Representation in the House of Commons', (1782), *Works*, Vol. 6.

[26] Op. cit., pp. 410, 446.

[27] Op. cit., pp. 10 ff.

[28] W. B. Gallie, 'Liberal Morality and Socialist Morality', in Laslett, *Philosophy, Politics and Society* (Oxford, 1956), pp. 116 ff. Each of us, in his view, is 'internally divided, pulled this way and that on different issues by the claims and counter-claims of two conflicting moralities' (p. 121), each of which has its 'own autonomous, i.e. not mutually corrigible, aims and standards' (p. 132).

analogy is not perfect, but it does give a rough idea of the lines along which we may concede justified exceptions to natural rights without jeopardizing the fundamental place they must hold in our scheme of justice, if we are to keep them there at all. And since all of them are equal rights (i.e. rights to equal treatment), a parallel observation may be made about the problem with which we started: an equalitarian concept of justice may admit just inequalities without inconsistency if, and only if, it provides grounds for equal human rights *which are also grounds for unequal rights of other sorts*. Such grounds, if we could find them, should carry right through all five of the maxims of distributive justice I listed above, showing how these maxims can be tied together as principles of justice and of the same concept of justice. I propose to identify these grounds in Section II, and then show, in Section IV, how on these grounds, supplemented by certain factual considerations, inequalities of merit may be recognized by the theory of equalitarian justice which I will expound in Section III.

II

Let me begin with the first on my list of maxims of distributive justice: 'To each according to his need.' Since needs are often unequal, this looks like a precept of unequal distribution. But this is wrong. It is in fact *the most perfect form of equal distribution*. To explain this let me take one of the best established rights in the natural law tradition: the right to the security of life and person. Believing that this is an equal right, what do we feel this means in cases of special need?

Suppose, for instance, New Yorker *X* gets a note from Murder, Inc., that looks like business. To allocate several policemen and plainclothesmen to guard him over the next few weeks at a cost a hundred times greater than the per capita cost of security services to other citizens during the same period, is surely *not* to make an exception to the equal distribution required by the equal right of all citizens to the security of their life and person; it is not done on the assumption that *X* has a greater right to security or a right to greater security. If the visitor from Mars drew this conclusion from the behaviour of the police, he would be told that he was just mistaken. The greater allocation of community resources in *X*'s favour, we would have to explain, is made precisely *because* *X*'s security rights are equal to those of other people in New York. This means that *X* is entitled to the same level of police-made security as is maintained for other New Yorkers. Hence in these special circumstances, where his security level would drop to zero without extra support, he should be given this to bring his security level nearer the normal. I say 'nearer', not 'up to' the normal, because I am talking of New York as of 1961. If I were thinking of New York with an ideal municipal government, ideally supplied with police resources, I *would* say 'up to the normal', because that is what equality of right would ideally mean. But as things are, perhaps the best than can be done for X without disrupting the general level of security maintained for all the other New Yorkers is to decrease his chances of being bumped off in a given week to, say one to ten thousand, while those of ordinary citizens, with ordinary protection are, say, one to ten million—no small difference.[29] Now if New York were more affluent, it would be able to buy more equality[30] of security for its citizens (as well as more security): by getting more, and perhaps also better paid, policemen, it would be able to close the gap between security maintained for people in ordinary circumstances and that supplied in cases of special need, like that of X in his present jam. Here we stumble on something of considerable interest: that approximation to the goal of completely equal security benefits for all citizens is a function of two variables: first, and quite obviously, of the pattern of distribution of the resources; second, and less obviously, of their size. If the distributable resources are so meagre that they are all used up to maintain a general level barely sufficient for ordinary needs, their reallocation to meet exceptional need will look too much like robbing Peter to pay Paul. In such conditions there is likely to be little, if any, provision for extremity of need and, what is more, the failure to meet the extremity will not be felt as a social injustice but as a calamity of fate. And since humanity has lived most of its life under conditions of general indigence, we can understand why it has been so slow to connect provision for special need with the notion of justice, and has so often made it a matter of charity; and why 'to each according to his need' did not become popularized as a precept of justice until the first giant increase in the productive resources, and then only by men like Blanc and Marx, who projected an image of a super-affluent, machine-run society on the grid of an austerely equalitarian conception of justice.[31]

[29] These figures, needless to say, are 'pulled out of a hat'.

[30] This point was first suggested to me by Professor Kenneth Boulding's striking remark that 'only a rich society can afford to be equalitarian'. *The Economics of Peace* (Englewood Cliffs, NJ, 1945), p. 111. The more guarded form in which I am stating the point will protect it against apparent counter-examples to Boulding's remark, e.g. the astonishing equalitarianism that was still practiced by the Eskimos of the Coronation Gulf and the Mackenzie River early in this century (see V. Stefansson's essay in *Freedom*, ed. Ruth N. Ashem, (New York, 1940)).

[31] The well-known maxim, 'from each according to his ability, to each according to his need' (Karl Marx, *Critique of the Gotha Programme*, 1875), echoes, without acknowledgement, a remark in the 9th ed. of Louis Blanc's *L'Organization du*

So we can see why distribution according to personal need, far from conflicting with the equality of distribution required by a human right, is so linked with its very meaning that under ideal conditions equality of right would coincide with distribution according to personal need. Our visitor misunderstood the sudden mobilization of New York policemen in favour of Mr *X*, because he failed to understand that it is benefits to persons, not allocation of resources as such, that are meant to be made equal; for then he would have seen at once that unequal distribution of resources would be required to equalize benefits in cases of unequal need. But if he saw this he might then ask, 'But why do you want this sort of equality?' My answer would have to be: because the human worth of all persons is equal, however unequal may be their merit. To the explanation of this proposition I shall devote the balance of this Section.

By 'merit' I shall refer throughout this essay to all the kinds of valuable qualities or performances in respect of which persons may be graded.[32] The concept will not be restricted to moral actions or dispositions.[33] Thus wit, grace of manner, and technical skill count as meritorious qualities fully as much as sincerity, generosity, or courage. Any valuable human characteristic, or cluster of characteristics, will qualify, provided only it is 'acquired', i.e. represents what its possessor has himself made of his natural endowments and environmental opportunities. Given the immense variety of individual differences, it will be commonly the case that of any two persons either may excel the other in respect of different kinds or sub-kinds of merit. Thus if *A* and *B* are both clever and brave men, *A* may be much the cleverer as a business man, *B* as a literary critic, and *A* may excel in physical, *B* in moral, courage. It should be clear from just this that to speak of 'a person's merit' will be strictly senseless except in so far as this is an elliptical way of referring to that person's merits, i.e. to those specifiable qualities or activities in which he rates well. So if there is a value attaching to the person himself as an integral and unique individual, *this* value will not fall under merit or be reducible to it. For it is of the

travail (Paris, 1850) that 'true equality is that which apportions work to ability and recompense to needs' (cited in D. O. Wagner, *Social Reformers* (New York, 1946), pp. 248).

[32] This is only one of the senses recognized by the dictionary (*The Shorter Oxford English Dictionary*, s.v., 4 and 6): 'Excellence', 'An Excellence', the latter being illustrated by "Would you ask for his merits? Alas! he has none" (from Goldsmith). In the other senses listed by the dictionary the word either *means* 'desert' or at least includes this in its meaning. On the present use of 'merit' the connection with 'desert' is synthetic.

[33] As is done by some philosophical moralists, e.g. Sir David Ross, op. cit., pp. 135 ff., where 'merit' and (moral) 'virtue' are coextensive.

essence of merit, as here defined, to be a grading concept; and there is no way of grading individuals as such. We can only grade them with respect to their qualities, hence only by abstracting from their individuality. If *A* is valued for some meritorious quality, *m*, his individuality does not enter into the valuation. As an individual he is then dispensable; his place could be taken without loss of value by any other individual with as good an *m*-rating. Nor would matters change by multiplying and diversifying the meritorious qualities with which *A* is endowed. No matter how enviable a package of well-rounded excellence *A* may represent, it would still follow that, if he is valued only for his merit, he is not being valued as an individual. To be sure individuals *may* be valued only for their merits. This happens all too commonly. *A* might be valued in just this way by *P*, the president of his company, for whom *A*, highly successful vice-president in charge of sales, amusing dinner-guest, and fine asset to the golf club, is simply high-grade equipment in various complexes of social machinery which *P* controls or patronizes. On the other hand, it is possible that, much as *P* prizes this conjunct of qualities (*M*), he values *A* also as an individual. *A* may be his son, and he may be genuinely fond of him. If so, his affection will be for *A*, not for his *M*-qualities. The latter *P* approves, admires, takes pride in, and the like. But his affection and good will are for *A*, and *not only because*, or *in so far as*, *A* has the *M*-qualities. For *P* may be equally fond of another son who rates well below *A* in *P*'s scoring system. Moreover, *P*'s affection for *A*, as distinct from his approval or admiration of him, need not fluctuate with the ups and downs in *A*'s achievements. Perhaps *A* had some bad years after graduating from college, and it looked then as though his brilliant gifts would be wasted. It does not follow that *P*'s love for *A* then lapsed or even ebbed. Constancy of affection in the face of variations of merit is one of the surest tests of whether or not a parent does love a child. If he feels fond of it only when it performs well, and turns coldly indifferent or hostile when its achievements slump, then his feeling for the child can scarcely be called *love*. There are many relations in which one's liking or esteem for a person are strictly conditional on his measuring up to certain standards. But convincing evidence that the relation is of this type is no evidence that the relation is one of parental love or any other kind of love. It does nothing to show that one has this feeling, or any feeling, for an *individual*, rather than for a place-holder of qualities one likes to see instantiated by somebody or other close about one.

Now if this concept of value attaching to a person's individual existence, over and above his merit—'individual worth',[34] let me call it

[34] That this is *intrinsic* worth goes without saying. But I do not put this term

—were applicable *only* in relations of personal love, it would be irrelevant for the analysis of justice. To serve our purpose its range of application must be coextensive with that of justice. It must hold in all human relations, including (or rather, especially in) the most impersonal of all, those to total strangers, fellow citizens or fellow men. I must show that the concept of individual worth does meet this condition.

Consider its role in our political community, taking the prescriptions of our laws for the treatment of persons as the index to our valuations. For merit (among other reasons) persons may be appointed or elected to public office or given employment by state agencies. For demerit they may lose licences, jobs, offices; they may be fined, gaoled, or even put to death. But in a large variety of law-regulated actions directed to individuals, either by private persons or by organs of the state, the question of merit and demerit does not arise. The 'equal protection of the laws' is due to persons not to meritorious ones, or to them in some degree above others.[35] So too for the right to vote. One does not have it for being intelligent and public-spirited, or lose it for being lazy, ignorant, or viciously selfish. One is entitled to exercise it as long as, having registered, one manages to keep out of jail. This kind of arrangement would look like whimsy or worse, like sheer immoralism, if the only values recognized in our political community were those of merit. For obviously there is nothing compulsory about our political system; we could certainly devise, if we so wished, workable alternatives which would condition fundamental rights on certain kinds of merit. For example, we might have three categories of citizenship. The top one might be for those who meet hgh educational qualifications and give definite evidence of responsible civic interest, e.g. by active participation in political functions, tenure of public office, record of leadership in civic organizations and support to them, and the like. People in this *A*-category might have multiple votes in all elections and exclusive eligibility for the more important political offices; they might also be entitled to a higher level of protection by the police and to a variety of other privileges and immunities. At the other end there would be a *C*-category, disfranchised and legally underprivileged, for those who do not meet some lower educational test or have had a record of law-infraction

into my label, since I want to distinguish this kind of value as sharply as possible from that of merit, and I include under 'merit' not only extrinsically, but also intrinsically, valuable qualities.

[35] A modicum of merit by way of self-help and law-obedience is generally presupposed. But it would be a mistake to think of the protection of the laws as a reward for good behaviour. Thus many legal protections are due as much to those who will not look out for themselves as to those who do, and to law-breakers as much as to law-observers.

or have been on the relief rolls for over three months. In between would be the *B*s with ordinary suffrage and intermediate legal status.

This '*M*-system' would be more complicated and cumbersome than ours. But something like it could certainly be made to work if we were enamoured of its peculiar scheme of values. Putting aside the question of efficiency, it gives us a picture of a community whose political valuations, conceived entirely in terms of merit, would never be grounded on individual worth, so that this notion would there be politically useless.[36] For us, on the other hand, it is indispensable.[37] We have to appeal to it when we try to make sense of the fact that our legal system accords to all citizens an identical status, carrying with it rights such as the *M*-system reserves to the *B*s or the *A*s, and some of which (like suffrage or freedom of speech) have been denied even to the nobility in some caste-systems of the past. This last comparison is worth pressing: it brings out the illuminating fact that in one fundamental respect our society is much more like a caste society (with a *unique* caste) than like the *M*-system. The latter has no place for a rank of dignity which descends on an individual by the purely existential circumstance (the 'accident') of birth and remains his unalterably for life. To reproduce this feature of our system we would have to look not only to caste-societies, but to extremely rigid ones, since most of them make some provision for elevation in rank for rare merit or degradation for extreme demerit. In our legal system no such thing can happen: even a criminal may not be sentenced to second-class citizenship.[38] And the fact that first-class citizenship, having been made common, is no longer a mark of distinction does not trivialize the privileges it entails. It is the simple truth, not declamation, to speak of it, as I have done, as a 'rank of dignity' in some ways comparable to that enjoyed by hereditary nobilities of the past. To see this one need only think of the position of groups in our society who have been cheated out of this status by the subversion of their constitutional rights. The difference in social position between Negroes and whites described in Dollard's classic[39] is not smaller than that between, say, bourgeoisie and aristocracy in the *ancien régime* of France. It might well be greater.

[36] Though it might have uses in the family or other relations.

[37] Even where a purely pragmatic justification is offered for democracy (e.g. Pendleton Herring, *Politics of Democracy* (New York, 1940) equality of worth must still be acknowledged, if only as a popular 'myth' or 'dogma'.

[38] No one, I trust, will confuse second-class citizenship with extreme punishments, such as the death penalty or a life sentence, or, for that matter, with *any* legal punishment in a democratic society. Second-class citizens are those deprived of rights without any presumption of legal guilt.

[39] John Dollard, *Castle and Class in a Southern Town* (New Haven, 1937).

Consider finally the role of the same value in the moral community. Here differences of merit are so conspicuous and pervasive that we might even be tempted to define the moral response to a person in terms of moral approval or disapproval of his acts or disposition, i.e. in terms of the response to his moral merit. But there are many kinds of moral response for which a person's merit is as irrelevant as is that of New Yorker *X* when he appeals to the police for help. If I see someone in danger of drowning I will not need to satisfy myself about his moral character before going to his aid. I owe assistance to any man in such circumstances, not merely to good men. Nor is it only in rare and exceptional cases, as this example might suggest, that my obligations to others are independent of their moral merit. To be sincere, reliable, fair, kind, tolerant, unintrusive, modest in my relations with my fellows is not due them because they have made brilliant or even passing moral grades, but simply because they happen to be fellow members of the moral community. It is not necessary to add, 'members in good standing'. The moral community is not a club from which members may be dropped for delinquency. Our morality does not provide for moral outcasts or half-castes. It does provide for punishment. But this takes place *within* the moral community and under its rules. It is for this reason that, for example, one has no right to be cruel to a cruel person. His offence against the moral law has not put him outside the law. He is still protected by its prohibition of cruelty—as much so as are kind persons. The pain inflicted on him as punishment for his offence does not close out the reserve of goodwill on the part of all others which is his birthright as a human being; it is a limited withdrawal from it. Capital punishment, if we believe in it, is no exception. The fact that a man has been condemned to death does not license his gaolers to beat him or virtuous citizens to lynch him.

Here, then, as in the single-status political community, we acknowledge personal rights which are not proportioned to merit and could not be justified by merit. Their only justification could be the value which persons have simply because they are persons: their 'intrinsic value as individual human beings', as Frankena calls it; the 'infinite value' or the 'sacredness' of their individuality, as others have called it. I shall speak of it as 'individual human worth'; or 'human worth', for short. What these expressions stand for is also expressed by saying that men are 'ends in themselves'. This latter concept is Kant's. Some of the kinks in his formulation of it[40] can be straightened out by explaining it as follows: everything other than a person can only have

[40] See, e.g., H. Sidgwick, *Methods of Ethics* (London, 1874), p. 363. For a parallel objection see the next note. Still another is that Kant, using the notion of

value *for* a person. This applies not only to physical objects, natural or man-made, which have only instrumental value, but also to those products of the human spirit which have also intrinsic, no less than extrinsic value: an epic poem, a scientific theory, a legal system, a moral disposition. Even such things as these will have value only because they can be (*a*) experienced or felt to be valuable by human beings and (*b*) chosen by them for competing alternatives. Thus of everything without exception it will be true to say: if x is valuable and is not a person, then x will have value for some individual other than itself. Hence even a musical composition or a courageous deed, valued for their own sake, as 'ends' not as means to anything else, will still fall into an entirely different category from that of the *valuers*, who do not need to be valued as 'ends' by someone else[41] in order to have value. In just this sense persons, and only persons, are 'ends in themselves'.

The two factors in terms of which I have described the value of the valuer—the capacities answering to (*a*) and (*b*) above—may not be exhaustive. But their conjunction offers a translation of 'individual human worth' whose usefulness for working purposes will speak for itself. To (*a*) I might refer as 'happiness', if I could use this term as Plato and Aristotle used *eudaimonia*, i.e. without the exclusively hedonistic connotations which have since been clamped on it. It will be less misleading to use 'well-being' or 'welfare' for what I intend here; that is, the enjoyment of value in all the forms in which it can be experienced by human beings. To (*b*) I shall refer as 'freedom' bringing under this term not only conscious choices and deliberate decisions but also those subtler modulations and more spontaneous expressions of individual preference which could scarcely be called 'choices' or 'decisions' without some forcing of language. So understood, a person's well-being and freedom are aspects of his individual existence as unique and unrepeatable as is that existence itself: if A and B are listening to the same symphony with similar tastes and dispositions, we may speak

intrinsic worth (*Würde* in contrast to *Preis*) to define *end in itself*, and hence as its sufficient condition, tends to conflate the value of persons as ends in themselves with that of their moral merit. Thus, though he says that 'Respect [the attitude due to a being which is an end in itself] always applies to persons only' (*Critique of Practical Reason*, trans. L. W. Beck (New York, 1956), p. 79) he illustrates by respect for a person's 'righteousness' (l.c.) and remarks: 'Respect is a tribute we cannot refuse to pay to merit . . .' (p. 80).

[41] Though, of course, they may be (if they are loved or respected as persons). In that case it will not be, strictly, the persons, but their welfare or freedom, which will be the 'end' of those who so love or respect them: since only that which can be realized by action can be an end, to speak of another *person* as my end is bad logical grammar.

of their enjoying the 'same' good, or having the 'same' enjoyment, and say that each has made the 'same' choice for this way of spending his time and money. But here 'same' will mean no more than 'very similar'; the two enjoyments and choices, occurring in the consciousness of *A* and *B* respectively, are absolutely unique. So in translating '*A*'s human worth' into 'the worth of *A*'s well-being and freedom' we are certainly meeting the condition that the former expression is to stand for whatever it is about *A* which, unlike his merit, has *individual* worth.

We are also meeting another condition: that the equality of human worth be justification, or ground, of equal human rights. I can best bring this out by reverting to the visitor from Mars who had asked a little earlier why we want equalization of security benefits. Let us conjure up circumstances in which his question would spring, not from idle curiosity, but from a strong conviction that this, or any other, right entailing such undiscriminating equality of benefits, would be entirely *un*reasonable. Suppose then that he hails from a strict meritarian community, which maintains the *M*-system in its political life and analogous patterns in other associations. And to make things simpler, let us also suppose that he is shown nothing in New York or elsewhere that is out of line with our formal professions of equality, so that he imagines us purer, more strenuous, equalitarians than we happen to be. The pattern of valuation he ascribes to us then seems to him fantastically topsy-turvey. He can hardly bring himself to believe that rational human beings should want equal personal rights, legal and moral, for their 'riff-raff' and their élites. Yet neither can he explain away our conduct as pure automatism, a mere fugue of social habit. 'These people, or some of them', he will be saying to himself, 'must have some reasons for this incredible code. What could these be?' If we volunteered an answer couched in terms of human worth, he might find it hard to understand us. Such an answer, unglossed, would convey to him no more than that we recognize, something which is highly and equally valuable in all persons, but has nothing to do with their merit, and constitutes the ground of their equal rights. But this might start him hunting—snark-hunting—for some special quality named by 'human worth' as honesty is named by 'honesty' and kindness by 'kindness,' wondering all the while how it could have happened that he and all his tribe have had no inkling of it, if all of them have always had it.[42]

But now suppose that we avail ourselves of the aforesaid translation. We could then tell him: 'To understand our code you should take into account how very different from yours is our own estimate of the relative worth of the welfare and freedom of different individuals. We agree

[42] Cf. Melden, *Rights and Right Conduct*, p. 80.

with you that not all persons are capable of experiencing the same values. But there is a wide variety of cases in which persons are capable of this. Thus, to take a perfectly clear case, no matter how *A* and *B* might differ in taste and style of life, they would both crave relief from acute physical pain. In that case we would put the same value on giving this to either of them, regardless of the fact that *A* might be a talented, brilliantly successful person, *B* 'a mere nobody'. On this we would disagree sharply. You would weigh the welfare of members of the élite more highly than that of 'riff-raff' as you call them. We would not. If *A* were a statesman, and giving him relief from pain enabled him to conclude an agreement that would benefit millions, while *B* an unskilled labourer, was himself the sole beneficiary of the like relief, we would, of course, agree that the *instrumental* value of the two experiences would be vastly different—but not their *intrinsic* value. In all cases where human beings are capable of enjoying the same goods, we feel that the intrinsic value of their enjoyment is the same. In just this sense we hold that (1) *one man's well-being is as valuable as any other's*. And there is a parallel difference in our feeling for freedom. You value it only when exercised by good persons for good ends. We put no such strings on its value. We feel that choosing for oneself what one will do, believe, approve, say, see, read, worship, has its own intrinsic value, the same for all persons, and quite independently of the value of the things they happen to choose. Naturally, we hope that all of them will make the best possible use of their freedom of choice. But we value their exercise of that freedom, regardless of the outcome; and we value it equally for all. For us (2) *one man's freedom is as valuable as any other's*.'

This sort of explanation, I submit, would put him in a position to resolve his dilemma. For just suppose that, taking this homily at face value, he came to think of us as believing (1) and (2).[43] No matter how unreasonable he might think of us he would feel it entirely reasonable that, since we do believe in equal *value* of human well-being and freedom, we should also believe in the prima-facie equality of men's *right* to well-being and to freedom. He would see the former as a good reason for the latter; or, more formally, he could think of (1) and (2) respectively as the crucial premisses in justification arguments whose respective conclusions would be: (3) One man's (prima-facie) right to well-being is equal to that of any other, and (4) One man's (prima-facie) right to freedom is equal to that of any other. Then, given (4), he could see how this would serve as the basis for a great variety of

[43] I am bypassing the factual question of the extent to which (1) and (2) are generally believed.

rights to specific kinds of freedom: freedom of movement, of association, of suffrage, of speech, of thought, of worship, of choice of employment, and the like. For each of these can be regarded as simply a specification of the general right to freedom, and would thus be covered by the justification of the latter. Moreover, given (3), he could see in it the basis for various welfare-rights, such as the right to education, medical care, work under decent conditions, relief in periods of unemployment, leisure, housing, etc.[44] Thus to give him (1) and (2) as justification for (3) and (4) would be to give him a basis for every one of the rights which are mentioned in the most complete of currently authoritative declarations of human rights, that passed by the Assembly of the United Nations in 1948. Hence to tell him that we believe in the equal worth of individual freedom and happiness would be to answer, in terms he can understand, his question, 'What is your reason for your equalitarian code?'[45]

Nowhere in this defence of the translation of 'equal human worth' into 'equal worth of human well-being and freedom' have I claimed that the former can be *reduced* to the latter. I offered individual well-being

[44] I am well aware of the incompleteness of this highly schematic account. It does not pretend to give the full argument for the justification of (3) and (4) (and see next note) or of their 'specifications'. Among other omissions, it fails to make allowance for the fact that the complex interrelations of these various rights would affect the justification of each.

[45] On p. 19 Frankena writes as though his own answer to the same question would be, 'because all men are similarly capable of enjoying a good life'; this, he says, is what 'justifies the *prima facie* requirement that they be treated as equals'. But that *A* and *B* are similarly capable of enjoying respectively good lives G(*A*) and G(*B*) is not a compelling reason for saying that *A* and *B* have equal right respectively to G(*A*) and G(*B*). The Brahmin who held (Sir Henry Maine, *Early History of Institutions* (New York, 1875), p. 399) that 'a Brahmin was entitled to 20 times as much happiness as anyone else' need not have held that the Brahmin's *capacity* for happiness (or, for 'enjoying a good life') differs in the same ratio from that of others. All he would have to deny would be the equal *value* of the happiness of Brahmins and of others. It is some such premisses as this that Frankena must affirm to bring off his justiciation argument. I might add that I am not objecting to listing capacity among the premisses. The only reason I did not is that I was only citing the 'crucial' premiss, the one that would be normally decisive for the acceptance or rejection of the justificandum. A reference to capacity would also be necessary, and I would follow Frankena in conceding that 'men may well be different in such a way that the best life of which one is capable simply is not as good as that of which another is capable' (op. cit., p. 20), adding a like concession in the case of freedom. *A*'s and *B*'s prima-facie equal rights to well-being and to freedom are in effect equal rights to that well-being and freedom of which *A* and *B* are equally capable. Thus where the capacity for freedom is severely limited (e.g. that of an idiot or anyone else in the *non compos mentis* class), the right to freedom would be correspondingly limited.

and freedom simply as two things which do satisfy the conditions defined by individual human worth. Are there others? For the purposes of this essay this may be left an open question. For if there are, they would provide, at most, additional grounds for human rights. The ones I have specified are grounds enough. They are all I need for the analysis of equalitarian justice as, I trust, will appear directly.

III

I offer the following definition: an action is *just* if, and only if, it is prescribed exclusively by regard for the rights of all whom it affects substantially.[46] This definition could be discussed at length. I shall make, and with the utmost brevity, just two general points by way of elucidation:

(*a*) The standard cases are clearly covered, e.g. that of the judge adjudicating a dispute. To perform justly this strictly judicial function[47] he must (i) seek to determine with scrupulous care what, in these circumstances, are the rights of the litigants and of others, if any, who are substantially affected,[48] and then (ii) render a verdict determined by regard for those rights and by nothing else. He may be unjust by failing at (i) through ignorance, carelessness, impatience, laziness, addiction to stereotypes of race or class, and the like; at (ii) by any sort of partiality, even if this is due to nothing so low as venality or prejudice, but perhaps even to humane and generous sentiments. Thus, if in the case before him an honest and upright man has trespassed on the rights of a well-known bully (perhaps only to protect one of the latter's victims), the judge will have no choice but to find for the bully: he must be 'blind' to anything but the relevant rights when making up his verdict. This is the common-sense view of the matter, and it accords perfectly with what follows from the definition.

(*b*) The definition does not flout common usage by making 'just' *interchangeable* with 'right', and 'unjust' with 'wrong'. Whenever the question of regard, or disregard, for substantially affected rights does not arise, the question of justice, or injustice, does not arise. We see a

[46] 'Substantially' is deliberately and unavoidably vague (as much so as is the '*minimis*' in the legal maxim *de minimis non curat lex*). No general rule can be given that would apply to all the cases that would have to be considered. As to the definition as a whole, there is nothing original about it. It is adapted from Ulpian's *justitia est constans et perpetua voluntas jus suum cuique tribuendi*, *Dig.* 1, 1, 10, pr., which is in turn adapted from the oldest one on record (the 'ancient formula' to which Frankena alludes), 'justice consists in rendering to every man his due' (Plato, *Republic* 331, paraphrasing the poet Simonides).

[47] I am not here concerned with the judge's quasi-legislative function.

[48] e.g. the public.

man wasting his property and talents in dissolute living. It would not occur to us to think of his conduct as unjust, unless we see it as having a substantial effect on somebody's rights, say, those of dependants: it is unfair or unjust to them.[49] Again, whenever one is in no position to govern one's action by regard for rights, the question of justice, or injustice, does not arise. Two strangers are in immediate danger of drowning off the dock on which I stand. I am the only one present, and the best I can do is to save one while the other drowns. Each has a right to my help, but I cannot give it to both. Hence regard for rights does not prescribe what I am to do, and neither 'just' nor 'unjust' will apply: I am not unjust to the one who drowns, nor just to the one I save.

A major feature of my definition of 'just' is that it makes the answer to 'is x just?' (where x is any action, decision, etc.) strictly dependent on the answer to another question: 'what are the rights of those who are substantially affected by x?'[50] The definition cannot, and does not pretend that it can, give the slightest help in answering the latter question, with but one exception: it does tell us that the substantially affected rights, whatever they may be, should all be impartially respected. Thus it does disclose one right, though a purely *formal* one: the right to have one's *other* rights respected as impartially as those of any other interested party. But what are these other rights? Are they equal or unequal? On this the definition is silent. It is thus completely neutral in the controversy between meritarians and equalitarians, and should prove equally acceptable to either party.[51] Its neutralism should not be held against it. The words 'just' and 'unjust' are not the private property of the equalitarians; they may be used as conscientiously by those who reject, as by those who share, their special view of justice. We are not compelled to provide for this in our definitions; but there are obvious advantages in doing so. For we thereby offer our opponents common ground on which they too may stand while making their case. We allow Aristotle, for instance, to claim, without misusing the language, that slavery and the disfranchisement of manual workers are just institutions. It allows us to rebut his claim, not by impugning its linguistic propriety, but by explaining that we affirm what his claim implicity denies: that all human beings have the right to personal and political freedom.

It should now be plain to the reader why I have been so heavily

[49] If we hold that every man has rights against himself, then there would be injustice to himself even if he had no dependants and no substantial obligations to others. Linguistic objections to this result would not affect the definition. If 'injustice to himself' is strained, it is no more so than 'rights against himself'.

[50] Cf. J. Pieper, *Justice*, trans. Lawrence Lynch (New York, 1955), pp. 13 ff.

[51] Unless, of course, each is bent on putting his special view of justice into the definition of the word.

preoccupied with the question of human rights throughout the first half of this essay, and content to write most of Section II without even mentioning the word 'justice'. I have done so precisely because my purpose in this essay is not to discuss justice in general, but equalitarian justice. As should now be obvious, had I tried to reason from the concept of justice to that of equalitarian justice I would have been reasoning in a circle. I did allude at the start to important historical and linguistic ties of justice with equality. But these, while perfectly relevant, are obviously not conclusive. They would be dismissed by a determined and clear-headed opponent, like Plato, as mere evidences of a widespread *mis*-conception of justice. I am not suggesting that we should yield him this point or that, conversely, there is any good reason to think that he would come around to our view if we presented him with the argument of Section II (or a stronger one to the same effect). My contention is rather that we would be misrepresenting our view of justice if we were to give him the idea that it is susceptible of proof by that kind of historical and linguistic evidence. To explain our position to him so that, quite apart from his coming to agree with it, he would at least have the chance to *understand* it, one thing would matter above all: to show that we believe in human rights, and why.

That is why the weight of the argument in the preceding Section II fell so heavily on the notion of human worth, understood to mean nothing less than the equal worth of the happiness and freedom of all persons. Given this, we have equal welfare rights and freedom rights; and this puts us in a position to cover the full range of human rights which the natural rights tradition left so perplexingly indeterminate. I did not stop to argue for this contention when I made it in Section II, and will not do so now, for I have more important business ahead of me. I have not forgotten the task I set myself at the close of Section I, and wish to proceed to it as soon as possible. But before proceeding to this in Section IV, there is a major item of still unfinished business that must be attended to. It concerns a feature of equalitarian justice that must be made fully explicit, if only because it will play an important role in the argument that is to follow in Section IV.

Consider the following very simple rule of just distribution: if A *and* B *have sole and equal right to* x, *they have a joint right to the whole of* x. This rule (R_1) would be normally taken as axiomatic. Thus if A and B had sole and equal right to an estate, no executor bent on making a just settlement of their claims would think of giving away a part of the estate to some other person, C. But why not? Can it be shown that the consequent of R_1 does follow from its antecedent? It can. *Only* A *and* B *have any right to* x entails *anyone other than*

A *or* B *has no right to* x and hence C *has no right to* x. Hence if some part of *x* were distributed to *C*, it would be going to someone who has no right to it. Such a distribution would not conform to our definition of 'just': it would not be the one prescribed by impartial regard for the relevant rights. Now what if the executor withheld some part of *x* from *A* or *B*, without giving it to a third party? But how could that happen? Did he perhaps abandon it in a deserted place? He has no right to do that with any property unless it happens to be *his own*. So if he did such a foolish thing with a part of the estate, he has acted as though *he* is the third party to whom this has been distributed, and most unjustly, since he has no right to it. But what if he actually destroyed a part, perhaps throwing it overboard in a strong-box stuffed with valuables to sink to the bottom of the ocean? This too he would have no right to do, unless this part of the property were already *his*. So this action would be as unjust as before and for the same reason. And there is no other possibility, unless a part of the estate were lost, or destroyed through some natural calamity, in which case the question of its being *withheld* by the executor from *A* and *B* would not arise.[52] If he does withhold it, he would have to give it to some third party or else act as though he had already given it to himself, hence in either case to someone who has no right to *x*, hence unjustly. To act justly he must give the whole of it to those who have sole right to it.

Now let us think of an allied case. A man leaves a will containing many marks of his affection for his two sons and sole heirs and of his wish to benefit them. The terms of his will provide, *inter alia*, that a large industrial property is to be used, at the direction of trustees, to produce income for the sole and equal benefit of *D* and *E*, the income to be divided annually between them. Here the annual distribution of the income will fall directly under R_1. But another decision, in which *D* and *E* have as big a stake, will not: how the property is to be used to yield the desired income. Let *L* and *M* be the only known feasible dispositions of the property for this purpose between which the trustees must decide at a given time: each, let us say, would involve a five-year commitment, but *L* would assure the estate twice the income, security, etc. being the same. *L* is obviously a windfall for the estate, and the trustees are not likely to waste a second thought on *M* as a possibly just decision in the circumstances. Why not? Why is it that in fairness to *D* and *E* they *should choose L*? Not in virtue of R_1, since that does not apply here: *L* is not a whole of which *M* is a part. What the trustees

[52] The only question then would be that of culpable negligence on the executor's part while the property was in his custody. And that is another matter.

must be invoking (or would be, if they were thinking out the basis of their decision) is an analogue to R_1, covering cases such as this, where the right is not to an already existing object but to a future benefit which may be secured at any one of several possible levels: *if* D *and* E *have sole and equal right to benefit from* x, *they have a joint right to the benefit at the highest level at which it may be secured*. If we were asked to justify this rule (R_2), how would we go about it? If the trustees' reason for preferring *M* to *L* were to benefit a third party, *C*, the reasoning would be the same as before: since only *D* and *E* have the right to benefit from *x, C* has no such right; hence *M* cannot be the disposition prescribed by regard for the relevant rights. But what if the trustees were to prefer *M*, without aiming to benefit a third party? This possibility would be analogous to the case above in which R_1 was violated by the wilful loss or destruction of part of *x*. For a preference for *M* would be fully as injurious to *D* and *E*, and as unjust to them, as if the trustees had voted for *L* with the diabolical rider that half the annual income during the next five years was to be withheld from *D* and *E* and destroyed. The loss to *D* and *E* would be exactly the same, and the injustice would be the same: the trustees might have the right to forgo a benefit to *themselves* equivalent to the difference between *L* and *M*, but only if *they* had the right to this benefit in the first place. In choosing *M* over *L* they would be acting as though they did have this right, hence in clear violation of *D*'s and *E*'s *sole* right.

Now the validity of R_2 is obviously unaffected by the number of those who have sole and equal right to a benefit. It would hold for any number; hence for the whole of humanity, or any lesser part of it. Consider then the total benefit derivable by humanity from men's use of what we may call 'the means of well-being', i.e. of their own bodies and minds and of the resources of the natural universe. Since men have an equal right to well-being[53] (apart from special property rights, and the like, with which we are not now concerned), they have an equal right to the means of well-being. And the right of humanity to these means is exclusive.[54] We are, therefore, entitled to assert that *men have sole and equal right to benefit from the means of well-being*. From this we may conclude, in conformity with R_2, that *men are jointly entitled to this benefit at the highest level at which it may be secured*.

[53] Proposition (3) near the close of sec. II.

[54] Or, at any rate, it may be so regarded for the purposes of this argument. To take account of the rights of other animals, we would only need to add 'except for the rights of other animals' before the italicized portion of the premiss and the conclusion of the ensuing argument, and the validity of the inference would be unaffected.

This conclusion affects importantly the concept of equalitarian justice. It implies that the fundamental and distinctive idea in its notion of just distribution is (i) not equal distribution of benefits, but (ii) their equal distribution at the highest obtainable level. (i) has already been argued for in Frankena's essay when he considered, and rejected, Hourani's attractive formula, 'Justice is equality, evident or disguised', as an over-simplification. But on Frankena's view neither can (ii) constitute the needed corrective. It is an obligation of beneficence, not of justice, he argues, 'to promote the greatest of possible good'. He writes: 'even if we allow . . . that society has an obligation to be beneficent, then we must insist that such beneficence, at least if it exceeds a certain minimum, is no part of social justice as such.'[55] Now there is no difference of opinion between us as to the importance of distinguishing sharply the concept of beneficence (or of benevolence) from that of equalitarian justice. But I submit that this can be done perfectly by adhering to the concept of equalitarian justice I have given here, and is in no way imperilled by my thesis here at (ii). To go back to the definition of 'just' at the start: this leaves plenty of scope for acts which might be beneficent but *un*just, as, for example, when *A* defrauds *B* to help *C*; or beneficent and *non*-just (neither just nor unjust: 'just' does not apply), as when *A* helps one needy person, disregarding the claim of millions of others for the simple reason that he is in no position to help more than one out of all these millions. Conversely, neither would it follow from my theory of equalitarian justice that every just act, decision, practice, etc., will be beneficent. A large number will be non-beneficent (neither beneficent nor maleficent; 'beneficent' will not apply): the repayment of debts, the rendering of ordinary judicial verdicts, or the enforcement of punishments. So *equalitarian justice* and *beneficence* will have different extensions, and their meanings will be as different as is that of *justice* on the present definition from that of *beneficence* on the usual view. Hence the concepts are entirely distinct, both intensionally and extensionally. But distinct concepts may, of course, overlap. And this is precisely what I maintain in the present case: (ii) above certainly falls under beneficence, but that, of itself, is no reason whatever why it *may* not *also* fall under equalitarian justice. That it does is what the foregoing argument for the validity of R_2, and its applicability to human rights, was designed to show.

One way of stating the thesis of that argument would be that equalitarian justice has a direct stake not only in equalizing the distribution of those goods whose enjoyment constitutes well-being, but also in promoting their creation. That it would have an indirect stake in the

[55] Op. cit., p. 6.

latter even if it were concerned *only* with equalizing their distribution could be argued independently by an obvious generalization of the point I made at the start of Section II, where I argued that a more affluent society could 'buy more equality'. The reasoning for and from R_2 provides a stronger and more general argument that *given any two levels of the production of good known to be possible in given circumstances, then*, other things being equal, *the higher should be preferred on grounds of justice*. 'Goods' here, as throughout this essay, is a general expression for a class of which economic goods would be a sub-class. We may thus use an economic test-case of the underlined proposition: suppose that the supreme policy-maker of the *N*s (whose economy resembles closely that of the USA) had to choose between two policies, P(*L*) and P(*M*), knowing that (a) the effect of P(*M*) would be to maintain throughout the next five years the current rate of annual increase of the gross national product (which is, say, 2.5 per cent), while that of P(*L*) would *double* that rate; (b) the pattern of distribution of the national income would remain the same; (c) the greater wealth produced under P(*L*) would not be offset by aggravation of the risk of war, cultural deterioration, corruption of morals, or of any other significant evil.[56] (c) is, of course, a strong restriction; but, like (b), it is built into the hypothesis to ensure that the *only* appreciable difference between the two policies would be in the lesser, or fuller, utilization and expansion of the economic resources of the nation. This, and the artificiality of the whole model, by no means trivializes the contention that in such circumstances equalitarian justice would leave the policy-maker no choice but P(*L*). To say that beneficence (or benevolence) would leave him no other choice *would* be trivial: no one would care to dispute this. But the same thing said for equalitarian justice can be, and is being, disputed. This asserts that the *N*s have *rights* in this matter which the policy-maker would violate if he were to choose P(*M*)—as much so as the trustees in the example would violate the rights of *D* and *E* if they chose *M*. That the rights of the *N*s, unlike those of *D* and *E*, are moral, not legal, is immaterial: *only* the moral justice of the decision is here in view. The moral rights in question are those of the *N*s to well-being, hence to the means of well-being: to anything which would enrich their life, save it from pain, disease, drudgery, emptiness, ugliness. Given (a) in the hypothesis, an enormously larger quantity of such means would be made available to the *N*s under P(*L*) in the course of the five-year period; and given

[56] Perhaps we should add (d), that P(*L*) would have no adverse effect on the economy of other nations and would not decrease the disposition of the *N*s to help needier nations.

(b) their distribution would be no more unequal than that of the smaller volume of goods produced under P(*M*). Hence the *N*s have jointly a right to P(*L*). They have this for just the reasons which justify the inference from the antecedent of R_2 to its consequent. The crux of the inference is that since the *N*s, and only they, have a right to the benefits obtainable under either alternative, they have a right to that alternative which produces the greater benefit. Only (and at most) if the policy-maker had *himself* the right to the aggregate benefit represented by the difference between P(*L*) and P(*M*) would he have that right. So if he were to choose P(*M*) he would violate the right of those who do. That is why that decision would be unjust.

Two more points:

(A) That not equality as such, but equality at the highest possible level, is the requirement of equalitarian justice may be argued as strongly in the case of the right to freedom.[57] Thus if a legislature had before it two bills, B(*L*) and B(*M*), such that B(*L*) would provide for greater personal freedom than would B(*M*), then, other things remaining equal, they would be voting unjustly if they voted for the second: they would be violating the human right to freedom of those affected by the legislation. A vote for B(*M*) would be tantamount to a vote for the needless[58] *restriction* of freedom. And since *freedom* is a personal (or individual) right, to equalize its restriction would be to aggravate, not to alleviate, its injustice. Would any of us feel that no injustice was suffered by Soviet citizens by the suppression of *Doctor Zhivago* if we were reliably informed that no one, not even Khrushchev, was exempted, and that the censors themselves had been foreign mercenaries?

(B) The conjunction of equalitarian justice and benevolence could have been argued at a still deeper level if we had gone down to the ultimate *reasons* for the equal right to well-being and freedom, i.e. to (1) and (2) at the close of Section II above. What could be a stronger expression of benevolence towards one's fellow men, than to say that the well-being and freedom of every one of them is worth as much as one's own and that of those few persons one happens to love? At this level equalitarian justice is as deeply committed to two notions which it does not display in its title, benevolence and freedom, as to the notion of

[57] Cf. the first principle of justice in J. B. Rawls, 'Justice as Fairness', *Philoophical Review*, 67 (1958), pp. 16 ff., at p. 165; reprinted in F. Olafson, *Justice and Social Policy* (Englewood Cliffs, NJ, 1961).

[58] Since we are stipulating that other things would be equal.

equality, which it does. It now remains to show how, given this threefold commitment, it can *also* recognize claims of *un*equal distribution.

IV

Why is it just to distribute good according to merit? I shall answer this for one distributable good which I shall call 'praise', using this word to cover all direct expressions of admiration, appreciation, or approval of merit which are subject to voluntary control. This is an extended use of the word, but it has definite limits. Thus if *A* and *B* are competing for an office, the mere fact of *C*'s appointing *A* is not to count as praise from *C* to *A*, no matter how emphatic be the approval of *A*'s merit it is understood to imply. To qualify as praise something more direct or express would be needed, though not necessarily in verbal form. Thus *C* would not have to congratulate *A* on the appointment, or tell him he has the good qualities the job calls for; it would be enough to convey as much to him by one's demeanour or facial expression.

A man should not be praised for merit he does not have. Indiscriminate praise is a fake; and to fake praise in special cases is to cheapen it, and hence to violate the equal right of all persons to be praised in a sound currency, if they are to be praised at all. It does not follow from this, nor is it true, that merit has to be the necessary *and* sufficient condition of giving praise. At times we would not praise a person unless we felt he needed a special reassurance or encouragement. But far more frequently merit *is* sufficient. Take our ordinary response to a delightful conversationalist, for example. In the various subtle, but unmistakable, ways in which we manifest our approval we measure out to him sizeable quantities of what some economists, without intending to be humorous, call 'psychic income'. We know that to give this is to please him. But the question of his need of it is not a factor in our giving it, any more than the landlord's need is a factor in the tenant's payment of the rent. And this is what happens in the majority of cases. This is 'the generally expected thing' when praise is given in our society, and this is what I shall call the practice of *praising for merit ('mp')* or *giving praise according to merit*. If we did not have *mp*, it would be understood that no person, or only some privileged persons (e.g. the monarch, the nobility, Aryans, members of the Communist Party, Platonic philosophers) have the right to praise any person they choose on the sole ground of his merit.

Mp is a 'practice' in the somewhat technical sense this term has acquired in recent moral philosophy.[59] For my present purpose two important points are involved here: (a) *mp* may be formulated in terms

[59] See especially, J. B. Rawls, 'Two Concepts of Rules', *Philosophical Review*,

of a set of rules, conformity to which depends on voluntary compliance with (or, obedience to) the rules. Thus one of the rules would be, 'Those in a position to praise both *A* and *B* should give more praise to *A* if his merit is the greater.' One's compliance with this rule is not forced by the *fact* that *A* has the greater merit, not by one's *belief* that he has. *C* might be well aware of the fact, yet lavish praise on *B*, cold-shouldering *A* (perhaps because he is fond of *B* and hates *A*). That the rule can be disobeyed in this and other ways proves that the usual compliance with it is voluntary. (b) In the absence of *mp*, actions which are now understood as praising for merit would be normally understood very differently even if they had, in all other respects, the same characteristics.[60] Thus suppose that *mp* did not exist, while praising for need did. In such a society the conduct by *C* just described would be construed very differently. No one would take it as an unfavourable reflection on *A*'s merit, and *A* could not feel slighted by it; from *C*'s excessive praise for *B, A* would merely gather that *C* has an exaggerated idea of *B*'s need of encouragement. *Not* to be praised in that society would be itself a kind of tribute.

If this is what *mp* means, then the distribution of praise under this practice is bound to reflect to some degree inequalities in the distribution of merit. To live with *mp* is to live in a world in which some people will get this kind of 'psychic income' in abundance, while others must subsist on miserable pittances of it.[61] For this reason equalitarian justice would have no choice but to condemn *mp* as an inherently unjust practice, *if* equality in the distribution of goods were its only concern. But from the account of it in Section III we know that it is also concerned that happiness and freedom be secured at the highest possible levels. Let us see what difference this makes.

But first let us take account of a matter of fact: that the effect of praising an achievement is generally to enhance the relevant creative effort. To say this is not to deny that sometimes praise has no effect and sometimes a bad effect. But if it were *generally* ineffective the argument I am about to make for it would fail. And *every* argument for it would fail if its normal effect were sufficiently bad—if, say, it were

64 (1955), pp. 3 ff; reprinted in F. Olafson, *Society, Law and Morality* (Englewood Cliffs, NJ, 1961).

[60] Cf. Rawls, op. cit., p. 25.

[61] In any society that puts a high premium on individual achievement something like this will always be true, so far as I can see, even after taking full account of mitigating factors, such as (a) that the varieties of merits are legion, so that some who fail at one kind of performance may shine at another, and (b) that praise may rightly be given not for absolute achievement but for achievement in some proportion to ability, so that a tiny success may rate high praise at times.

like that of alcohol on alcoholics. If it demoralized all, or most, people, praise would be as vile as flattery, or viler; only a few poisonous individuals would indulge in it. The actual facts are reassuringly different, in spite of occasional swelled heads. What happens for the most part is that in praising a meritorious performance we give its merit our backing. We thereby help the performer, giving him the incentive to attain again the same merit, or a higher one. We even help ourselves: by going on record in favour of the meritorious performance we are more likely to emulate it ourselves in the future. This being the case, the proponent of equalitarian justice cannot judge *mp* fairly unless he connects it with his interest in getting all human beings to be as creative as possible, i.e. to bring into existence, to the best of their ability, those values which will enrich their own life and that of others. This gives him at once a strong initial interest in *mp* as a practice generating incentives to creative effort. And since *mp* can exist *alongside* of other incentive-generating practices (and always has in every known society), its presence in a given society represents a net addition (and a substantial one) to the aggregate stimuli to creative effort. A society with *mp*, therefore, would have a higher level of production of good than it would have without *mp*. But as has been argued in Section III,

> given any two levels of production of good known to be possible in given circumstances, then, other things being equal, the higher should be preferred on grounds of justice.

This would provide a utilitarian argument for the justice of *mp* (justifying it as a means to an end which justice approves), *if* the 'other things being equal' clause can be made good.

To make up our minds on this 'if', let us first be clear about the fact that *mp* as such does not require, or even favour, inequality in the distribution of any of the *other* goods (goods other than praise) whose creation it tends to enhance. How equally or unequally these are going to be distributed will depend on decisions which are entirely distinct from the decision to maintain *mp*. Thus it would be sheer confusion to think that there would be any incompatibility between deciding to distribute praise according to merit and economic goods according to need. The most starry-eyed equalitarian, intent on running his whole economy on the latter maxim, could afford to be as much of an enthusiast for *mp* as anyone else; indeed he would have good reason to be much more of one: having denied himself the usual economic incentives, he would have to work this one for all it was worth. As this example may suggest, *mp* fits a generally equalitarian society not only as well as a meritarian one, but better. But I do not wish to make anything of this last point. All that is needed for the present argument is that the practice of *mp* as such cannot be held *generally* responsible for inequalities in the distribution of goods in the society, but only for those inherent in its own operation, i.e. inequalities in the distribution of praise itself. The question then is whether *these* inequalities will be so repugnant to justice as to constitute offsetting factors against the tonic effect of *mp* on human productivity which our concept of justice approves. When we narrow down the question in this way I think it can be shown that they will not be repugnant to justice at all, and will not only leave 'other things equal', but better than equal.

To simplify the problem to the utmost let us think of a purely economic society of two individuals, *A* and *B*, *A* being the more efficient producer. An angel is set over them, whose goodwill for each of them is boundless. If he could measure out to them well-being directly from some celestial storehouse, he would be giving vast and equal measures to each. Such direct munificence is unfortunately denied him. He has been told that whatever well-being is to come to *A* and *B* must reach them entirely through their own efforts; all the angel can do for them is to propose to them new practices. He now puts his mind on whether or not he should offer them *mp*, which they have hitherto done without. To isolate the probable effect of *mp* itself on their lives, he pegs the solution on two assumptions: (*a*) that they will operate it fairly (for if they did not, the results would not be an indication of the use of *mp*, but of its misuse); (*b*) the expected increment in their joint product is to be divided in the same ratio as at present (for there is nothing about *mp* to require any special ratio, hence any ratio different from the present). He then sees that, on these conditions, *A* and *B* have both much to gain from the new arrangement: the economic income of each will increase; and each will get some of the newly-created 'psychic income', though *A* the more meritorious producer, will get more of this than *B*.[62] If these were the only results of the change, the angel would have no reason to hesitate between leaving them in their present state or giving them *mp*. He would give it to them, and not because of having any preference, even the slightest, for the well-being of *A* over that of *B*, but precisely because he has the same desire to increase the happiness of both as much as possible in the circumstances of his choice, i.e. circumstances in which he must choose either for the status quo or for their present way of life as modified by *mp*.[63]

[62] The reader should not be offended by the psychological crudity of this and ensuing remarks. I am trying to get this model to answer just one kind of question.

[63] The reader may want to know why the angel is limiting his decision-problem

But, of course, there may be another result from the change: the mere fact that *A* will be made happier than *B* (*A* can count on getting the larger share of the praise) may make *B* unhappy, and so much so that his unhappiness from just this source might be great enough to outbalance his gains and even (if we allow the angel some way of determining such things) *A*'s gains as well. This possibility could be quite enough to disrupt totally the angel's calculations. Whether or not *mp* will prove a blessing or a curse will now turn on how *B* takes it; and *B* knowing this could use it to blackmail the angel against even making the offer: *B* need only announce that he would make himself miserable enough to offset the expected gains. Fortunately the situation has a saving feature: *A* and *B* are moral beings. This has not been stated; but it is certainly implied in assumption (*a*), for only moral beings could operate this practice fairly. Our angel then can ask *B* to look at *mp* as a moral being should, hence with equal regard for *A*'s well-being as for his own. If he did so, *B* would not be made unhappy merely because *A* became happier than himself, that is to say, out of envy. To say this to *B* is not, alas, to assure him that he will react to the effects of the practice as a moral being should, thereby saving himself the misery of jealousy. No one can ensure this for *B* except (at most) *B* himself and by his own effort; but that, in any case, *B* cannot bring up any unfavourable results due to *envy* as a reason against the *justice* of the proposed institution. To allow such reasons to count would ruin the prospects of giving a moral justification of any practice: by the same token unhappiness due to arrogance (i.e. to the demand for special privilege) would also count, and that would be the end of justice.

The upshot of the argument is simply this: *because* (not in spite) of his equal concern for the happiness of all persons, a proponent of equalitarian justice would have good reason to approve *mp, given* its stimulating effect on the creation of those goods whose enjoyment constitutes happiness, *unless* the effect were offset by others repugnant to his sense of justice. But there are no such effects. The fact that envious people are made unhappy by an institution is no evidence of its injustice.

This is not the only argument for *mp*, or even the strongest. There are two others which deserve at least as full a treatment, but fortunately

in just this way and is giving no consideration to other alternatives to the status quo. The answer has already been given in my earlier remark that *mp* can exist alongside of other incentive-generating practices; therefore the question of introducing it need not be complicated by giving it a comparative rating against such practices; *A* and *B* may have a variety of other practices and *mp* as well.

do not require it. I shall make them in the most summary fashion to compensate for the unavoidable length of the one I have just finished. Both of them argue from the right to freedom.

(1) Praising for merit is something people like to do, and do spontaneously when they are left free to talk and laugh and applaud without restraints from political or clerical or domestic martinets. It is thus a direct expression of human freedom, and such a pervasive one that it spreads over every area of life, private or public. To try to suppress this practice would involve enormous inroads on personal liberty.

(2) Over and above its coincidence, for the reason just given, with one of the major *ends* of freedom (that of expressing without impediment one's actual feelings about one's fellows' character and conduct), it is also an indispensable *means* for another such end: that of diffusing widely among the population free choices between competing values. It is like 'consumer's vote' in a free economy: it gives the consumer of the values produced in a society a means of influencing the producers, and thus a share in determining which values are produced and in what proportions. Its obvious disadvantage is its lack of any facilities for aggregating and recording the results of individual decisions, either directly, as through elections, or indirectly, as through the market. But it has the advantage of being as equally distributed as the suffrage, while extending, and more flexibly, to even larger and more varied sets of choices than those of the market.

With this case for the justice of the practice of praising for merit thus laid out before us, let us take stock of what has been accomplished and how. I have taken the maxim, 'to each according to his merit', as in need of justification, and have undertaken to derive it from a set of propositions which includes only equalitarian value-premisses (those from which the equal right of human beings to well-being and freedom is derived) plus one or more factual premisses. Since I limited the demonstration to the special proposition, 'to each *praise* according to his merit', I needed such factual premisses as that the general effect of so distributing praise enhances the production of value and offers a useful device for its control by the free responses of private individuals. From each of these we get an instrumental, or utilitarian, justification: we justify this way of distributing praise because it is a means to the advancement of those ends which are stated in our value-premisses, such as the well-being and the freedom to which all persons have a severally equal and jointly exclusive right. We also get a collateral non-instrumental justification in terms of freedom: praising for merit is itself one of the forms in which persons choose to express their freedom. Since merit is unequal, to justify *mp* is to justify unequal rights in respect of praise. The whole argument then falls into the following form: because persons have *equal* rights to well-being and to freedom, then, in the special circumstances of distributing praise for merit (those noticed in the factual premisses of the argument) their right to this particular good is *un*equal. If we then think of the latter as an exception, or as a whole class of exceptions, to men's equal right to enjoyable good, we are in a position to justify the exception in the way in which I said earlier (at the close of Section I) exceptions to natural rights should be justified. The moral (as distinct from the factual) reasons given in this exception to the equal right to good have been only such reasons as were built into our concept of equalitarian justice and would be given as the reasons for all our natural rights: men's joint and equal right to well-being and freedom at the highest obtainable level.

But apart from the theoretical import of this argument, it has useful practical implications. In telling us why we *may* justly distribute praise unequally according to merit, it tells us also what we may *not* do. In general it warns us against confusing merit with human worth, and against allowing merit to swamp human worth. It reminds us that terms like 'superior' and 'inferior', properly applicable to a person's merit, are inapplicable to the person: there can be strictly and literally superior or inferior poets, teachers, bankers, garage-mechanics, actresses, statesmen; but there can be strictly and literally no superior or inferior persons, individuals, men. From this it follows that when we praise a man we must not praise him *as* a man. His humanity is not a fit subject for praise. To think otherwise is to incur a 'category mistake', and one fraught with grave moral consequences. For given men's sensitiveness to honour and dishonour, when merit is made the measure of their human dignity, their own sense of dignity tends to become distorted. If they are talented and successful, praise misdirected from their achievements to their person will foster the illusion that they are superior persons, belong to a higher moral caste, and may claim on moral grounds a privileged status for their own well-being and freedom.[64] Conversely, if low achievement stores are not kept wholly

[64] The best example of this among philosophical moralists is Nietzsche: 'Egoism belongs to the nature of a distinguished soul. I mean that immovable faith that other beings are by nature subordinate to a being such as 'we are', that they should sacrifice themselves to us'. *Beyond Good and Evil*, trans. Marianne Cowan (Chicago, 1935), p. 265. A little earlier (p. 258) he had praised that 'good and healthy aristrocracy' which 'accepts with a clear conscience the sacrifice of an enormous number of men who must *for its sake* [that of the aristocracy] be suppressed and reduced to incomplete human beings, to slaves, to tools' (Nietzsche's italics).

distinct from personal worth, which does not register on any score, men may be made to feel that they are the human inferiors of others, that their own happiness or freedom has inferior worth. This would be a grave injustice. Any practice which tends to so weaken and confuse the personal self esteem of a group of persons—slavery, serfdom, or, in our own time, racial segregation—may be morally condemned on this one ground, even if there were no other for indicting it. Some such ground is alluded to in the Court opinion in the decision which finally struck down segregation in the public schools.[65] That verdict could be reached more directly and extended to every form of racial segregation,[66] by applying the ideas that have been sketched in this essay. If one thinks of human worth as the moral foundation of all rights, one will see that the equal honour of persons is presupposed by the unequal honour that may be given to unequal merit and, hence, that no practice which habitually humiliates persons can be defended by differences of merit, real or imagined.

Along similar lines I believe it may be argued that other differentials—in particular those of economic reward, economic power, and political power—can be justified on the terms of equalitarian justice. Given certain propositions which, if true, are true on empirical grounds, recording observable uniformities of human nature and conduct with which every moral philosophy must reckon, good *moral* reasons may be offered for inequalities of various kinds, which would be 'just-making' reasons, the very same as those which would be offered for equalizing benefits of other kinds. And the very procedure which led to these results would contain built-in protections of human equality, limiting the differentials in income and in power by the very machinery which certifies their justice within the permissible range. To accomplish this would be to answer Plato's question, the one that started us off on this whole enquiry early in Section I. It would be to show him over

[65] *Brown* v. *Topeka Board of Education*, 347 US (1954), pp. 483 ff., 'To separate them from others of similar age and qualifications solely because of their race generates a feeling of inferiority as to their status in the community that may affect their hearts and minds in a way unlikely ever to be undone.'

[66] The context in which the above citation is imbedded leaves one uncertain as to whether, in the opinion of the Court, (a) this evil was *per se* a reason for outlawing segregation in public schools, or (b) constituted such a reason merely because the 'feeling of inferiority' reduced the children's chances of getting equal benefit from their schooling and thus disturbed the equality of their educational opportunities. The ensuing citation from the earlier finding in the Kansas case makes it look as though (*b*) expressed the Court's opinion; and (*b*), unlike (*a*), is not immediately generalizable to other forms of segregation.

what special form the three maxims of unequal distribution, ‘to each according to his merit, his work, and the agreements he has made’, may be joined without theoretical inconsistency or moral compromise to the two maxims of equal distribution, ‘to each according to his need, and to his [human] worth’.

III

ARE THERE ANY NATURAL RIGHTS?[1]

H. L. A. HART

I SHALL advance the thesis that if there are any moral rights at all, it follows that there is at least one natural right, the equal right of all men to be free. By saying that there is this right, I mean that in the absence of certain special conditions which are consistent with the right being an equal right, any adult human being capable of choice (1) has the right to forbearance on the part of all others from the use of coercion or restraint against him save to hinder coercion or restraint and (2) is at liberty to do (i.e. is under no obligation to abstain from) any action which is not one coercing or restraining or designed to injure other persons.[2]

I have two reasons for describing the equal rights of all men to be free as a *natural* right; both of them were always emphasized by the classical theorists of natural rights. (1) This right is one which all men

Reprinted by permission of the author and *The Philosophical Review* from the *Philosophical Review*, Vol. LXIV, No. 2 (April 1955), pp. 175–91.

[1] I was first stimulated to think along these lines by Mr Stuart Hampshire, and I have reached by different routes a conclusion similar to his.

[2] Further explanation of the perplexing terminology of freedom is, I fear, necessary. *Coercion* includes, besides preventing a person from doing what he chooses, making his choice less eligible by threats; *restraint* includes any action designed to make the exercise of choice impossible and so includes killing or enslaving a person. But neither coercion nor restraint includes *competition*. In terms of the distinction between 'having a right to' and 'being at liberty to', used above and further discussed in sect. I, B, all men say have, consistently with the obligation to forbear from coercion, the *liberty* to satisfy if they can such at least of their desires as are not designed to coerce or injure others, even though in fact, owing to scarcity, one man's satisfaction causes another's frustration. In conditions of extreme scarcity this distinction between competition and coercion will not be worth drawing; natural rights are only of importance 'where peace is possible' (Locke). Further, freedom (the absence of coercion) can be *valueless* to those victims of unrestricted competition too poor to make use of it; so it will be pedantic to point out to them that though starving they are free. This is the truth exaggerated by the Marxists whose *identification* of poverty with lack of freedom confuses two different evils.

have if they are capable of choice: they have it *qua* men and not only if they are members of some society or stand in some special relation to each other. (2) This right is not created or conferred by men's voluntary action; other moral rights are.[3] Of course, it is quite obvious that my thesis is not as ambitious as the traditional theories of natural rights; for although on my view all men are *equally* entitled to be free in the sense explained, no man has an absolute or unconditional right to do or not to do any particular thing or to be treated in any particular way; coercion or restraint of any action may be justified in special conditions consistently with the general principle. So my argument will not show that men have any right (save the equal right of all to be free) which is 'absolute', 'indefeasible', or 'imprescriptible'. This may for many reduce the importance of my contention, but I think that the principle that all men have an equal right to be free, meagre as it may seem, is probably all that the political philosophers of the liberal tradition need have claimed to support any programme of action even if they have claimed more. But my contention that there is this one natural right may appear unsatisfying in another respect; it is only the conditional assertion that *if* there are any moral rights then there must be this one natural right. Perhaps few would now deny, as some have, that there are moral rights; for the point of that denial was usually to object to some philosophical claim as to the 'ontological status' of rights, and this objection is now expressed not as a denial that there are any moral rights but as a denial of some assumed logical similarity between sentences used to assert the existence of rights and other kinds of sentences. But it is still important to remember that there may be codes of conduct quite properly termed moral codes (though we can of course say they are 'imperfect') which do not employ the notion of *a* right, and there is nothing contradictory or otherwise absurd in a code or morality consisting wholly of prescriptions or in a code which prescribed only what should be done for the realization of happiness or some ideal of personal perfection.[4] Human actions in such systems would be evaluated or criticized as compliances with prescriptions or as *good* or *bad, right* or *wrong, wise* or *foolish, fitting* or *unfitting*, but no one in such a system would have, exercise, or claim rights, or

[3] Save those general rights (cf. sect. II, B) which are particular exemplifications of the right of all men to be free.

[4] Is the notion of *a* right found in either Plato or Aristotle? There seems to be no Greek word for it as distinct from 'right' or 'just' (*δικαίον*), thought expressions like *τὰ ἐμὰ δικαία* are I believe fourth-century legal idioms. The natural expressions in Plato are *τὸ ἑαυτὸν* (*ἔχειν*) or *τὰ τινι ὀφειλόμενα*, but these seem confined to property or debts. There is no place for a moral right unless the moral value of individual freedom is recognized.

violate or infringe them. So those who lived by such systems could not of course be committed to the recognition of the equal right of all to be free; nor, I think (and this is one respect in which the notion of a right differs from other moral notions), could any parallel argument be constructed to show that, from the bare fact that actions were recognized as ones which ought or ought not to be done, as right, wrong, good, or bad, it followed that some specific kind of conduct fell under these categories.

I

(A) Lawyers have for their own purposes carried the dissection of the notion of a legal right some distance, and some of their results[5] are of value in the elucidation of statements of the form 'X has a right to . . .' outside legal contexts. There is of course no simple identification to be made between moral and legal rights, but there is an intimate connection between the two, and this itself is one feature which distinguishes a moral right from other fundamental moral concepts. It is not merely that as a matter of fact men speak of their moral rights mainly when advocating their incorporation in a legal system, but that the concept of a right belongs to that branch of morality which is specifically concerned to determine when one person's freedom may be limited by another's[6] and so to determine what actions may appropriately be made the subject of coercive legal rules. The words '*droit*', '*diritto*', and '*Recht*', used by continental jurists, have no simple English translation and seem to English jurists to hover uncertainly between law and morals, but they do in fact mark off an area of morality (the morality of law) which has special characteristics. It is occupied by the concepts of justice, fairness, rights, and obligation (if this last is not used as it is by many moral philosophers as an obscuring general label to cover every action that morally we ought to do or forbear from doing). The most important common characteristic of this group of moral concepts is that there is no incongruity, but a special congruity in the use of force or the threat of force to secure that what is just or fair or

[5] As W. D. Lamont has seen: cf. his *Principles of Moral Judgement* (Oxford, 1946); for the jurists, cf. Hohfeld's *Fundamental Legal Conceptions* (New Haven, 1923).

[6] Here and subsequently I use 'interfere with another's freedom', 'limit another's freedom', 'determine how another shall act', to mean either the use of coercion or demanding that a person shall do or not do some action. The connection between these two types of 'interference' is too complex for discussion here; I think it is enough for present purposes to point out that having a justification for demanding that a person shall or shall not do some action is a necessary though not a sufficient condition for justifying coercion.

someone's right to have done shall in fact be done; for it is in just these circumstances that coercion of another human being is legitimate. Kant, in the *Rechtslehre*, discusses the obligations which arise in this branch of morality under the title of *officia juris*, 'which do not require that respect for duty shall be of itself the determining principle of the will', and contrasts them with *officia virtutis*, which have no moral worth unless done for the sake of the moral principle. His point is, I think, that we must distinguish from the rest of morality those principles regulating the proper distribution of human freedom which alone make it morally legitimate for one human being to determine by his choice how another should act; and a certain specific moral value is secured (to be distinguished from moral virtue in which the goodwill is manifested) if human relationships are conducted in accordance with these principles even though coercion has to be used to secure this, for only if these principles are regarded will freedom be distributed among human beings as it should be. And it is I think a very important feature of a moral right that the possessor of it is conceived as having a moral justification for limiting the freedom of another and that he has this justification not because the action he is entitled to require of another has some moral quality but simply because in the circumstances a certain distribution of human freedom will be maintained if he by his choice is allowed to determine how that other shall act.

(B) I can best exhibit this feature of a moral right by reconsidering the question whether moral rights and 'duties'[7] are correlative. The contention that they are means, presumably, that every statement of the form 'X has a right to . . .' entails and is entailed by 'Y has a duty (not) to . . .', and at this stage we must not assume that the values of the name-variables 'X' and 'Y' must be different persons. Now there is certainly one sense of 'a right' (which I have already mentioned) such that it does not follow from X's having a right that X or someone else has any duty. Jurists have isolated rights in this sense and have referred to them as 'liberties' just to distinguish them from rights in the centrally

[7] I write 'duties' here because one factor obscuring the nature of a right is the philosophical use of 'duty' and 'obligation' for all cases where there are moral reasons for saying an action ought to be done or not done. In fact 'duty', 'obligation', 'right', and 'good' come from different segments of morality, concern different types of conduct, and make different types of moral criticism or evaluation. Most important are the points (1) that obligations may be voluntarily incurred or created, (2) that they are *owed* to special persons (who have rights), (3) that they do not arise out of the character of the actions which are obligatory but out of the relationship of the parties. Language roughly though not consistently confines the use of 'having an obligation' to such cases.

important sense of 'right' which has 'duty' as a correlative. The former sense of 'right' is needed to describe those areas of social life where competition is at least morally unobjectionable. Two people walking along both see a ten-dollar bill in the road twenty yards away, and there is no clue as to the owner. Neither of the two are under a 'duty' to allow the other to pick it up; each has in this sense a right to pick it up. Of course there may be many things which each has a 'duty' not to do in the course of the race to the spot—neither may kill or wound the other—and corresponding to these 'duties' there are rights to forbearances. The moral propriety of all economic competition implies this minimum sense of 'a right' in which to say that 'X has a right to' means merely that X is under no 'duty' not to. Hobbes saw that the expression 'a right' could have this sense but he was wrong if he thought that there is no sense in which it does follow from X's having a right that Y has a duty or at any rate an obligation.

(C) More important for our purpose is the question whether for all moral 'duties' there are correlative moral rights, because those who have given an affirmative answer to this question have usually assumed without adequate scrutiny that to have a right is simply to be capable of benefiting by the performance of a 'duty'; whereas in fact this is not a sufficient condition (and probably not a necessary condition) of having a right. Thus animals and babies who stand to benefit by our performance of our 'duty' not to ill-treat them are said *therefore* to have rights to proper treatment. The full consequence of this reasoning is not usually followed out; most have shrunk from saying that we have rights against ourselves because we stand to benefit from our performance of our 'duty' to keep ourselves alive or develop our talents. But the moral situation which arises from a promise (where the legal-sounding terminology of rights and obligations is most appropriate) illustrates most clearly that the notion of having a right and that of benefiting by the performance of a 'duty' are not identical. X promises Y in return for some favour that he will look after Y's aged mother in his absence. Rights arise out of this transaction, but it is surely Y to whom the promise has been made and not his mother who *has* or *possesses* these rights. Certainly Y's mother is a person concerning whom X has an obligation and a person who will benefit by its performance, but the person *to whom* he has an obligation to look after her is Y. This is something *due to* or *owed to* Y, so it is Y, not his mother, whose right X will disregard and to whom X will have done *wrong* if he fails to keep his promise, though the mother may be physically injured. And it is Y who has a moral *claim* upon X; is *entitled* to have his mother looked after, and who can *waive* the claim and *release* Y from the obligation.

Y is, in other words, morally in a position to determine by his choice how X shall act and in this way to limit X's freedom of choice; and it is this fact, not the fact that he stands to benefit, that makes it appropriate to say that he has a *right*. Of course often the person to whom a promise has been made will be the only person who stands to benefit by its performance, but this does not justify the identification of 'having a right' with 'benefiting by the performance of a duty'. It is important for the whole logic of rights that, while the person who stands to benefit by the performance of a duty is discovered by considering what will happen if the duty is not performed, the person who has a right (to whom performance is *owed* or *due*) is discovered by examining the transaction or antecedent situation or relations of the parties out of which the 'duty' arises. These considerations should incline us not to extend to animals and babies whom it is wrong to ill-treat the notion of a right to proper treatment, for the moral situation can be simply and adequately described here by saying that it is wrong or that we ought not to ill-treat them or, in the philosopher's generalized sense of 'duty', that we have a duty not to ill-treat them.[8] If common usage sanctions talk of the rights of animals or babies it makes an idle use of the expression 'a right', which will confuse the situation with other different moral situations where the expression 'a right' has a specific force and cannot be replaced by the other moral expressions which I have mentioned. Perhaps some clarity on this matter is to be gained by considering the force of the preposition 'to' in the expression 'having a duty to Y' or 'being under an obligation to Y' (where 'Y' is the name of a person); for it is significantly different from the meaning of 'to' in 'doing something to Y' or 'doing harm to Y', where it indicates the person affected by some action. In the first pair of expressions, 'to' obviously does not have this force, but indicates the person to whom the person morally bound is bound. This is an intelligible development of the figure of a bond (*vinculum juris: obligare*); the precise figure is not that of two persons bound by a chain, but of *one* person bound, the other end of the chain lying in the hands of another to use if he chooses.[9] So it appears absurd to speak of having duties or owing obligations to ourselves—of course we may have 'duties' not to do harm to ourselves, but what could be meant (once the distinction between these different meanings of 'to' has been grasped) by insisting that we have duties or obligations *to* ourselves not to do harm to ourselves?

[8] The use here of the generalized 'duty' is apt to prejudice the question whether animals and babies have rights.

[9] Cf. A. H. Campbell, *The Structure of Stair's Institutes* (Glasgow, 1954), p. 31.

(D) The essential connection between the notion of a right and the justified limitation of one person's freedom by another may be thrown into relief if we consider codes of behaviour which do not purport to confer rights but only to prescribe what shall be done. Most natural law thinkers down to Hooker conceived of natural law in this way: there were natural duties compliance with which would certainly benefit man—things to be done to achieve man's natural end—but not natural rights. And there are of course many types of codes of behaviour which only prescribe what is to be done, e.g. those regulating certain ceremonies. It would be absurd to regard these codes as conferring rights, but illuminating to contrast them with rules of games, which often create rights, though not, of course, moral rights. But even a code which is plainly a moral code need not establish rights; the Decalogue is perhaps the most important example. Of course, quite apart from heavenly rewards human beings stand to benefit by general obedience to the Ten Commandments: disobedience is wrong and will certainly harm individuals. But it would be a surprising interpretation of them that treated them as conferring rights. In such an interpretation obedience to the Ten Commandments would have to be conceived as due to or owed to individuals, not merely to God, and disobedience not merely as wrong but as *a wrong to* (as well as harm to) individuals. The Commandments would cease to read like penal statutes designed only to rule out certain types of behaviour and would have to be thought of as rules placed at the disposal of individuals and regulating the extent to which *they* may demand certain behaviour from others. Rights are typically conceived of as *possessed* or *owned by* or *belonging to* individuals, and these expressions reflect the conception of moral rules as not only prescribing conduct but as forming a kind of moral property of individuals to which they are as individuals entitled; only when rules are conceived in this way can we speak of *rights* and *wrongs* as well as right and wrong actions.[10]

II

So far I have sought to establish that to have a right entails having a moral justification for limiting the freedom of another person and for determining how he should act; it is now important to see that the moral justification must be of a special kind if it is to constitute a right, and this will emerge most clearly from an examination of the circumstances in which rights are asserted with the typical expression 'I have

[10] Continental jurists distinguish between '*subjektives*' and '*objektives Recht*', which corresponds very well to the distinction between *a* right, which an individual has, and what it is right to do.

a right to . . .'. It is I think the case that this form of words is used in two main types of situations: (A) when the claimant has some special justification for interference with another's freedom which other persons do not have ('*I* have a right to be paid what you promised for my services'); (B) when the claimant is concerned to resist or object to some interference by another person as having no justification ('*I* have a right to say what I think').

(A) *Special rights*. When rights arise out of special transactions between individuals or out of some special relationship in which they stand to each other, both the persons who have the right and those who have the corresponding obligation are limited to the parties to the special transaction or relationship. I call such rights special rights to distinguish them from those moral rights which are thought of as rights against (i.e. as imposing obligations upon)[11] everyone, such as those that are asserted when some unjustified interference is made or threatened as in (B) above.

(i) The most obvious cases of special rights are those that arise from promises. By promising to do or not to do something, we voluntarily incur obligations and create or confer rights on those to whom we promise; we alter the existing moral independence of the parties' freedom of choice in relation to some action and create a new moral relationship between them, so that it becomes morally legitimate for the person to whom the promise is given to determine how the promisor shall act. The promisee has a temporary authority or sovereignty in relation to some specific matter over the other's will which we express by saying that the promisor is under an obligation *to* the promisee to do what he has promised. To some philosophers the notion that moral phenomena—rights and duties or obligations—can be brought into existence by the voluntary action of individuals has appeared utterly mysterious; but this I think has been so because they have not clearly seen how special the moral notions of a right and an obligation are, nor how peculiarly they are connected with the distribution of freedom of choice; it would indeed be mysterious if we could make actions morally good or bad by voluntary choice. The simplest case of promising illustrates two points characteristic of all special rights: (1) the right and obligation arise not because the promised action has itself any particular moral quality, but just because of the voluntary transaction between the parties; (2) the identity of the parties concerned is vital—only *this* person (the promisee) has the moral justification for determining how the promisor shall act. It is

[11] Cf. sect. (B) below.

his right; only in relation to him is the promisor's freedom of choice diminished, so that if he chooses to release the promisor no one else can complain.

(ii) But a promise is not the only kind of transaction whereby rights are conferred. They may be *accorded* by a person consenting or authorizing another to interfere in matters which but for his consent or authorization he would be free to determine for himself. If I consent to your taking precautions for my health and happiness or authorize you to look after my interests, then you have a right which others have not, and I cannot complain of your interference if it is within the sphere of your authority. This is what is meant by a person surrendering his rights to another; and again the typical characteristics of a right are present in this situation: the person authorized has the right to interfere not because of its intrinsic character but because *these* persons have stood in *this* relationship. No one else (not similarly authorized) has any *right*[12] to interfere in theory even if the person authorized does not exercise his right.

(iii) Special rights are not only those created by the deliberate choice of the party on whom the obligation falls, as they are when they are accorded or spring from promises, and not all obligations to other persons are deliberately incurred, though I think it is true of all special rights that they arise from previous voluntary actions. A third very important source of special rights and obligations which we recognize in many spheres of life is what may be termed mutuality of restrictions, and I think political obligation is intelligible only if we see what precisely this is and how it differs from other right-creating transactions (consent, promising) to which philosophers have assimilated it. In its bare schematic outline it is this: when a number of persons conduct any joint enterprise according to rules and thus restrict their liberty, those who have submitted to these restrictions when required have a right to a similar submission from those who have benefited by their submission. The rules may provide that officials should have authority to enforce obedience and make further rules, and this will create a structure of legal rights and duties, but the moral obligation to obey the rules in such circumstances is *due to* the co-operating members of the society, and they have the correlative moral right to obedience. In social situations of this sort (of which political society is the most complex example) the obligation to obey the rules is something distinct from whatever other moral reasons there may be for obedience in terms of good consequences (e.g. the prevention of suffering); the obligation

[12] Though it may be *better* (the lesser of two evils) that he should: cf. below.

is due to the co-operating members of the society as such and not because they are human beings on whom it would be wrong to inflict suffering. The utilitarian explanation of political obligation fails to take account of this feature of the situation both in its simple version that the obligation exists because and only if the direct consequences of a particular act of disobedience are worse than obedience, and also in its more sophisticated version that the obligation exists even when this is not so, if disobedience increases the probability that the law in question or other laws will be disobeyed on other occasions when the direct consequences of obedience are better than those of disobedience.

Of course to say that there is such a moral obligation upon those who have benefited by the submission of other members of society to restrictive rules to obey these rules in their turn does not entail either that this is the only kind of moral reason for obedience or that there can be no cases where disobedience will be morally justified. There is no contradiction or other impropriety in saying 'I have an obligation to do X, someone has a right to ask me to, but I now see I ought not to do it'. It will in painful situations sometimes be the lesser of two moral evils to disregard what really are people's rights and not perform our obligations to them. This seems to me particularly obvious from the case of promises: I may promise to do something and thereby incur an obligation just because that is one way in which obligations (to be distinguished from other forms of moral reasons for acting) are created; reflection may show that it would in the circumstances be wrong to keep this promise because of the suffering it might cause, and we can express this by saying '*I ought not* to do it though *I have an obligation to him* to do it' just because the italicized expressions are not synonyms but come from different dimensions of morality. The attempt to explain this situation by saying that our real obligation here is to avoid the suffering and that there is only a prima-facie obligation to keep the promise seems to me to confuse two quite different kinds of moral reason, and in practice such a terminology obscures the precise character of what is at stake when 'for some greater good' we infringe people's rights or do not perform our obligations to them.

The social-contract theorists rightly fastened on the fact that the obligation to obey the law is not merely a special case of benevolence (direct or indirect), but something which arises between members of a particular political society out of their mutual relationship. Their mistake was to identify *this* right-creating situation of mutual restrictions with the paradigm case of promising; there are of course important similarities, and these are just the points which all special rights have in common, viz. that they arise out of special relationships between human beings and not out of the character of the action to be done or its effects.

(iv) There remains a type of situation which may be thought of as creating rights and obligations: where the parties have a special natural relationship, as in the case of parent and child. The parent's moral right to obedience from his child would I suppose now be thought to terminate when the child reaches the age 'of discretion', but the case is worth mentioning because some political philosophies have had recourse to analogies with this case as an explanation of political obligation, and also because even this case has some of the features we have distinguished in special rights, viz. the right arises out of the special relationship of the parties (though it is in this case a natural relationship) and not out of the character of the actions to the performance of which there is a right.

(v) To be distinguished from special rights, of course, are special liberties, where, exceptionally, one person is *exempted* from obligations to which most are subject but does not thereby acquire a *right* to which there is a correlative obligation. If you catch me reading your brother's diary, you say, 'You have no right to read it'. I say, 'I have a right to read it—your brother said I might unless he told me not to, and he has not told me not to.' Here I have been specially *licensed* by your brother who had a right to require me not to read his diary, so I am exempted from the moral obligation not to read it. Cases where *rights*, not liberties, are accorded to manage or interfere with another person's affairs are those where the licence is not revocable at will by the person according the right.

(B) *General rights*. In contrast with special rights, which constitute a justification peculiar to the holder of the right for interfering with another's freedom, are general rights, which are asserted defensively, when some unjustified interference is anticipated or threatened, in order to point out that the interference is unjustified. 'I have the right to say what I think.'[13] 'I have the right to worship as I please.' Such rights share two important characteristics with special rights. (1) to have them is to have moral justification for determining how another shall act, viz. that he shall not interfere.[14] (2) The moral justification

[13] In speech the difference between general and special rights is often marked by stressing the pronoun where a special right is claimed or where the special right is denied. 'You have no right to stop him reading that book' refers to the reader's general right. '*You* have no right to stop him reading that book' denies that the person addressed has a special right to interfere though others may have.

[14] Strictly, in the assertion of a general right both the *right* to forbearance from coercion and the *liberty* to do the specified action are asserted, the first in the face of actual or threatened coercion, the second as an objection to an actual

does not arise from the character of the particular action to the performance of which the claimant has a right; what justifies the claim is simply—there being no special relation between him and those who are threatening to interfere to justify that interference—that this is a particular exemplification of the equal right to be free. But there are of course striking differences between such defensive general rights and special rights. (1) General rights do not arise out of any special relationship or transaction between men. (2) They are not rights which are peculiar to those who have them but are rights which all men capable of choice have in the absence of those special conditions which give rise to special rights. (3) General rights have as correlatives obligations not to interfere to which everyone else is subject and not merely the parties to some special relationship or transaction, though of course they will often be asserted when some particular persons threaten to interfere as a moral objection to the interference. To assert a general right is to claim in relation to some particular action the equal right of all men to be free in the absence of any of those special conditions which constitute a special right to limit another's freedom; to assert a special right is to assert in relation to some particular action a right constituted by such special conditions to limit another's freedom. The assertion of general rights directly invokes the principle that all men equally have the right to be free; the assertion of a special right (as I attempt to show in Section III) invokes it indirectly.

III

It is, I hope, clear that unless it is recognized that interference with another's freedom requires a moral justification the notion of a right could have no place in morals; for to assert a right is to assert that there is such a justification. The characteristic function in moral discourse of those sentences in which the meaning of the expression 'a right' is to be found—'I have a right to . . .', 'You have no right to . . .', 'What right have you to . . .?'—is to bring to bear on interferences with another's freedom, or on claims to interfere, a type of moral evaluation or criticism specially appropriate to interference with freedom and characteristically different from the moral criticism of actions made with the use of expressions like 'right', 'wrong', 'good', and 'bad'. And this is only one of many different types of moral ground for saying 'You ought . . .' or 'You ought not . . .'. The use of the expression 'What

or anticipated demand that the action should not be done. The first has as its correlative an obligation upon everyone to forbear from coercion. the second the absence in any one of a justification for such a demand. Here, in Hohfeld's words, the correlative is not an obligation but a 'no-right'.

right have you to . . .?' shows this more clearly, perhaps, than the others; for we use it, just at the point where interference is actual or threatened, to call for the moral *title* of the person addressed to interfere; and we do this often without any suggestion at all that what he proposes to do is otherwise wrong and sometimes with the implication that the same interference on the part of another person would be unobjectionable.

But though our use in moral discourse of 'a right' does presuppose the recognition that interference with another's freedom requires a moral justification, this would not itself suffice to establish, except in a sense easily trivialized, that in the recognition of moral rights there is implied the recognition that all men have a right to equal freedom; for unless there is some restriction inherent in the meaning of 'a right' on the type of moral justification for interference which can constitute a right, the principle could be made wholly vacuous. It would, for example, be possible to adopt the principle and then assert that some characteristic or behaviour of some human beings (that they are improvident, or atheists, or Jews, or Negroes) constitutes a moral justification for interfering with their freedom; *any* differences between men could, so far as my argument has yet gone, be treated as a moral justification for interference and so constitute a right, so that the equal right of all men to be free would be compatible with gross inequality. It may well be that the expression 'moral' itself imports some restriction on what can constitute a moral justification for interference which would avoid this consequence, but I cannot myself yet show that this is so. It is, on the other hand, clear to me that the moral justification for interference which is to constitute a *right* to interfere (as distinct from merely making it morally good or desirable to interfere) is restricted to certain special conditions and that this is inherent in the meaning of 'a right' (unless this is used so loosely that it could be replaced by the other moral expressions mentioned). Claims to interfere with another's freedom based on the general character of the activities interfered with (e.g. the folly or cruelty of 'native' practices) or the general character of the parties ('We are Germans. They are Jews') even when well founded are not matters of moral right or obligation. Submission in such cases even where proper is not *due to* or *owed to* the individuals who interfere, it would be equally proper whoever of the same class of persons interfered. Hence other elements in our moral vocabulary suffice to describe this case, and it is confusing here to talk of rights. We saw in Section II that the types of justification for interference involved in special rights was independent of the character of the action to the performance of which there was a right but depended upon certain previous transactions and relations between individuals (such as promises, consent, authorization, submission to mutual restrictions). Two questions here suggest themselves: (1) On what intelligible principle could these bare forms of promising, consenting, submission to mutual restrictions, be either necessary or sufficient, irrespective of their content, to justify interference with another's freedom? (2) What characteristics have these types of transaction or relationship in common? The answer to both these questions is I think this: if we justify interference on such grounds as we give when we claim a moral right, we are in fact indirectly invoking as our justification the principle that all men have an equal right to be free. For we are in fact saying in the case of promises and consents or authorizations that this claim to interfere with another's freedom is justified because he has, in exercise of his equal right to be free, freely chosen to create this claim; and in the case of mutual restrictions we are in fact saying that this claim to interfere with another's freedom is justified because it is fair; and it is fair because only so will there be an equal distribution of restrictions and so of freedom among this group of men. So in the case of special rights as well as of general rights recognition of them implies the recognition of the equal right of all men to be free.

IV

ARE THERE ANY ABSOLUTE RIGHTS?

ALAN GEWIRTH

IT IS a widely held opinion that there are no absolute rights. Consider what would be generally regarded as the most plausible candidate: the right to life. This right entails at least the negative duty to refrain from killing any human being. But it is contended that this duty may be overridden, that a person may be justifiably killed if this is the only way to prevent him from killing some other, innocent person, or if he is engaged in combat in the army of an unjust aggressor nation with which one's own country is at war. It is also maintained that even an innocent person may justifiably be killed if failure to do so will lead to the deaths of other such persons. Thus an innocent person's right to life is held to be overridden when a fat man stuck in the mouth of a cave prevents the exit of speleologists who will otherwise drown, or when a child or some other guiltless person is strapped onto the front of an aggressor's tank, or when an explorer's choice to kill one among a group of harmless natives about to be executed is the necessary and sufficient condition of the others' being spared, or when the driver of a runaway trolley can avoid killing five persons on one track only by killing one person on another track.[1] And topping all such tragic examples is the catastrophic situtation where a nuclear war or some other

Reprinted by permission of the author and the *Philosophical Quarterly* from *Philosophical Quarterly*, 31 (1981), pp. 1–16.

[1] For the cave example, see Philippa Foot, 'The Problem of Abortion and the Doctrine of Double Effect', *Oxford Review*, no. 5 (1967), p. 7. For the 'innocent shield' and the tank, see Robert Nozick, *Anarchy, State, and Utopia* (New York, 1974), p. 35, and Judith J. Thomson, *Self-Defense and Rights* (Lindley Lecture, University of Kansas, 1976), p. 11. For the explorer and the natives, see Bernard Williams, 'A Critique of Utilitarianism', in J. J. C. Smart and B. Williams, *Utilitarianism For and Against* (Cambridge, 1973), pp. 98–9. For the trolley example, see Foot, op. cit., p. 8, and Judith J. Thomson, 'Killing, Letting Die, and the Trolley Problem', *The Monist*, 59 (1976), pp. 206 ff. I have borrowed from Thomson's *Self-Defense and Rights*, p. 10, the terminological distinction used below between 'infringing' and 'violating' a right.

unmitigated disaster can be avoided only by infringing some innocent person's right to life.

Despite such cases, I shall argue that certain rights can be shown to be absolute. But first the concept of an absolute right must be clarified.

I

1. I begin with the Hohfeldian point that the rights here in question are claim-rights (as against liberties, powers, and so forth) in that they are justified claims or entitlements to the carrying out of correlative duties, positive or negative. A duty is a requirement that some action be performed or not be performed; in the latter, negative case, the requirement constitutes a prohibition.

A right is *fulfilled* when the correlative duty is carried out, i.e. when the required action is performed or the prohibited action is not performed. A right is *infringed* when the correlative duty is not carried out, i.e. when the required action is not performed or the prohibited action is performed. Thus someone's right to life is infringed when the prohibited action of killing him is performed; someone's right to medical care is infringed when the required action of providing him with medical care is not performed. A right is *violated* when it is unjustifiably infringed, i.e. when the required action is unjustifiably not performed or the prohibited action is unjustifiably performed. And a right is *overridden* when it is justifiably infringed, so that there is sufficient justification for not carrying out the correlative duty, and the required action is justifiably not performed or the prohibited action is justifiably performed.

A right is *absolute* when it cannot be overridden in any circumstances, so that it can never be justifiably infringed and it must be fulfilled without any exceptions.

The idea of an absolute right is thus doubly normative: it includes not only the idea, common to all claim-rights, of a justified claim or entitlement to the performance or non-performance of certain actions, but also the idea of the exceptionless justifiability of performing or not performing those actions as required. These components show that the question whether there are any absolute rights demands for its adequate answer an explicit concern with criteria of justification. I shall here assume what I have elsewhere argued for in some detail: that these criteria, in so far as they are valid, are ultimately based on a certain supreme principle of morality. the Principle of Generic Consistency (*PGC*).[2] This principle requires of every agent that he act in accord with

[2] Alan Gewirth, *Reason and Morality* (Chicago, 1978), pp. 135 ff., 197–8, 343–4.

the generic rights of his recipients as well as of himself, i.e., that he fulfil these rights. The generic rights are rights to the necessary conditions of action, freedom, and well-being, where the latter is defined in terms of the various substantive abilities and conditions needed for action and for successful action in general. The *PGC* provides the ultimate justificatory basis for the validity of these rights by showing that they are equally had by all prospective purposive agents, and it also provides in general for the ordering of the rights in cases of conflict. Thus if two moral rights are so related that each can be fulfilled only by infringing the other, that right takes precedence whose fulfilment is more necessary for action. This criterion of degrees of necessity for action explains, for example, why one person's right not to be lied to must give way to another person's right not to be killed when these two rights are in conflict. In some cases the application of this criterion requires a context of institutional rules.

2. The general formula of a right is as follows: 'A has a right to X against B by virtue of Y.' In addition to the right itself, there are four elements here: the *subject* of the right, the right-holder (A); the *object* of the right (X); the *respondent* of the right, the person who has the correlative duty (B); and the *justificatory basis* or *ground* of the right (Y). I shall refer to these elements jointly as the *contents* of the right. Each of the elements may vary in generality. Various rights may conflict with one another as to one or another of these elements, so that not all rights can be absolute.

One aspect of these conflicts is especially important for understanding the question of absolute rights. Although, as noted above, the *objects* of moral rights are hierarchically ordered (according to the degree of their necessity for action), this is not true of the *subjects* of the rights. If one class or group of persons inherently had superior moral rights over another class or group (as was held to be the case throughout much of human history), any conflict between their respective rights would be readily resoluble: the rights of the former group would always take precedence, they would never be overridden (at least by the rights of members of other groups), and to this extent they would be absolute.[3] It is because (as is shown by the *PGC* as well as by other moral principles) moral rights are equally distributed among all human persons as prospective purposive agents that some of the main conflicts of rights arise. This is most obviously the case

[3] Cf. Friedrich Nietzsche, *The Will to Power*, sect. 872: 'The great majority of men have no right to existence, but are a misfortune to higher men' (trans. Walter Kaufmann (New York, 1967), p. 467). See also Nietzsche, *Beyond Good and Evil*, sect. 260 (trans. Kaufmann (New York, 1966), p. 206).

where one person's right to life conflicts with another person's, since in the absence of guilt on either side, it is assumed that the two person's have equal rights. Thus the difficulty of supporting the thesis that there are absolute rights derives much of its force from its connection with the principle that all persons are equal in their moral rights.

3. The differentiation of the elements of rights serves to explicate the various levels at which rights may be held to be absolute. We may distinguish three such levels. The first is that of *Principle Absolutism*. According to this, what is absolute, and thus always valid and never overridden, is only some moral principle of a very high degree of generality which, referring to the subjects, the respondents, and especially the objects of rights in a relatively undifferentiated way, presents a general formula for all the diverse duties of all respondents or agents toward all subjects or recipients. The *PGC* is such a principle; so too are the Golden Rule, the law of love, Kant's categorical imperative, and the principle of utility. Principle Absolutism, however, may leave open the question whether any specific rights are always absolute, and what is to be done in the cases of conflict. Even act-utilitarianism might be an example of Principle Absolutism, for it may be interpreted as saying that those rights are absolute whose fulfilment would serve to maximize utility overall. These rights, whatever they may be, might of course vary in their specific contents from one situation to another.

At the opposite extreme is *Individual Absolutism*, according to which an individual person has an absolute right to some particular object, at a particular time and place when all grounds for overriding the right in the particular case have been overcome. But this still leaves open the question of what are the general grounds or criteria for overriding any right, and what are the other specific contents of such rights.

It is at the intermediate level, that of *Rule Absolutism*, that the question of absolute rights arises most directly. At this level, the rights whose absoluteness is in question are characterized in terms of specific objects with possible specification also of subjects and respondents, so that a specific rule can be stated describing the content of the right and the correlative duty. The description will not use proper names and other individual referring expressions, as in the case of Individual Absolutism, nor will it consist only in a general formula applicable to many specifically different kinds of rights and duties and hence of objects, subjects, and respondents, as in the case of Principle Absolutism. It is at this level that one asks whether the right to life of all persons or of all innocent persons is absolute, whether the rights to freedom of speech and of religion are absolute, and so forth.

The rights whose absoluteness is considered at the level of Rule Absolutism may vary in degree of generality, in that their objects, their subjects, and their respondents may be given with greater or lesser specificity. Thus there is greater specificity as we move along the following scale: the right of all persons to life, the right of all innocent persons to life, the right of all innocent persons to an economically secure life, the right of children to receive an economically secure and emotionally satisfying life from their parents, and so forth.

This variability raises the following problem. For a right to be absolute, it must be conclusively valid without any exceptions. But, as we have seen, rights may vary in generality, and all the resulting specifications of their objects, subjects, or respondents may constitute exceptions to the more general rights in which such specifications are not present. For example, the right of innocent persons to life may incorporate an exception to the right of all persons to life, for the rule embodying the former right may be stated thus: all persons have a right not to be killed except when the persons are not innocent, or except when such killing is directly required in order to prevent them from killing somebody else. Similarly, when it is said that all persons have a right to life, the specification of 'persons' may suggest (although it does not strictly entail) the exception-making rule that all animals (or even all organisms) have a right to life except when they are not persons (or not human). Hence, since an absolute right is one that is valid without any exceptions, it may be concluded either that no rights are absolute because all involve some specification or that all rights are equally absolute because once their specifications are admitted they are entirely valid without any further exceptions.

The solution to this problem consists in seeing that not all specifications of the subjects, objects, or respondents of moral rights constitute the kinds of exception whose applicability to a right debars it from being absolute. I shall indicate three criteria for permissible specifications. First, when it is asked concerning some moral right whether it is absolute, the kind of specification that may be incorporated in the right can only be such as results in a concept that is recognizable to ordinary practical thinking. This excludes rights that are 'overloaded with exceptions', as well as those whose application would require intricate utilitarian calculations.[4]

[4] See R. M. Hare, 'Principles', *Proceedings of the Aristotelian Society*, 73 (1972–73), pp. 7 ff. This paper is also relevant to some of the other issues of 'exceptions' discussed above. See also Marcus G. Singer, *Generalization in Ethics* (New York, 1961), pp. 100–3, 124–33, and David Lyons, 'Mill's Theory of Morality', *Noûs*, 10 (1976), pp. 112–13.

Second, the specifications must be justifiable through a valid moral principle. Since, as we saw above, the idea of an absolute right is doubly normative, a right with its specification would not even begin to be a candidate for absoluteness unless the specification were morally justified and could hence be admitted as a condition of the justifiability of the moral right. There is, for example, a good moral justification for incorporating the restriction of innocence on the subjects of the right not to be killed; but there is not a similarly good moral justification for incorporating racial, religious, and other such particularist specifications. It must be emphasized, however, that this moral specification guarantees only that the right thus specified is an appropriate candidate for being absolute; it is, of itself, not decisive as to whether the right *is* absolute.

A third criterion is that the permissible specification of a right must exclude any reference to the possibly disastrous consequences of fulfilling the right. Since a chief difficulty posed against absolute rights is that for any right there can be cases in which its fulfilment may have disastrous consequences, to put this reference into the very description of the right would remove one of the main grounds for raising the question of absoluteness.

The relation between rights and disasters is complicated by the fact that the latter, when caused by the actions of persons, are themselves infringements of rights. This point casts a new light on the consequentialist's thesis that there are no absolute rights. For when he says that every right may be overridden if this is required in order to avoid certain catastrophes—such as when torture alone will enable the authorities to ascertain where a terrorist has hidden a fused charge of dynamite—the consequentialist is appealing to basic rights. He is saying that in such a case one right—the right not to be tortured—is overridden by another right: the right to life of the many potential victims of the explosion. This raises the following question. Can the process of one right's overriding another continue indefinitely or does the process come to a stop with absolute rights?

In order to deal with this question, two points must be kept in mind. First, even when catastrophes threatening the infringement of basic rights are invoked to override other rights, at least part of the problem created by such conflict depends, as was noted above, on the assumption that all the persons involved here have equal moral rights. There would be no serious conflict of rights and no problem about absolute rights if, for example, the rights of the persons threatened by the catastrophe were deemed inferior to those of persons not so threatened.

Second, despite the close connection between rights in general and the rights threatened by disastrous consequences, it is important to distinguish them. For if the appeal to avoidance of disastrous consequences were to be construed simply as an appeal for the fulfilment or protection of certain basic rights, then, on the assumption that certain disasters must always be avoided when they are threatened, the consequentialist would himself be an absolutist. We can escape this untoward result and render more coherent the opposition between absolutism and consequentialism if we recognize a further important assumption of the question whether there are any absolute rights. Amid the various possible specifications of Rule Absolutism, the rights in question are the normative property of *distinct individuals*.[5] In referring to some event as a 'disaster' or a 'catastrophe', on the other hand, what is often meant is that a large mass of individuals *taken collectively* loses some basic good to which they have a right. It is their *aggregate* loss that constitutes the catastrophe. (This, of course, accounts for the close connection between the appeal to disastrous consequences and utilitarianism.) Thus the question whether there are any absolute rights is to be construed as asking whether distinct individuals, each of whom has equal moral rights (and who are to be characterized, according to the conditions of Rule Absolutism, by specifications that are morally justifiable and recognizable to ordinary practical thinking), have any rights that may never be overridden by any other considerations, including even their catastrophic consequences for collective rights.

II

4. We must now examine the merits of the prime consequentialist argument against the possibility of absolute moral rights: that circumstances can always be imagined in which the consequences of fulfilling the rights would be so disastrous that their requirements would be overridden. The formal structure of the argument is as follows: (1) if R, then D. (2) O (~D). (3) Therefore, O(~R). For example, (1) if some person's right to life is fulfilled in certain circumstances, then some great disaster may or will occur. But (2) such disaster ought never to (be allowed to) occur. Hence, (3) in such circumstances the right ought not to be fulfilled, so that it is not absolute.

Proponents of this argument have usually failed to notice that a parallel argument can be given in the opposite direction. If exceptions to the fulfilment of any moral right can be justified by imagining the possible disastrous consequences of fulfilling it, why cannot exceptionless

[5] Cf. H. L. A. Hart, 'Are There Any Natural Rights?', *Philosophical Review*, 64 (1955), p. 182 (reprinted here), and Hart, 'Bentham on Legal Rights', in *Oxford Essays in Jurisprudence*, 2nd Series, ed. A. W. B. Simpson (Oxford, 1973), p. 193.

moral rights be justified by giving them such contents that their infringement would be unspeakably evil? The argument to this effect may be put formally as follows: (1) If ~R, then E. (2) O(~E). (3) Therefore, O(R). For example, (1) if a mother's right not to be tortured to death by her own son is not fulfilled, then there will be unspeakable evil. But (2) such evil ought never to (be allowed to) occur. Hence, (3) the right ought to be fulfilled without any exceptions, so that it is absolute.

Two preliminary points must be made about these arguments. First, despite their formal parallelism, there is an important difference in the meaning of 'then' in their respective first premisses. In the first argument, 'then' signifies a consequential causal connection: if someone's right to life is fulfilled, there may or will ensue as a result the quite distinct phenomenon of a certain great disaster. But in the second argument, 'then' signifies a moral conceptual relation: the unspeakable evil is not a causal *consequence* of a mother's being tortued to death by her own son; it is rather a central moral constituent of it. Thus the second argument is not consequentialist, as the first one is, despite the fact that each of their respective first premisses has the logical form of antecedent and consequent.

A related point bears on the second argument's specification of the right in question as a mother's right not to be tortured to death by her own son. This specification does not transgress the third requirement given above for permissible specifications: that reference to disastrous consequences must not be included in the formulation of the right. For the torturing to death is not a disastrous causal consequence of infringing the right; it is directly an infringement of the right itself, just as not being tortured to death by her own son is not a consequence of fulfilling the right but *is* the right. This distinction can perhaps be seen more clearly in such a less extreme case as the right not to be lied to. Being told a lie is not a causal *consequence* of infringing this right; rather, it just is an infringement of the right. In each case, moreover, the first two requirements for permissible specifications of moral rights are also satisfied: their contents are recognizable to ordinary practical thinking and they are justified by a valid moral principle.

5. Let us now consider the right mentioned above: a mother's right not to be tortured to death by her own son. Assume (although these specifications are here quite dispensable) that she is innocent of any crime and has no knowledge of any. What justifiable exception could there be to such a right? I shall construct an example which, though fanciful, has sufficient analogues in past and present thought and action to make it relevant to the status of rights in the real world.[6]

[6] Cf. Aristotle, *Nicomachean Ethics*, III. 1. 1110a5, 27, and H. V. Dicks,

Suppose a clandestine group of political extremists have obtained an arsenal of nuclear weapons; to prove that they have the weapons and know how to use them, they have kidnapped a leading scientist, shown him the weapons, and then released him to make a public corroborative statement. The terrorists have now announced that they will use the weapons against a designated large distant city unless a certain prominent resident of the city, a young politically active lawyer named Abrams, tortures his mother to death, this torturing to be carried out publicly in a certain way at a specified place and time in that city. Since the gang members have already murdered several other prominent residents of the city, their threat is quite credible. Their declared motive is to advance their cause by showing how powerful they are and by unmasking the moralistic pretensions of their political opponents.

Ought Abrams to torture his mother to death in order to prevent the threatened nuclear catastrophe? Might he not merely pretend to torture his mother, so that she could then be safely hidden while the hunt for the gang members continued? Entirely apart from the fact that the gang could easily pierce this deception, the main objection to the very raising of such questions is the moral one that they seem to hold open the possibility of acquiescing and participating in an unspeakably evil project. To inflict such extreme harm on one's mother would be an ultimate act of betrayal; in performing or even contemplating the performance of such an action the son would lose all self-respect and would regard his life as no longer worth living.[7] A mother's right not to be tortured to death by her own son is beyond any compromise. It is absolute.

Licensed Mass Murder: A Socio-Psychological Study of Some S.S. Killers (London, 1972). For similar extreme examples, see I. M. Crombie, 'Moral Principles' in *Christian Ethics and Contemporary Philosophy*, ed. Ian T. Ramsey (New York, 1966), p. 258; Paul Ramsey, 'The Case of the Curious Exception', in *Norm and Context in Christian Ethics*, ed. Gene H. Outka and P. Ramsey (New York, 1968), pp. 101, 127 ff; Donald Evans, 'Paul Ramsey on Exceptionless Moral Rules', *American Journal of Jurisprudence*, 16 (1971), pp. 204, 207; John M. Swomley, Jr., in *The Situation Ethics Debate*, ed. Harvey Cox (Philadelphia, 1968), p. 87; I have elsewhere argued for another absolute right: the right to the non-infliction of cancer. See Alan Gewirth, 'Human Rights and the Prevention of Cancer', *American Philosophical Quarterly*, 17 (1980), pp. 117–25.

[7] This reference to the minimal moral conditions of a worthwhile life is, of course, an ancient theme; see Aristotle, *Nichomachean Ethics*, III. 1. 1110a 27; IV. 3. 1124b 7; IX. 8. 1169a 20 ff. For an excellent contemporary statement, see Alan Donagan, *The Theory of Morality* (Chicago, 1977), especially pp. 156–57, 183. For other recent discussions of the relation of the agent's character and intentions to moral absolutism, see John Casey 'Actions and Consequences', in

This absoluteness may be analysed in several different interrelated dimensions, all stemming from the supreme principle of morality. The principle requires respect for the rights of all persons to the necessary conditions of human action, and this includes respect for the persons themselves as having the rational capacity to reflect on their purposes and to control their behaviour in the light of such reflection. The principle hence prohibits using any person merely as a means to the well-being of other persons. For a son to torture his mother to death even to protect the lives of others would be an extreme violation of this principle and hence of these rights, as would any attempt by others to force such an action. For this reason, the concept appropriate to it is not merely 'wrong' but such others as 'despicable', 'dishonourable', 'base', 'monstrous'. In the scale of moral modalities, such concepts function as the contrary extremes of concepts like the supererogatory. What is supererogatory is not merely good or right but goes beyond these in various ways; it includes saintly and heroic actions whose moral merit surpasses what is strictly required of agents. In parallel fashion, what is base, dishonourable, or despicable is not merely bad or wrong but goes beyond these in moral demerit since it subverts even the minimal worth or dignity both of its agent and of its recipient and hence the basic presuppositions of morality itself. Just as the supererogatory is superlatively good, so the despicable is superlatively evil and diabolic, and its moral wrongness is so rotten that a morally decent person will not even consider doing it. This is but another way of saying that the rights it would violate must remain absolute.

6. There is, however, another side to this story. What of the thousands of innocent persons in the distant city whose lives are imperilled by the threatened nuclear explosion? Don't they too have rights to life which, because of their numbers, are far superior to the mother's right? May they not contend that while it is all very well for Abrams to preserve his moral purity by not killing his mother, he has no right to purchase this at the expense of their lives, thereby treating them as mere means to his ends and violating their own rights? Thus it may be argued that the morally correct description of the alternative confronting Abrams is not simply that it is one of not violating or violating an innocent person's right to life, but rather not violating one innocent person's right to life and thereby violating the right to life of thousands of other innocent persons through being partly responsible for their deaths, or violating one innocent person's

Morality and Moral Reasoning, ed. J. Casey (London, 1971), pp. 155–7, 195 ff.; R. A. Duff, 'Absolute Principles and Double Effect', *Analysis*, 36 (1976), pp. 73 ff.; P. T. Geach, *The Virtues* (Cambridge, 1977), pp. 113–17.

right to life and thereby protecting or fulfilling the right to life of thousands of other innocent persons. We have here a tragic conflict of rights and an illustration of the heavy price exacted by moral absolutism. The aggregative consequentialist who holds that the action ought always to be performed which maximizes utility or minimizes disutility would maintain that in such a situation the lives of the thousands must be preferred.

An initial answer may be that terrorists who make such demands and issue such threats cannot be trusted to keep their word not to drop the bombs if the mother is tortured to death; and even if they now do keep their word, acceding in this case would only lead to further escalated demands and threats. It may also be argued that it is irrational to perpetrate a sure evil in order to forestall what is so far only a possible or threatened evil. Philippa Foot has sagely commented on cases of this sort that if it is the son's duty to kill his mother in order to save the lives of the many other innocent residents of the city, then 'anyone who wants us to do something we think wrong has only to threaten that otherwise he himself will do something we think worse'.[8] Much depends, however, on the nature of the 'wrong' and the 'worse'. If someone threatens to commit suicide or to kill innocent hostages if we do not break our promise to do some relatively unimportant action, breaking the promise would be the obviously right course, by the criterion of degrees of necessity for action. The special difficulty of the present case stems from the fact that the conflicting rights are of the same supreme degree of importance.

It may be contended, however, that this whole answer, focusing on the probable outcome of obeying the terrorists' demands, is a consequentialist argument and, as such, is not available to the absolutist who insists that Abrams must not torture his mother to death whatever the consequences.[9] This contention imputes to the absolutist a kind of indifference or even callousness to the sufferings of others that is not warranted by a correct understanding of his position. He can be concerned about consequences so long as he does not regard them as possibly superseding or diminishing the right and duty he regards as absolute. It is a matter of priorities. So long as the mother's right not to be tortured to death by her son is unqualifiedly respected, the absolutist can seek ways to mitigate the threatened disastrous consequences and possibly to avert them altogether. A parallel case is found in the theory of legal punishment: the retributivist, while asserting

[8] 'The Problem of Abortion and the Doctrine of Double Effect' (see n. 1), p. 10.

[9] See Jonathan Bennett, 'Whatever the Consequences', *Analysis*, 26 (1966), pp. 89–91.

that punishment must be meted out only to the persons who deserve it because of the crimes they have committed, may also uphold punishment for its deterrent effect so long as the latter, consequentialist consideration is subordinated to and limited by the conditions of the former, antecedentalist consideration.[10] Thus the absolutist can accommodate at least part of the consequentialist's substantive concerns within the limits of his own principle.

Is any other answer available to the absolutist, one that reflects the core of his position? Various lines of argument may be used to show that in refusing to torture his mother to death Abrams is not violating the rights of the multitudes of other residents who may die as a result, because he is not morally responsible for their deaths. Thus the absolutist can maintain that even if these others die they still have an absolute right to life because the infringement of their right is not justified by the argument he upholds. At least three different distinctions may be added for this purpose. In the unqualified form in which they have hitherto been presented, however, they are not successful in establishing the envisaged conclusion.

One distinction is between direct and oblique intention. When Abrams refrains from torturing his mother to death, he does not directly intend the many ensuing deaths of the other inhabitants either as end or as means. These are only the foreseen but unintended side-effects of his action or, in this case, inaction. Hence, he is not morally responsible for those deaths.

Apart from other difficulties with the doctrine of double effect, this distinction as so far stated does not serve to exculpate Abrams. Consider some parallels. Industrialists who pollute the environment with poisonous chemicals and manufacturers who use carcinogenic food additives do not directly intend the resulting deaths; these are only the unintended but foreseen side-effects of what they do directly intend, namely, to provide profitable demand-fulfilling commodities. The entrepreneurs in question may even maintain that the enormous economic contributions they make to the gross national product outweigh in importance the relatively few deaths that regrettably occur. Still, since they have good reason to believe that deaths will occur from causes under their control, the fact that they do not directly intend the deaths does not remove their causal and moral responsibility for them. Isn't this also true of Abrams's relation to the deaths of the city's residents?

A second distinction drawn by some absolutists is between killing

[10] See Gewirth, *Reason and Morality*, pp. 294–9.

and letting die. This distinction is often merged with others with which it is not entirely identical, such as the distinctions between commission and omission, between harming and not helping, between strict duties and generosity or supererogation. For the present discussion, however, the subtle differences between these may be overlooked. The contention, then, is that in refraining from killing his mother, Abrams does not kill the many innocent persons who will die as a result; he only lets them die. But one does not have the same strict moral duty to help persons or to prevent their dying as one has not to kill them; one is responsible only for what one does, not for what one merely allows to happen. Hence, Abrams is not morally responsible for the deaths he fails to prevent by letting the many innocent persons die, so that he does not violate their rights to life.

The difficulty with this argument is that the duties bearing on the right to life include not only that one not kill innocent persons but also that one not let them die when one can prevent their dying at no comparable cost. If, for example, one can rescue a drowning man by throwing him a rope, one has a moral duty to throw him the rope. Failure to do so is morally culpable. Hence, to this extent the son who lets the many residents die when he can prevent this by means within his power is morally responsible for their deaths.

A third distinction is between respecting other persons and avoiding bad consequences. Respect for persons is an obligation so fundamental that it cannot be overridden even to prevent evil consequences from befalling some persons. If such prevention requires an action whereby respect is withheld from persons, then that action must not be performed, whatever the consequences.

One of the difficulties with this important distinction is that it is unclear. May not respect be withheld from a person by failing to avert from him some evil consequence? How can Abrams be held to respect the thousands of innocent persons or their rights if he lets them die when he could have prevented this? The distinction also fails to provide for degrees of moral urgency. One fails to respect a person if one lies to him or steals from him; but sometimes the only way to prevent the death of one innocent person may be by stealing from or telling a lie to to some other innocent person. In such a case, respect for one person may lead to disrespect of a more serious kind for some other innocent person.

7. None of the above distinctions, then, serves its intended purpose of defending the absolutist against the consequentialist. They do not show that the son's refusal to torture his mother to death does not violate the other persons' right to life and that he is not morally

responsible for their deaths. Nevertheless, the distinctions can be supplemented in a way that does serve to establish these conclusions.

The required supplement is provided by the principle of the intervening action. According to this principle, when there is a causal connection between some person A's performing some action (or inaction) X and some other person C's incurring a certain harm Z, A's moral responsibility for Z is removed if, between X and Z, there intervenes some other action Y of some person B who knows the relevant circumstances of his action and who intends to produce Z or who produces Z through recklessness. The reason for this removal is that B's intervening action Y is the more direct or proximate cause of Z, and, unlike A's action (or inaction), Y is the sufficient conditon of Z as it actually occurs.[11]

An example of this principle may help to show its connection with the absolutist thesis. Martin Luther King Jr. was repeatedly told that because he led demonstrations in support of civil rights, he was morally responsible for the disorders, riots, and deaths that ensued and that were shaking the American Republic to its foundations.[12] By the principle of the intervening action, however, it was King's opponents who were responsible because their intervention operated as the sufficient conditions of the riots and injuries. King might also have replied that the Republic would not be worth saving if the price that had to be paid was the violation of the civil rights of black Americans. As for the rights of the other Americans to peace and order, the reply would be that these rights cannot justifiably be secured at the price of the rights of blacks.

If follows from the principle of the intervening action that it is not the son but rather the terrorists who are morally as well as causally responsible for the many deaths that do or may ensue on his refusal to torture his mother to death. The important point is not that he lets these persons die rather than kills them, or that he does not harm them but only fails to help them, or that he intends their deaths only obliquely but not directly. The point is rather that is only through the intervening of lethal actions of the terrorists that his refusal eventuates in the many deaths. Since the moral responsibility is not the son's, it does not affect his moral duty not to torture his mother to death, so that her correlative right remains absolute.

[11] Cf. H. L. A. Hart and A. M. Honoré, *Causation in the Law* (Oxford, 1959), pp. 69 ff., 127 ff., 292 ff. For an application of this principle in a related context, see Gewirth, 'Human Rights and the Prevention of Cancer' (n. 6 above), pp. 118–19.

[12] See, e.g., Charles E. Whittaker in Whittaker and William Sloane Coffin Jr., *Law, Order and Civil Disobedience* (Washington, DC, 1967), pp. 11 ff.

This point also serves to answer some related questions about the rights of the many in relation to the mother's right. Since the son's refusal to torture his mother to death is justified, it may seem that the many deaths to which that refusal will lead are also justified, so that the rights to life of these many innocent persons are not absolute. But since they are innocent, why aren't their rights to life as absolute as the mother's? If, on the other hand, their deaths are unjustified, as seems obvious, then isn't the son's refusal to torture his mother to death also unjustified, since it leads to those deaths? But from this it would follow that the mother's right not to be tortured to death by her son is not absolute, for if the son's not infringing her right is unjustified, then his infringing it would presumably be justified.

The solution to this difficulty is that it is a fallacy to infer, from the two premisses (1) the son's refusal to kill his mother is justified and (2) many innocent persons die as a result of that refusal, to the conclusion (3) their deaths are justified. For, by the principle of the intervening action, the son's refusal is not causally or morally responsible for the deaths; rather, it is the terrorists who are responsible. Hence, the justification referred to in (1) does not carry through to (2). Since the terrorists' action in ordering the killings is unjustified, the resulting deaths are unjustified. Hence, the rights to life of the many innocent victims remain absolute even if they are killed as a result of the son's justified refusal, and it is not he who violates their rights. He may be said to intend the many deaths obliquely, in that they are a foreseen but unwanted side-effect of his refusal. But he is not responsible for that side-effect because of the terrorists' intervening action.

It would be unjustified to violate the mother's right to life in order to protect the rights to life of the many other residents of the city. For rights cannot be justifiably protected by violating another right which, according to the criterion of degrees of necessity for action, is at least equally important. Hence, the many other residents do not have a right that the mother's right to life be violated for their sakes. To be sure, the mother also does not have a right that their equally important rights be violated in order to protect hers. But here too it must be emphasized that in protecting his mother's right the son does not violate the rights of the others; for by the principle of the intervening action, it is not he who is causally or morally responsible for their deaths. Hence too he is not treating them as mere means to his or his mother's ends.

8. Where, then does this leave us? From the absoluteness of the mother's right not to be tortured to death by her son, does it follow that in the described circumstances a nuclear explosion should be permitted to occur over the city so that countless thousands of

innocent persons may be killed, possibly including Abrams and his mother?

Properly to deal with this question, it is vitally important to distinguish between abstract and concrete absolutism. The abstract absolutist at no point takes account of consequences or of empirical or causal connections that may affect the subsequent outcomes of the two alternatives he considers. He views the alternatives as being both mutually exclusive and exhaustive. His sole concern is for the moral guiltlessness of the agent, as against the effects of the agent's choices for human weal or woe.

In contrast, as I suggested earlier, the concrete absolutist is concerned with consequences and empirical connections, but always within the limits of the right he upholds as absolute. His consequentialism is thus limited rather than unlimited. Because of his concern with empirical connections, he takes account of a broader range of possible alternatives than the simple dualism to which the abstract absolutist confines himself. His primary focus is not on the moral guiltlessness of the agent but rather on the basic rights of persons not to be subjected to unspeakable evils. Within this focus, however, the concrete absolutist is also deeply concerned with the effects of the fulfilment of these rights on the basic well-being of other persons.

The significance of the distinction can be seen by applying it to the case of Abrams. If he is an abstract absolutist, he deals with only two alternatives which he regards as mutually exclusive as well as exhaustive: (1) he tortures his mother to death; (2) the terrorists drop a nuclear bomb killing thousands of innocent persons. For the reasons indicated above, he rejects (1). He is thereby open to the accusation that he chooses (2) or at least that he allows (2) to happen, although the principle of the intervening action exempts him from moral guilt or responsibility.

If, however, Abrams is a concrete absolutist, then he does not regard himself as being confronted only by these two terrible alternatives, nor does he regard them or their negations as mutually exclusive. His thought-processes include the following additional considerations. In accordance with a point suggested above, he recognizes that his doing (1) will not *assure* the non-occurrence of (2). On the contrary, his doing (1) will probably *lead* to further threats of the occurrence of (2) unless he or someone else performs further unspeakably evil actions (3), (4), and so forth. (A parallel example may be found in Hitler's demand for Czechoslovakia at Munich after his taking over of Austria, his further demand for Poland after the capitulation regarding Czechoslovakia, and the ensuing tragedies). Moreover, (2) may occur even if Abrams does (1). For persons who are prepared to threaten that they will do (2) cannot be trusted to keep their word.

On the other hand, Abrams further reasons, his not doing (1) may well not lead to (2). This may be so for several reasons. He or the authorities or both must try to engage the terrorists in a dialogue in which their grievances are publicized and seriously considered. Whatever elements of rationality may exist among the terrorists will thereby be reinforced, so that other alternatives may be presented. At the same time, a vigorous search and preventive action must be pursued so as to avert the threatened bombing and to avoid any recurrences of the threat.

It is such concrete absolutism, taking due account of consequences and of possible alternatives, that constitutes the preferred pattern of ethical reasoning. It serves to protect the rights presupposed in the very possibility of a moral community while at the same time it gives the greatest probability of averting the threatened catastrophe. In the remainder of this paper, I shall assume the background of concrete absolutism.

III

9. I have thus far argued that the right of the mother not to be tortured to death by her son is absolute. But the arguments would also ground an extension of the kind of right here at issue to many other subjects and respondents, including fathers, daughters, wives, husbands, grandparents, cousins, and friends. So there are many absolute rights, on the criterion of plurality supplied by Rule Absolutism.

It is sometimes held that moral obligations are 'agent-relative' in that, at least in cases of conflict, one ought to give priority to the welfare of those persons with whom one has special ties of family or affection.[13] Applied to the present question, this view would suggest that the subjects having the absolute right that must be respected by respondents are limited to the kinds of relations listed above. It may also be thought that as we move away from familial and affectional relations, the proposed subjects of rights come to resemble more closely the anonymous masses of other persons who would be killed by a nuclear explosion, so that a quantitative measure of numbers of lives lost would become a more cogent consideration in allocating rights.

These conclusions, however, do not follow. Most of the arguments I have given above for the mother's absolute right not to be tortured to death apply to other possible human subjects without such

[13] See Derek Parfit, 'Innumerate Ethics', *Philosophy and Public Affairs*, 7 No. 4 (1978), p. 287.

specifications. My purpose in beginning with such an extreme case as the mother-son relation was to focus the issue as sharply as possible; but, this focus once gained, it may be widened in the ways just indicated. Although the mother has indeed a greater right to receive effective concern from her son than from other, unrelated persons, the unjustifiability of violating rights that are on the same level of necessity for action is not affected either by degrees of family relationship or by the numbers of persons affected. Abrams would not be justified in torturing to death some other innocent person in the described circumstances, and in failing to murder he would not be morally responsible for the deaths of other innocent persons who might be murdered by someone else as a consequence.

These considerations also apply to various progressively less extreme objects of rights than the not being tortued to death to which I have so far confined the discussion. The general content of these objects may be stated as follows: all innocent persons have an absolute right not to be made the intended victims of a homicidal project. This right, despite its increase in generality over the object, subject, and respondents of the previous right, still conforms to the requirements of Rule Absolutism. The word 'intended' here refers both to direct and to oblique intention, with the latter being subject to the principle of the intervening action. The word 'project' is meant to indicate a definite, deliberate design; hence, it excludes the kind of unforeseeable immediate crisis where, for example, the unfortunate driver of a trolley whose brakes have failed must choose between killing one person or five. The absolute right imposes a prohibition on any form of active participation in a homicidal project against innocent persons, whether by the original designers or by those who would accept its conditions with a view to warding off what they would regard as worse consequences. The meaning of 'innocent' raises many questions of interpretation into which I have no space to enter here, but some of its main criteria may be gathered from the first paragraph of this paper. As for 'persons', this refers to all prospective purposive agents.

The right not to be made the intended victim of a homicidal project is not the only specific absolute right, but it is surely one of the most important. The general point underlying all absolute rights stems from the moral principle presented earlier. At the level of Principle Absolutism, it may be stated as follows: agents and institutions are absolutely prohibited from degrading persons, treating them as if they had no rights or dignity. The benefit of this prohibition extends to all persons, innocent or guilty; for the latter, when they are justly punished, are still treated as responsible moral agents who are capable of understanding the principle of morality and acting accordingly, and the punishment must not be cruel or arbitrary. Other specific absolute rights may also be generated from this principle. Since the principle requires of every agent that he act in accord with the generic rights of his recipients as well as of himself, specific rights are absolute in so far as they serve to protect the basic presuppositions of the valid principle of morality in its equal application to all persons.

V
UTILITY AND RIGHTS*

DAVID LYONS

TWO NOTIONS concerning the relation of rights to utilitarianism seem widely accepted, by both utilitarians and their critics. The first is that utilitarianism is hostile to the idea of moral rights. The second is that utilitarianism is capable of providing a normative theory about legal and other institutional rights. This chapter chiefly concerns the second thesis, and argues against it. But it also says something about the first. In previous writings I have challenged the first thesis,[1] but here I shall suggest that it is sound. The upshot is that utilitarianism has a great deal of trouble accommodating rights.

I. SCOPE AND PLAN OF THE ARGUMENT

By 'Utilitarianism' I mean the theory that the only sound, fundamental basis for normative (or moral) appraisal is the promotion of human

Reprinted by permission of New York University Press from *Ethics, Economics and the Law: NOMOS XXIV*, edd. J. Roland Pennock and John W. Chapman, copyright © 1982 by New York University Press, pp. 107–38.

* This is a revised version of a paper presented to the annual meeting of the American Society for Political and Legal Philosophy on 4 January 1980. An earlier version with a narrower focus, entitled 'Utility as a Possible Ground of Rights', published in *Noûs*, 14 (March 1980), 17–28. In arriving at the views developed in these articles, as well as in revising them, I have been helped considerably by comments I have received from a number of individuals. These articles developed out of earlier presentations on the subject of utility and rights at the University of Texas, the University of Virginia, Colgate University, and Cornell University. On those occasions I sought to extend the utilitarian account of rights I had earlier extracted from John Stuart Mill's writings. Criticism of Mill's theory of moral rights led me to question the less controversial assumption about legal rights that is principally discussed here. I wish especially to thank John Bennett, Jules Coleman, Stephen Massey, Richard Miller, and Robert Summers for their comments on previous drafts.

[1] See my 'Human Rights and the General Welfare', *Philosophy & Public Affairs*, 6 (1977), pp. 113–29, and 'Mill's Theory of Justice', in *Values and Morals*, edd. I. Goldman and J. Kim (Dordrecht, 1978), pp. 1–20.

welfare. But my argument has implications beyond utilitarianism in this limited sense. It extends in the first place to a number of normative views that are closely associated with utilitarianism but not equivalent to it, such as normative 'economic analysis' in the law. Second, it extends to many other 'goal-based' theories and perhaps to other normative theories as well. All of these theories have trouble with legal as well as with moral rights.

Outside ethical theory—in economics and fields that economics has influenced strongly[2]—traditional utilitarian terminology and doctrines have sometimes been displaced by new ones. To a great extent, this change represents an attempt to secure behaviouristic foundations for normative doctrines. Sometimes, utilitarian terms have been given a self-consciously behaviouristic interpretation, as when references to 'pleasure' and 'pain' are replaced by a concern for individuals 'preferences' or one's 'willingness to pay'. In other cases, normative doctrines have departed from traditional utilitarianism, largely because of worries about 'interpersonal comparisons of utility'. For example, the utilitarian requirement that the overall net balance of pleasure over pain be maximized has been replaced, in some quarters, by notions of 'economic efficiency', some versions of which do not require us (even in principle) to compare the benefits conferred and imposed on others. The result is a doctrine that is by no means equivalent to traditional utilitarianism. I believe, nevertheless, that my argument applies to these modifications and descendants of utilitarianism. Economists and theorists working in other fields frequently take normative positions that are, for present purposes, similar to those found within the utilitarian tradition. The problems that I discuss in this chapter are, so far as I can see, problems for their theories as much as they are for utilitarianism.

Later on I shall suggest how these problems beset a much wider class of theories, including some that are opposed to utilitarianism. These problems concern rights. My argument requires, however, that we distinguish two broad categories of rights, which I shall call 'moral rights' and 'legal rights'.

Some rights are thought to exist independently of social recognition and enforcement. This is what I think we usually mean by 'moral rights'. These include the rights that are sometimes called 'natural' or 'human', but are not limited to them. Natural or human rights are rights we are all said to have (by those who believe we have them) just by

[2] See, e.g., Richard A. Posner, 'Utilitarianism, Economics, and Legal Theory', *J. Legal Stud*, 8 (1979), pp. 103–40, which also provides references to some of the relevant legal and economic literature.

virtue of our status as human beings. They are independent of particular circumstances and do not depend on any special conditions. The class of moral rights is broader, since it includes rights that depend on particular circumstances or special conditions, such as promises. Moral rights, in general, do not depend on social recognition or enforcement, as is shown by the fact that they are appealed to even when it is not believed that they are enforced or recognized by law or by prevailing opinion.

Utilitarians are seen as hostile to moral rights; I shall call this *The Moral Rights Exclusion Thesis* (*Exclusion Thesis* for short). Economic theorists who embrace doctrines similar to utilitarianism tend to ignore (rather than reject) the idea of moral rights. Moral rights have little, if anything, to do with normative doctrines of this kind.[3]

Other rights presuppose some sort of social recognition or enforcement, the clearest case being rights conferred by law, including constitutional rights. I restrict my attention here to legal rights within this general class.

It is generally assumed that utilitarians have no difficulty accommodating legal rights and providing a normative theory about them; I shall call this *The Legal Rights Inclusion Thesis* (*Inclusion Thesis* for short). Normative theorists working within economics and policy studies are concerned with telling us which legal rights should be conferred, and take for granted that their theories are capable of accommodating such rights. I shall argue that they are mistaken.[4]

The main part of my argument may be summarized as follows. The

[3] It is sometimes suggested that economic analysis is capable of taking full account of competing normative claims, such as claims about justice or moral rights, by treating them as expressions of individual's preferences (preferences frustrated when institutions would be regarded by such individuals as violating moral rights or breaching other moral principles). See, e.g., Guido Calabresi and A. Douglas Melamed, 'Property Rules, Liability Rules, and Inalienability: One View of the Cathedral', *Harv. L. Rev.* 85 (1972), pp. 1089–1128. But this is inadequate. Someone who claims, for example, that slavery is morally unacceptable because it violates basic human rights may be expressing a preference against slavery, but he is doing more than that. He is claiming in the context that considerations of efficiency alone *could not justify* slavery. The question to be faced is not whether slavery will frustrate preferences but whether that claim is true. To understand this as a question about preferences (even enlarging it to include the preferences of people other than those who embrace the claim) is to look at these matters from the standpoint of economic analysis, and thus to beg the very question at issue, namely, whether economically efficient institutions can be morally unacceptable *because* they violate rights.

[4] It is sometimes suggested that when we speak of 'moral' rights we are referring to rights that ought to be conferred and enforced by social institutions. On this view, a utilitarian's normative theory of institutional rights is equivalent to a theory of moral rights. This notion does not affect the present

Exclusion Thesis assumes that moral rights make a difference to evaluation of conduct by excluding a range of direct utilitarian arguments that might militate against conduct (but not when it involves the exercise of rights) or that might justify conduct (but not when it would interfere with the exercise of rights). I call this the normative force of moral rights. The Inclusion Thesis assumes, by contrast, that legal rights are morally neutral and lack such force. But when legal rights are regarded as justifiable or morally defensible, they are regarded as having moral force. In other words, the idea that legal rights are morally defensible entails the idea of a moral presumption in favour of respecting them, even though it may not be useful to exercise them or may be useful to interfere with them in particular cases. The problem for utilitarianism then, is whether it can somehow accommodate the moral force of justified legal rights. I argue that it cannot do so satisfactorily. Although there are often utilitarian reasons for respecting justified legal rights, these reasons are not equivalent to the moral force of such rights, because they do not exclude direct utilitarian arguments against exercising such rights or for interfering with them. Specifically, utilitarian arguments for institutional design (the arguments that utilitarians might use in favour of establishing or maintaining certain legal rights) do not logically or morally exclude direct utilitarian arguments concerning the exercise of, or interference with, such rights. As a consequence, evaluation of conduct from a utilitarian standpoint is dominated by direct utilitarian arguments and therefore ignores the moral force of justified legal rights. The utilitarian is committed to ignoring the moral force of those very rights that he is committed to regarding as having moral force by virtue of the fact that he regards them as morally justifiable.

II. BENTHAM'S APPROACH

Of the classical utilitarians, Bentham is the one whose approach is most directly analogous to that of contemporary economic theorists as well as that of utilitarians who wish to provide a normative theory of legal rights. He accepted The Exclusion and Inclusion Theses. And so it is useful to begin with his ideas.

We are often reminded that Bentham dismissed the very idea of

argument. I believe it, however, to be mistaken. To say that rights ought to be *respected* is not to imply that they ought to be *enforced* (even by extra-legal institutions). Respect for rights can simply amount to doing what the corresponding obligations require, and from the fact that one is under an obligation (even an obligation correlative with another person's rights) it does not follow that any sort of coercion, strictly speaking, is justified for the purpose of ensuring obligatory performances or penalizing non-performance.

natural rights as 'nonsense'. One reason, of course, was his rejection of certain doctrines associated with natural rights, such as the notion that they are conferred by nature or discovered by the pure light of natural reason. But Bentham in effect rejected moral rights generally, that is, rights that do not presuppose social recognition or enforcement.[5]

Bentham's most direct, official reason for rejecting moral rights derives from his analysis of statements about rights and obligations. He held that meaningful statements about rights must be understood as statements about beneficial obligations, and he held that statements about obligations concern the requirements of coercive legal rules. He held that one has a right if and only if one is supposed to benefit from another person's compliance with a coercive legal rule. It follows that he could not recognize rights that are independent of social recognition or enforcement, that is, moral rights.

These analytical doctrines have no straightforward relation to Bentham's utilitarianism. His analysis of rights neither follows from a principle of utility nor entails it. Nevertheless, it is arguable that, given his utilitarianism, Bentham could not have accepted the idea that we have any moral rights. It would seem that his utilitarianism committed him to The Exclusion Thesis.

One might argue for the incompatibility of utilitarianism and moral rights as follows. Moral rights are not merely *independent of* social recognition and enforcement but also provide *grounds for appraising* law and other social institutions. If social arrangements violate moral rights, they can be criticized accordingly. Moral rights imply the establishment of institutions that respect them. But Bentham held that institutions are to be evaluated *solely* in terms of human welfare. Unless we assume that arguments based on moral rights converge perfectly with those based on welfare, it would seem that a utilitarian like Bentham would be obliged to reject moral rights.

This reasoning appears, however, to assume rather than prove The Exclusion Thesis. Why should we suppose that arguments based on moral rights diverge from welfare considerations? The answer has to do with the normative character of rights. If I have a right to do something, this provides *an argumentative threshold* against objections to my doing it, as well as a presumption against others' interference.

[5] For Bentham's analysis of rights, see my 'Rights, Claimants, and Beneficiaries', *American Philosophical Quarterly*, (1969), pp. 173–85, and H. L. A. Hart, 'Bentham on Legal Rights', in A. W. B. Simpson, ed., *Oxford Essays in Jurisprudence* (Second Series) (Oxford, 1973), pp. 171–201. Bentham did accept the idea of 'natural liberties', but only in the sense that one is 'free' to do whatever is not restricted by coercive social rules.

Considerations that might otherwise be sufficient against my so acting, in the absence of my having the right, or that might justify others' interference, are ineffective in its presence.

Consider, for example, the idea that I have a right to life. This entails that I may act so as to save it and that others may not interfere, even if these acts or the results would otherwise be subject to sound criticism. I need not show that my life is valuable or useful, and the fact that my defending it would have bad overall consequences or is otherwise objectionable does not show that my defending it is wrong, or that others' interference is not wrong. My right provides a measure of justification for certain actions of my own, as well as limits to interference. I call this argumentative threshold character the *normative force* of moral rights.

This point is sometimes distorted by exaggeration. Note, however, that my right to life does not automatically justify any course of action whatsoever that may be needed to save it; nor does it absolutely block justification for other's taking my life. Rights are not necessarily 'absolute'. That is why I speak of thresholds that need to be surmounted.[6]

Let us apply this to utilitarianism. From the standpoint of this theory we are entitled to assume that considerations of welfare are morally relevant, so that the promotion of welfare to a minimal degree provides justification for a course of action. Considerations like these are incremental. However, minimal increments of utility are incapable of surmounting the argumentative threshold of my rights. I may defend my life even at *some* cost to overall welfare, and others may not interfere *just* because it would promote overall welfare to *some* degree if they did. If one accepts moral rights, one cannot accept absolute guidance by welfare arguments. And so we have The Moral Rights Exclusion Thesis.

[6] The sort of exaggeration cautioned against here is unfortunately suggested by Ronald Dworkin's speaking of rights as 'trumps' against utilitarian arguments. See his 'Taking Rights Seriously', in *Taking Rights Seriously* (Cambridge, Mass., 1978), pp. 184–205. But, as Dworkin meakes clear, he does not assume that rights are generally 'absolute'; see, e.g. pp. 191–2. My suggestion that rights have normative (or moral) force derives from Dworkin's discussion, but differs from it in several ways. (1) I distinguish moral from legal rights and attribute moral force to legal rights only when they are morally defensible or justified. (2) The normative force of rights cannot be understood simply in terms of their relation to utilitarian arguments but must be considered more generally; my discussion attempts to allow that. (3) Dworkin's distinction between 'strong' and 'weak' rights corresponds roughly to the two aspects of normative force in my discussion: 'strong' rights provide obstacles to the justification of other's interference, while 'weak' rights provide justifications for one's own behaviour. Dworkin's argument seems to rely on both aspects of the normative force of rights.

Similar considerations apply to normative doctrines in economics and other fields that are developed in terms like 'economic efficiency'. If one believes that institutions are to be evaluated solely in terms of their promotion of such values, and not in terms of independent rights, one cannot accept the idea that we have any moral rights.

Bentham's attitude toward legal rights was of course different. His analysis of rights in terms of the beneficial requirements of coercive legal rules allows for the possibility of legal rights. And the general idea that utilitarianism is compatible with legal rights is hardly controversial, being widely assumed in law, economics, and political theory. Much the same idea is presupposed by what is called 'the economic analysis of law' (though only the normative versions of 'economic analysis' interest us here).

The Legal Rights Inclusion Thesis assumes that institutions serving the general welfare or economic efficiency are capable of conferring rights. Critics of utilitarianism as well as critics of normative economic analysis (including those who believe we have moral rights) do not challenge this assumption. They may claim that utilitarian or economically efficient institutions would establish some rights that ought not to be established (such as certain property rights) or would violate some rights that ought to be respected (such as rights to privacy or to personal autonomy), but they do not claim that such institutions are incapable of conferring any rights at all.

This is a plausible assumption, at least when it is coupled with a morally neutral conception of legal rights, by which I mean a conception that generates no moral presumption that those rights should be respected. Furthermore, the idea that utilitarian and efficient institutions confer rights leaves plenty of room for opponents of utilitarianism and of normative economic analysis to criticize those institutions, on the basis of moral rights or other values.

I am sympathetic to the morally neutral conception of legal rights, for reasons such as the following. The law of a society may be understood as implying that people have certain rights. But the law may be outrageously unjust and hence the rights it confers morally indefensible. There is absolutely no moral presumption favouring respect for those legal rights conferred by chattel slavery. Circumstances may of course provide some reasons for respecting morally objectionable entitlements. Those on whom such rights may be conferred are, after all, human beings who can claim some measure of respect and consideration from others too. But, while these considerations may affect what we ought to do in the context of morally outrageous institutions, they do not show anything about the moral force of legal rights themselves.

So I am prepared to say that, from the fact that I have a right conferred on me by law, *nothing follows* concerning what I or others may do. We might put this point by saying that *merely* legal rights have *no moral force*.

Some writers do not share my view of legal rights, though their reasons are unclear.[7] In any case, if I am wrong about legal rights in this respect, then all have moral force. If we could assume that, my argument would be simpler. Since I deny it, I must limit my attention to those legal rights with moral force. These are legal rights that are taken to be morally defensible, the rights conferred by laws that are supposed to be justified. Let us see what this amounts to.

III. LEGAL RIGHTS WITH MORAL FORCE

Suppose that Mary rents a house that comes with a garage for her car. Access to the garage is provided by a private driveway, which she alone is authorized to use. Sometimes, however, she finds someone else's car parked in the driveway, which prevents her from parking or leaving with her own car. This may be inconvenient or it may not. Whenever it happens, however, Mary's rights are not being respected by other individuals.

Mary's rights depend on social arrangements, and they are enforceable by legal means. They thus qualify as legal rights. I shall assume, however, that these rights are *not merely* legal. I am supposing, in other words, that the social arrangements presupposed by Mary's rights and their enforceability are justifiable; those institutions or their relevant parts are morally defensible. This does not seem an implausible assumption to adopt. From the fact that Mary's rights are not shared by others, for example, we cannot infer that they are morally objectionable. I would suppose that ordinary rights like Mary's can arise and be justified in otherwise unjust as well as just societies, though this is not required for the argument. Within a society in which people have fair shares of the resources and considerable freedom to decide how to use their respective shares, for example, some individuals, with needs that are different from Mary's, may reasonably decide to make arrangements that are different from hers. And in such a society there may be good reason to have rights like Mary's made enforceable by law. Of course, Mary's rights are meant only as an example. If one has objections to private parking arrangements, it should be possible to substitute another example for the purpose. It is useful, however, to choose

[7] Dworkin seems to assume that all legal rights have moral force. See his 'Reply to Critics', *Taking Rights Seriously*, pp. 326–7.

very ordinary rights, which clearly depend on institutional arrangements and legal recognition or enforcement. What I think we can agree about Mary's rights applies to many other routine legal rights, that is, to those we think of as morally defensible.

Given the arrangements that Mary has made, she may use the garage and driveway as she wishes. She may permit others to use them or refuse to do so. Others may not use them without her permission. In other words, Mary's rights make a difference to what she and others may justifiably do.

The principal assumption I shall make is this. When we regard Mary's rights as morally defensible, on any basis whatsoever, we also regard them as having moral force. The differences that her rights make to evaluation of conduct obtain, not just in the eyes of the law, but also from a moral point of view. We may disagree about the conditions that must be satisfied if legal rights are to be morally defensible. But if we hold that Mary's rights are morally defensible, then we are committed to agreeing that they have such force. Utilitarians and non-utilitarians will disagree about the conditions that justify legal rights. This is compatible, however, with their agreeing that certain legal rights are morally defensible. And the latter entails, as I shall assume, that such rights have moral force. To deny that Mary's legal rights have such force is to deny that they are morally defensible.

Mary's rights make a difference even when they are infringed. If others encroach upon her rights thoughtlessly or for their own private convenience, for example, it is incumbent on them to apologize or even, perhaps, to compensate her for any inconvenience she has suffered as a consequence. If they fail to do so, then they act wrongly. If compensation should be offered, then Mary is free to accept it or refuse it, as she prefers.

Of course, Mary's rights are limited. The driver of an emergency vehicle on an urgent errand might justifiably block Mary's driveway without first obtaining Mary's permission—even, perhaps, in the face of her refusal to give permission. This holds from both a legal as well as a moral standpoint. And, to simplify matters here, I shall assume that the legal limits of Mary's rights correspond perfectly to what we should regard on reflection as their proper limits from a moral point of view. Limits like these on Mary's rights are compatible with the idea that her rights make a difference to moral arguments. We need not assume that Mary's rights are 'absolute' and overwhelm all conflicting considerations. My point is simply that Mary's rights entail an argumentative or justificatory threshold. Certain considerations are capable of justifying encroachments on Mary's rights, but not all are. Let us look at this more closely.

If one regards Mary's moral position from a utilitarian standpoint, then one might be presumed to reason as follows. Mary is fully justified in exercising her legal rights only when and in a manner in which she can promote human welfare to the maximum degree possible, and others are fully justified in encroaching on Mary's rights in the same sort of circumstances and for the same sort of reason.

This reasoning may be framed in probabilistic terms. What may be thought required, then, is not that human welfare actually be promoted to the maximum degree possible, but that Mary's acts, when she exercises her rights, or the acts of those who encroach on them, be *most likely* to maximize human welfare (or something of the sort). This type of qualification will not, I think, affect the present argument, and I shall generally ignore it hereafter.

The utilitarian pattern of reasoning that I have sketched seems to clash with the idea that Mary's rights are morally defensible and thus have moral force. For it assumes that Mary's rights *make no difference* to what she and others may justifiably do, except in so far as the legal recognition of those rights changes circumstances so that certain possible courses of action have added utility or disutility. But this is not the way Mary's moral position is ordinarily viewed when it is assumed that her legal rights are morally defensible.

Suppose, for example, that a neighbour decides late at night to park his car in Mary's driveway, without obtaining her permission, in order to save himself a long cold walk from the nearest legal parking space. He might reason soundly that Mary is unlikely to be inconvenienced, since he shall move his car early the next morning. And that might turn out to be the case. Nevertheless, Mary might justifiably resent and complain of his presumption. Of course, Mary could reflect that she might have been seriously inconvenienced if an emergency had arisen during the night and she was unable to use her car. But it should not be assumed that her resentment would be justified solely by the possible inconvenience she might have suffered. For that might have happened even if she had given permission beforehand for him to use the driveway, in which case her resentment would not be warranted. Her belief is that her neighbour acted unjustifiably—that his action could not be justified simply by calculations of actual or probable utilities.

We can generalize these points as follows. Mary has the moral freedom to exercise her rights, within certain limits. Neither this freedom nor its limits can be explained by the utilitarian line of reasoning we have described. For example, Mary may act to her own disadvantage, without the prospect of compensating advantages to anyone else.

Her rights also permit her some indifference to the effects of her choices upon others. They permit her, for example, to inconvenience others while exercising her rights, without the prospect of compensating advantages to anyone, including herself. She need not act so as to maximize utility when she exercises her rights. Similarly, others may not act in certain ways without her permission, even if their doing so would maximize utility.

A utilitarian might object that he is not interested in Mary's rights as such but only in evaluation of her conduct and that of others. He might suggest that I have ignored the distinction between Mary's having rights and the conditions under which she justifiably exercises them. But I have framed my argument so as to respect that distinction. My point is not that Mary's rights completely determine what she and others may justifiably do but that her rights make a difference to the evaluation of her and others' conduct, a difference that unrestricted utilitarian reasoning cannot accept. The difference is not simple, since we cannot assume that Mary's rights are 'absolute'. In the present context, the difference amounts to this: from the mere fact that net utility would not be maximized by her exercising her rights, we cannot infer that her exercise of them is not justified; similarly, from the mere fact that net utility would be maximized by encroaching on her rights, we cannot infer that one is justified in encroaching on them.

One thing that complicates matters here is that Mary's rights, to be morally defensible, must have some foundation in human interests, needs, or welfare and are limited in turn by similar considerations. For this reason, utilitarian considerations are, *within limits*, relevant to a final determination of what Mary and others may justifiably do, which is bounded by a decent regard for others' welfare. Mary's decisions must give some respect to the interests of others, and what others may justifiably do is determined in part by the effects of their conduct upon people generally. Thus, despite her rights, Mary may not deny access to her driveway to someone in dire need, and others may use it without her permission if the need is pressing. But this is not to say that utilitarian reasoning *generally* determines how Mary and others may justifiably act. Let us suppose that *very substantial* utilities or disutilities outweigh the moral force of Mary's rights. We cannot infer from this that *minimal increments* of utility are sufficient to outweigh those arguments. To reason in that way would assume that Mary's rights make no difference to moral argument, or in other words, that her rights lack moral force. But, if I am right, Mary's legal rights have moral force if they are morally defensible.

It should be emphasized that I am assuming there is no moral objection to Mary's having such special control over her garage and driveway. I do not mean to suggest (and I have explicitly denied) that any arbitrary arrangements that Mary might secure under the law would have similar moral consequences. I would not suggest, for example, that if the law gave Mary comparable control over another human being—if, in other words, it regarded her as the owner of a chattel slave—then she would be morally free to decide, in a similar way, how to use that person. Even if the law regarded Mary in that way, we might reasonably deny that the legal arrangements make any difference to the way that Mary may justifiably behave, from a moral point of view. But our example is not like that. I have deliberately chosen to focus on an ordinary, mundane legal right that might plausibly be regarded as morally defensible.

It is also important to emphasize that I have not been discussing moral rights, that is, rights we are supposed to have independently of social recognition or enforcement. Nor is it suggested that Mary's rights arise of their own accord, without any foundation in fact. What is suggested, rather, is that, given the relevant facts in the social circumstances, which have to do with Mary's unobjectionably renting a house with a garage serviced by a driveway, she assumes a new moral position. She acquires rights, and her acquired rights appear to function as more or less stable moral factors with characteristic implications.

I have not claimed that there can be no utilitarian foundation for Mary's rights. It might be argued, for example, that the general welfare can be served by institutional arrangements that provide Mary with such special control over her garage and driveway. Let us now see how this argument would proceed, and what it might prove.

IV. UTILITARIAN INSTITUTIONS

Although Bentham is widely thought to be committed to the pattern of utilitarian reasoning I have been discussing, he does not seem to deal with problems of the sort we have considered. Bentham and those who follow in his footsteps, including those wedded to normative economic analysis, are concerned with the evaluation of law and social institutions. In this connection, Bentham applies the standard of utility, not to individual acts taken separately, but rather to the rules and institutions that he thinks of as conferring rights. Those favouring economic analysis use a standard of efficiency in a similar way. They criticize, evaluate, and recommend legal rules in terms of some value that the rules are supposed to serve. These theorists assume, in accordance with

The Inclusion Thesis, that rights would be conferred by institutions they regard as justified.

It does seem plausible to suppose that institutions conforming to utilitarian requirements or to the dictates of economic efficiency would incorporate rights. In the first place, when we consider possible institutions, we naturally tend to model them on those with which we are familiar, and these are generally assumed to confer rights. In the second place, and most importantly for present purposes, it seems reasonable to suppose that institutions designed to serve the general welfare or economic efficiency are capable of satisfying a *necessary* condition for incorporating rights. That is, the rules of such institutions might confer the proper range of freedom and impose the appropriate restrictions upon others' behaviour that correspond to rights like Mary's. I know of no general argument that could deny this possibility.

When Bentham assumed that rights would be incorporated in utilitarian institutions, he proceeded on the assumption that rights exist whenever coercive restrictions upon behaviour serve the interests of determinate individuals. It is difficult to imagine how institutions supported by the best utilitarian arguments could fail to create some useful restrictions, and it is natural to suppose that some of these restrictions would be useful by serving or securing the interests of specific persons. So, on Bentham's theory, it would seem that such institutions confer rights.

Economic theorists have not devoted much attention to the question of what it is to have a right. But it is reasonable to suppose that they have been guided by some conception of rights like Bentham's.

But we cannot pursue the basic issue here within the framework constructed by Bentham. Our question is not whether rights as Bentham conceived of them can be reconciled to utilitarianism, nor whether rights as economic analysts conceive of them can be reconciled with the principles of economic efficiency. This is so for two distinct reasons.

In the first place, it could be said that Bentham took rights a bit too seriously. He inflated their normative force into coercive power. He imagined that, when I have a right, existing legal rules provide for their enforcement. But enforcement is not an essential feature of rights, not even legal rights. Rights can be recognized by law even when no legal provisions are made for their enforcement. Consider, for example, those civil rights of US citizens that are based upon the 'equal protection clause' of the Constitution. These rights went without enforcement for many years. The Civil Rights Acts and the Civil Rights Division of the US Department of Justice were intended as means for securing these rights. Enforcement enhances these rights and establishes new 'secondary' rights, but it does not create the basic constitutional rights themselves. Legal rights are not necessarily enforced, and their enforcement not its authorization is an essential feature of legal rights. Bentham was mistaken. In consequence, at least part of the reason theorists sometimes think they have for concentrating upon legal rights while ignoring moral rights is an illusion.

In the second place, Bentham's analysis ignores the moral force of rights under justified institutions. The question that we face is whether utilitarianism or comparable theories can accommodate legal rights with moral force.

This qualification is important, and it does not prejudice our enquiry in any way that is unfair to utilitarianism or normative economic analysis. The institutions that a utilitarian or an economic analyst regards as fully justified are, presumably, his best candidates for institutions that create rights with moral force. If such a theorist regards some institutions as *justified* but he *cannot* accommodate the moral force of legal rights conferred by those institutions, then his theory is in trouble, faced with a kind of incoherence. On the one hand, he wishes to claim that the institutions he can justify would confer some rights. On the other hand, his basic theory does not allow him to accommodate the moral force possessed by legal rights in justified or morally defensible institutions. This is what I shall now try to show.

V. THE RELEVANCE OF DIRECT UTILITARIAN ARGUMENTS

The strategy of my argument is this. I shall suppose that a utilitarian or economic analyst believes that certain rights would be conferred by legal institutions that are justified by his basic normative principles. I take this to imply that the rights are to be regarded as morally defensible and thus that we can consider them as having moral force. I shall then try to show that this force cannot be accommodated by a normative position developed on the foundation of welfare or some comparable value such as economic efficiency.

For purposes of illustration, let us suppose that a utilitarian or economist believes that we can justify a set of institutions like those assumed in our example. Under the rules of those institutions, Mary has exclusive use of the garage and driveway attached to the house she is renting (though others' use of them is permitted under special circumstances, even without her permission). We shall assume, furthermore, that the freedom conferred by the rules on Mary and the obligations imposed by them on others match precisely what we should regard on reflection as the proper extent and limits of her rights when viewed from a moral standpoint. Mary is not required to worry generally about the utility of her actions or about economic efficiency when deciding how to use her garage or driveway or whether to permit others to use them. Nor are others expected to decide whether to use Mary's garage or driveway just on the basis of the utility of such conduct or its efficiency. And officials are not expected to decide on such grounds when they are called upon to apply or enforce the relevant, clear legal rules.

Unless something like this can be assumed, the idea that legal rights with moral force can be accommodated by a theory based on welfare or efficiency is defeated at the start. But the assumption appears reasonable. At least, I know of no general argument that could deny the possibility that such institutions as would be preferred by a utilitarian or by an economist might confer the proper range of freedom and the appropriate restrictions on others' behaviour that correspond to the moral force of ordinary legal rights like Mary's. It should be emphasized, of course, that we are not supposing that such institutions would respect all rights that ought to be respected, including moral rights, which are independent of social recognition and enforcement, or that such institutions satisfy any other normative standards that a critic of utilitarianism or of normative economic analysis may endorse. These are concerns that a utilitarian or an economic analyst cannot be thought to share. Our strategy is to accept the normative approach of utilitarians and of economic analysts and to see where that leads us.

It must also be emphasized, however, that these assumptions do not settle the present issue. They imply only that such theories are capable of satisfying a *necessary* condition for accommodating legal rights with moral force. But our question is not whether utilitarianism or efficiency analysis could regard such institutions as justified or morally defensible. Our question is *what significance* such a theorist must attach to that fact when it comes to *evaluating conduct* in the context of those rules; for example, in determining how an official in such a system should behave.

A utilitarian or policy analyst might be thought to reason now as follows: 'Institutions are justified if, or to the extent that, they promote human welfare or economic efficiency. Institutions ought to be designed so that official as well as private decisions will by and large promote such a value to the extent that this can be contrived. When that has been accomplished, conduct that is subject to the rules of those institutions can be justified only by reference to those rules. In other words, utilitarian and comparable arguments have their place, but they have no monopoly on justification. They do not always control the evaluation of conduct. When the rules are justified, they are to be followed. Their justified legal impact thus translates into moral force.

This is the approach John Rawls has suggested that a utilitarian would take to institutions that are justified on utilitarian grounds. In replying to the objection that utilitarianism allows the punishment of innocent persons, for example, he supposes that a utilitarian official who understands the utilitarian justification of the rules that he is charged with administering would abide by the rules.[8]

But the pattern of reasoning just sketched ignores some of the utilitarian considerations that are inevitably at work in particular cases that arise under such rules. For it is predictable that real social rules that are supported by the best utilitarian and economic arguments will require decisions in particular cases that would not most effectively promote welfare or efficiency. Such goals can sometimes be promoted more effectively by departing from the rules, or by changing them, than by following them. When that happens, a direct utilitarian or economic argument supports deviation from the rules.[9]

Suppose that a utilitarian official, or one who has adopted the precepts of normative economic analysis, is called upon to enforce the rules on Mary's behalf. He can understand perfectly the justification that he accepts for those rules. And his legal duty may be transparent. The rules vindicate Mary's claim, and he is legally bound to decide in her favour.

I do not see how such reasoning can settle matters for a utilitarian or economic-minded official. Suppose there are direct utilitarian or economic considerations on the other side—considerations sufficient to be appreciated by such officials, but not sufficient to surmount the justificatory threshold of Mary's rights. I do not see how our utilitarian or economic-minded official can regard these considerations

[8] See John Rawls, 'Two Concepts of Rules', *Philosophical Review*, 64 (1955), pp. 3–32.

[9] This point does not depart from the main thesis of *Forms and Limits of Utilitarianism* (Oxford, 1965), in which I argued for the 'extensional equivalence' of certain principles that I called 'simple' and 'general' utilitarianism. The extensional equivalence argument was extended to cover a limiting case of rule-utilitarianism—a theory (dubbed 'primitive' rule-utilitarianism) in which no consideration is given to such things as the complexity or cost of rules. Rule-utilitarian theories that concern themselves with ordinary, manageable social rules were explicitly excluded from the scope of that argument. Thus, *Forms and Limits* argues, in effect, that direct and indirect utilitarian arguments are *sometimes* equivalent. Along with this chapter, however, it assumes that they are *not always* equivalent.

as irrelevant to what he ought, ultimately, to do. He must regard them as providing arguments for deviating from existing rules, or for changing them, despite their justification. His primary aim, after all, is the promotion of welfare or efficiency. He must always consider arguments for promoting it directly, when he has the opportunity to do so. If so, he must be understood as prepared to violate Mary's legal rights—even though they are supposed to be morally defensible, from which it seems to follow that they have moral force and thus rule out unrestricted, direct, incremental utilitarian reasoning.

That is, a utilitarian official must be willing to reason as follows: 'Mary's legal rights are clear, as is the utilitarian justification for allowing her to acquire such rights and to have them made enforceable by law. Even if this is an exceptional case, the same indirect utilitarian arguments continue to hold. Utilitarian legislators would be well advised not to modify the rules, should they have occasion to do so. These rules are as well designed, from a utilitarian standpoint, as any such rules can be. They cannot usefully be adjusted to take into account every special case that may arise under them. And, taking the utilitarian risks into account, it seems equally clear that welfare would be better served by not enforcing Mary's rights in this particular case.' Acceptance of reasoning like this shows that such a theorist cannot fully accept the normative implications of his claim that Mary's legal rights are morally defensible. He cannot regard Mary's rights as making that difference to the evaluation of conduct that we supposed those rights do. For such reasoning cannot justify an infringement upon Mary's rights, though he is prepared to entertain it.

One might try to answer this objection in the following way: 'An official who faces such a decision has more utilitarian reason to adhere to the rules then he has to depart from them. For an official who understands the utilitarian arguments for the rules appreciates that they assume general compliance on the part of officials as well as private citizens. This provides him with a general reason for believing that a departure from the rules is likely to do more harm than good. Furthermore, in any particular case it is likely that the direct utilitarian gains will be seen to be outweighed by the direct utilitarian costs of departing from the rules, resulting, for example, from frustrated expectations. It is therefore unreasonable to believe that a utilitarian official would depart from the rules instead of enforcing Mary's rights.'

This argument requires that two points be made. In the first place, from the fact that a sound utilitarian argument is available for a legal rule it does not follow that utility will be maximized by adhering to the rules in each and every case. Conditions vary, and a sensitive utilitarian official will presumably be flexible. In the second place, the original argument can be understood as implying that officials *have an obligation* to comply with morally defensible rules that establish rights—an obligation that is not equivalent to the implications of direct utilitarian reasoning. Like Mary's rights, this obligation is not 'absolute'; it can be overridden by substantial countervailing considerations. But, given Mary's rights and this corresponding obligation, direct, unrestricted, incremental utilitarian reasoning on the part of officials is ruled out. It is of course quite possible that direct utilitarian reasoning would yield conclusions that conform to Mary's rights; but this cannot be assumed. And the two modes of reasoning should not be confused.

A utilitarian might now reply in either of two ways. He might reject the pattern of reasoning that is entailed by talk of rights and obligations and maintain that we would be better off not to think in such terms. I do not address this issue here. My argument is meant to show certain difficulties that arise for utilitarian and comparable theories when they seek to *accommodate* rights (and obligations) under institutions they endorse.

Alternatively, a utilitarian might claim that a responsible utilitarian official would adopt a secondary principle (or perhaps a 'rule of thumb') that requires him to adhere to the rules of utilitarian institutions. Such a principle, it may be said, is functionally equivalent to the idea that an official is under an obligation to adhere to the rules and to respect the rights they confer.

This line of reasoning seems, however, to concede the point at issue. To make it plausible, one must suppose that experience demonstrates that utility is best served in the long run if one reasons just as if one was under such an obligation. But systematic evidence to this effect is rarely, if ever, offered. A utilitarian who argues in this way appreciates the force of the original objection but retains the hope of *somehow* finding utilitarian arguments to meet it. He offers us no more than a promissory note, without any assurance that it can be honoured.

Bentham never faced this issue squarely, and I do not think that Mill did either. They seem to assume either of two things: either that, once the rules are justified, they must be followed; or else that particular cases simply cannot arise such that the justified rules require one thing and the direct application of the utilitarian standard to those cases requires another. Bentham and Mill were, perhaps, prevented from considering such difficulties by the assumption that, once justified rules are established, the legal recognition of the rights they confer change circumstances so that certain possible courses of action have added utility or disutility. Thus, it may be thought that there is always sufficient utilitarian reason of a direct kind to argue against deviation from justified rules. But this, as I have already suggested, cannot be assumed. Moreover, reasoning like this does not meet the point of the objection, which is that once those morally defensible rights are established, certain modes of reasoning are *illicit*.

Economists have not faced this issue squarely either. This is because they have not generally considered the implications of their economic 'analysis' when it becomes a normative position. They are thus faced with a significant theoretical decision. Either they shall consider efficiency the sole fundamental basis for normative appraisals, of conduct as well as of institutions, in which case they must accept the consequences of the foregoing argument. Or they must accept the idea that there are other values to be served, beyond economic efficiency, in which case they must entertain the possibility of rights and obligations that are independent of social recognition and enforcement, rights and obligations that justified legal institutions ought to respect.

The problem I have sketched may be summarized as follows. Normative theories that are founded on certain values, such as welfare or efficiency, quite naturally regard legal rules or institutions as justified if they are supported by the best arguments in those terms. But such theories do not generate any obligation to adhere to the rules that they regard as justified. And they cannot do so unless they are restricted for just such a purpose.

VI. THE RELEVANCE OF RULE-UTILITARIANISM

A type of theory that might seem to meet this objection is 'rule-utilitarianism'. In its relevant forms, rule-utilitarianism *limits* the application of the standard of utility to rules or social institutions and *requires compliance* with rules that are certified as having the requisite utilitarian justification. I do not mean to suggest that such a theory is incoherent. But, before proceeding further, we should distinguish two types of rule-utilitarian theory, only one of which is directly relevant to the present argument.

One type of rule-utilitarian theory seeks to accommodate the idea of moral obligations (and, derivatively, moral rights). It concerns itself with the 'ideal moral rules' for a community or an 'ideal moral code'.[10] Another type of rule-utilitarian theory is concerned with established laws that can be defended on utilitarian grounds. It concerns itself

[10] See, e.g. R. B. Brandt, 'Some Merits of One Form of Rule-Utilitarianism', *University of Colorado Studies, Series in Philosophy* (1967), pp. 39–65.

with obligations to comply with useful social institutions. The latter, not the former, is most relevant here. For we are concerned with the question what difference it makes, from a moral point of view, to have laws and social institutions that are morally defensible. A rule-utilitarian of the first type does not address himself to this question, at least not in any direct way. But a rule-utilitarian of the second type in effect addresses himself to this question. This is the sort of rule-utilitarianism suggested (though not endorsed) by Rawls.[11]

My point about this sort of theory is that it represents a qualified utilitarian position. It does not follow from the more basic idea, common to all forms of utilitarianism, that human welfare is to be promoted. Nor does it follow from the more specific idea that social rules are to be evaluated in utilitarian terms.

What can be understood to follow from the fact that an institution can be supported by the best utilitarian arguments? If it follows that the rules must be respected (or at least that there is a moral obligation to respect them), then the utilitarian has a basis for claiming that his theory accommodates legal rights with moral force. But not so otherwise. The question may be understood as follows. If a utilitarian believes that certain rules are justified on utilitarian grounds, does he *contradict* himself by supposing that direct utilitarian arguments for deviating from the rules may be entertained? I see no contradiction here. If so, the utilitarian cannot understand the legal impact of such rules automatically to translate into moral force, not even when those rules are supported by the best utilitarian arguments. He cannot regard the morally defensible rights under *utilitarian* institutions as having moral force.

If so, The Legal Rights Inclusion Thesis must be qualified drastically, so that it becomes a morally uninteresting platitude. It cannot be understood to say that utilitarianism and comparable theories accommodate legal rights with their moral force intact, even when those rights are conferred by rules regarded as justified under such theories. It can be understood to say only that utilitarianism and comparable theories accept the possibility of justified institutions with rights that must be regarded as *merely* legal, devoid of moral force. For these theories do not allow the rights conferred by justified institutions to make the requisite difference to the evaluation of conduct that such rights are ordinarily assumed to do.

We can apply this to Rawls's argument, in which he suggested that a utilitarian official would abide by the rules of institutions he regards

[11] In 'Two Concepts of Rules', 8, *supra*.

as justified. We can understand Rawls's argument in either of two ways. He might be taken as suggesting that regarding rules as justified on utilitarian grounds *logically commits* one to abiding by their implications in particular cases. I have just tried to show that this is a mistake. Alternatively, Rawls might be understood as proposing that utilitarians *restrict their theory* so that it applies to rules or institutions but not to conduct under them. This is, I believe, a reasonable way of reading Rawls's suggestion, and the foregoing argument implies that it is the more generous of these two alternative readings.

For nothing in the idea that welfare is to be promoted restricts the application of the standard of utility to social rules or institutions. If such a restriction is *adopted* by a theorist who sees himself as working within the utilitarian tradition, that involves the *addition* of a factor that a utilitarian is not obliged to accept, either by the constraints of logic or by the normative implications of his theory. In the absence of such a factor, a utilitarian cannot ignore direct utilitarian arguments.

Imposing such a restriction on the idea that human welfare is to be promoted is either arbitrary or else is motivated by a desire to accommodate the moral force of rights and obligations under justified rules. In its relevant forms, rule-utilitarianism represents a compromise—a recognition that the utilitarian approach is incomplete at best and, unless it is restricted, cannot accommodate the moral force of morally defensible legal rights and obligations.

Similar considerations apply to normative theories based on the goal of economic efficiency. If the moral force of legal rights and obligations under justified institutions is to be accommodated, then those theories must be restricted. And restricting them reopens general questions about the standards to be used in evaluating institutions themselves.

It may be thought that I have overstated my case. I have suggested that a utilitarian (unless he restricts his theory to accommodate objections) will evaluate conduct by means of direct utilitarian considerations —in effect, by 'act-utilitarian' reasoning. But, it may be objected, from the fact that an institution is supported by the best utilitarian arguments it must be thought by a utilitarian to follow that one has reason to conform to the rules of that institution. I have ignored, it may be said, the direct practical implications that the utilitarian justification of social rules or institutions has for a utilitarian.

If this were correct, then the most that could be claimed is that utilitarianism gives rise in such contexts to *conflicting* considerations. The foregoing reasoning would not show that direct utilitarian arguments concerning conduct are *excluded* by a utilitarian justification of the institutions within the context of which that conduct may take place. It would show only that such arguments must be weighed within utilitarianism against arguments flowing from the utilitarian justification of those institutions. Then the most that could be said for utilitarianism is either that one who follows its dictates would not violate the rights it regards as justified as often as my argument implies (though he would violate them sometimes) or else that utilitarianism is indeterminate in such cases, in which event it would not require that such rights as it regards as morally defensible ought to be respected.

If they are sound, such consequences cannot offer much comfort to the utilitarian. But are they sound? I think not. To see this, we must distinguish between (1) a reason for maintaining an institution and (2) a reason for conforming to institutional rules. It is reasonable to suppose that the utilitarian justification of an institution provides a utilitarian with a reason of type (1), that is, a reason for maintaining that institution. But we cannot assume that a reason of type (2) likewise follows. The utilitarian justification of an institution provides a reason for conforming to that institution *only if* conformity to its rules is required. in the circumstances, for maintaining that institution. But this is just what we cannot assume. For it is possible for the rules to be violated (by officials or private individuals) without threatening the institution —more precisely, without threatening its utility. In such a case, the utilitarian justification of the institution provides the utilitarian himself with no reason for conforming to its rules—not when greater utility accrues to deviation from them.

Someone might approach this issue differently. One reason why indirect utilitarian considerations, concerning rules and institutions, do not converge with direct utilitarian considerations, concerning individuals' conduct, is that real social rules must be simple enough for the practical guidance of ordinary mortals and also typically involve social costs. These costs include sanctions designed to coerce officials and private individuals into following the law when they may be tempted to act otherwise. A person might therefore reason that an official would be strongly constrained to follow rules that are predicated upon serving human welfare when those rules have been properly designed. One might suppose that a utilitarian institution would be contrived so as to make it very undesirable for an official to depart from rules that he is charged with administering. Useful sanctions might seem to ensure that Mary's rights would be respected.

But we cannot assume that such expedients will do the trick. In the first place, we cannot assume that maximally useful rules, or rules supported by the best utilitarian arguments, would always be sufficiently constraining to prevent deviation from them. In the second place, someone who is guided by utilitarian considerations should not be influenced so decisively by considerations of self-interest as this suggestion assumes. He should be willing to accept a risk himself, for the sake of serving the *general* welfare more effectively, as the direct utilitarian arguments that counsel infringements on Mary's rights show possible.

Alternatively, one might assume that an official would not deviate from rules that he is charged with administering, because he would think it *wrong* to do so. One might suppose, for example, that an official would regard himself as having accepted a position of public trust, which involves obligations that he cannot in good conscience ignore. He might see himself as morally bound by his commitment to adhere to the rules as he finds them. But, if we suppose that such a factor is at work in our example, then we are assuming, in effect, the influence of *non*-utilitarian arguments. If the argument suggested here is to make any difference, it must be based on the idea of an independent obligation that does not follow from the considerations already canvassed. To have recourse to such obligations, however, is to concede that utilitarian principles need supplementation before we can secure a normative theory that is capable of accommodating ordinary legal rights with moral force.

VII. EXTENSION OF THE ARGUMENT

As we have already observed, this argument would not seem limited to utilitarianism, but concerns also the relationship of rights to other closely related theories, such as economic analysis when offered as a normative approach to law or social policy. But the considerations that extend the argument that far suggest that it must extend much further.[12] The argument would seem to concern all 'goal-based' theories that satisfy two conditions: (1) the goal or goals accepted by the theory as the basis for appraising institutions are capable of being served not only through institutional design but also by the action of individuals when their conduct falls under the scope of the institutional rules; (2) the goal or goals do not (separately or together) entail some value that demands respect for rules that are favourably appraised in relation to them. The latter condition is vague, and I am not sure what sort of goal might fail to meet it. It simply seems necessary to allow that some goals might satisfy condition (1) but would also require respect for the rights conferred by institutions that serve those goals, in the way that welfare, happiness, economic efficiency, and the like do not.

To illustrate the way the argument might be extended—imagine

[12] I owe this suggestion to Jules Coleman.

that we dedicate a legal system to the service of social and economic equality—a useful example, since this value is often contrasted with utility and is believed to conflict with the latter in practice. The same sorts of problems concerning rights accrue to a theory based on promoting substantive equality as attach to one based on human welfare or economic efficiency. For the rules of institutions might be contrived to serve social and economic equality as far as it is possible for rules to do, but it would still be possible for social and economic equality to be served (perhaps in small ways) by deviation from those rules in particular cases. There is nothing about the basic value to be served that requires respect for all the rights that may be conferred by such institutions.

If we explored this issue further, we might find a very wide range of goal-based normative theories have the same trouble with legal rights. We might also find that other sorts of theories (e.g. 'right-based' and 'duty-based' theories) face similar difficulties.

What all of this seems to show is that normative theories require a more complex character than those we have considered if they are to accommodate the moral force of legal rights under justified institutions. Many theories fail to account for an obligation to adhere to rules that are regarded by them as justified. From the assumption that rules serve appropriate values it does not seem to follow that there is the requisite sort of obligation to adhere to them, an obligation that gives due respect to the morally defensible rights conferred by those rules.

If a utilitarian (or other goal-based) theory of *moral* obligations were possible, it might fill the gap just noted. It might explain how we have moral obligations to comply with social institutions that are predicated on serving the general welfare, for example. We cannot assume that a utilitarian theory of moral obligations would generate precisely this obligation, but the possibility of a normative utilitarian theory of legal rights would be revived.

This development is ironic, for it rests the possibility of a normative theory of *legal* rights upon the possibility of a theory of *moral* obligations, though the former is usually thought to be much less problematic than the latter. In any case, it brings us round full circle. We began by noting the traditional utilitarian attitude toward moral rights, embraced by Bentham, which is similar to the traditional utilitarian attitude toward moral obligations (when obligations are not confused with whatever happens to be required by some sort of normative principle). Like rights, obligations have a normative life of their own, with implications that are neither reducible to, nor traceable by, direct considerations of utility. It does not follow, however, that a utilitarian theory of moral rights or obligations is impossible.

VIII. MILL'S THEORY OF MORAL RIGHTS AND OBLIGATIONS

In previous works I have offered a sympathetic reading of Mill's theory of morality and justice, in order to challenge the usual view that utilitarianism is incapable of accommodating either moral rights or moral obligations. (In recent years emphasis has been placed on rights, but obligations received more, and similar, attention a half century ago.) I would like now to summarize that argument briefly and show why it seems to fail. Considerations relevant to the main argument, concerning legal rights, apply here too.

Mill's theory is promising because (under the interpretation I have offered) his way of trying to accommodate moral rights and obligations is not a form of *ad hoc* revisionism motivated by the desire to evade substantive objections to utilitarianism. It is not a form of revisionism at all, but turns on a theory of the moral concepts, the relations among which establish constraints upon any normative theory. Instead of adopting (what has since been thought of as) the standard utilitarian approach to moral reasoning—instead of assuming that one is always required to promote a certain value to the maximum degree possible—Mill begins by sketching a stratified analysis of normative concepts.

Mill's general idea can be understood as follows. We can distinguish three levels of normative concepts and judgement. For present purposes, the bottom (most concrete) level concerns the rightness or wrongness, justice or injustice, morality or immorality of particular acts. The intermediate, second level consists of moral principles, which concern (general) moral rights and obligations. Judgements of right and wrong conduct at the bottom level are functions of moral rights and obligations, and of nothing else. (Since moral rights are assumed to be correlative to obligations, but not vice versa, this can be put solely in terms of obligations.) A particular act is right if and only if it does not breach a moral obligation, unless that obligation has been overridden by another obligation. But moral principles are not self-certifying; they turn upon values they somehow serve (Mill is least clear about this relation). The topmost level of normative judgements and concepts concerns the values that may be invoked to establish moral principles (which concern general moral rights and obligations). For Mill, of course, the value at work at this topmost level is human happiness or welfare. So, moral principles about general rights and obligations are supposed to have a direct relationship to the principle of utility. But judgements concerning the rightness or wrongness of particular actions have *no* such relation. Acts must be judged as right or wrong depending on whether they respect moral rights and obligations, and *never* on the basis of direct utilitarian reasoning.

This feature of Mill's reconstructed analytic theory is vital to the possibility of a utilitarian account of moral rights and obligations. It ensures that Mill's theory does not collapse into act-utilitarianism. It ensures, more generally, that the evaluation of conduct in his theory is not dominated by direct utilitarian considerations. Mill's way of ensuring this is by conceptual analysis, which leads to the claim that moral concepts are so stratified that interactions are possible between adjacent levels but are absolutely prohibited between the top and bottom levels. Without this conceptual foundation, his theory would either collapse into act-utilitarianism or amount to just another, more or less arbitrary, revision of utilitarianism.

Mill's conceptual claims provide a necessary (though not a sufficient) condition for accommodating moral rights and obligations, if we assume that moral rights and obligations possess normative force (which Mill suggests). In the present context, that makes possible the hope that his theory will generate a moral obligation to conform to the actual rules of institutions that can be defended on utilitarian grounds, so that the theory will require respect for the rights conferred by such rules.

The success of Mill's theory thus turns upon the truth of his conceptual claims. But these seem stronger than the moral concepts can bear. It is plausible to hold that what is right or wrong is at least in part a function of moral rights and obligations (this is what is meant by the normative force of moral rights and obligations). But it is not so plausible to hold that the concepts involved *completely prohibit* the direct appeal to ultimate values, such as human welfare, when evaluating conduct. On the view I have ascribed to Mill—the one that promises a way of accommodating moral rights and obligations—someone who evaluates conduct by means of direct utilitarian arguments is guilty of a conceptual mistake. He is not reasoning unsoundly; he is reasoning *fallaciously*. But this appears excessive, to say the least; and yet nothing short of this will secure Mill's moral principles from being dominated by direct utilitarian considerations.

Consider, for example, our imaginary utilitarian official. When he takes into account the effects of his conduct on human welfare while trying to decide what to do, he does not seem to be confused or to be violating the contraints of the moral concepts. If he places too much weight upon direct utilitarian considerations, that may be a moral error, but it does not look like a conceptual mistake. As a utilitarian, it seems incumbent on him to consider the effects of his conduct on welfare. If so, we have no reason to believe that direct utilitarian considerations will not dominate his moral reasoning. Thus, we have no reason to believe that a satisfactory utilitarian theory of *moral* rights and obligations can be developed. So we have no reason to believe that a utilitarian would be obliged to respect the moral force of justified *legal* rights and obligations.

IX. SUMMARY

A utilitarian might be assumed to reason as follows: 'I will have no truck with "moral rights", which are figments of unenlightened moralists' imaginations. I am concerned with human welfare, with promoting it as far as possible, and I approve of social institutions to the extent they serve that purpose. Those institutions are morally defensible, and no others are. Under them, people have rights—not imaginary, toothless rights, but real, enforceable rights.'

This was Bentham's attitude (though not Mill's), and it fits the normative thinking found most generally in the literature of 'economic analysis'. The trouble is, it ignores a central normative issue, what conduct is required or permitted by the theory that endorses those allegedly justifiable rights.

Economists might be excused for neglecting this issue—at least until it is pointed out to them—since they tend to think only about rules and regulations and to ignore how principles apply directly to individuals' conduct, perhaps because they have not approached their normative conclusions from a self-consciously normative standpoint. But utilitarians have no such excuse. As Bentham was aware, the aim of promoting some value like human welfare is as relevant to individual acts as it is to social institutions; the latter application does not rule out the former. But, unless utilitarianism is restricted, its direct application to conduct undermines respect for the very rights it wishes to endorse.

VI

RIGHTS, GOALS, AND FAIRNESS*

T. M. SCANLON

CRITICS of utilitarianism frequently call attention to the abhorrent policies that unrestricted aggregative reasoning might justify under certain possible, or even actual, circumstances. They invite the conclusion that to do justice to the firm intuition that such horrors are clearly unjustifiable one must adopt a deontological moral framework that places limits on what appeals to maximum aggregate well-being can justify. As one who has often argued in this way, however, I am compelled to recognize that this position has its own weaknesses. In attacking utilitarianism one is inclined to appeal to individual rights, which mere considerations of social utility cannot justify us in overriding. But rights themselves need to be justified somehow, and how other than by appeal to the human interests their recognition promotes and protects? This seems to be the uncontrovertible insight of the classical utilitarians. Further, unless rights are to be taken as defined by rather implausible rigid formulae, it seems that we must invoke what looks very much like the consideration of consequences in order to determine what they rule out and what they allow. Thus, for example, in order to determine whether a given policy violates the right of freedom of expression it is not enough to know merely that it restricts speech. We may need to consider also its effects: how it would affect access to the means of expression and what the consequences would be of granting to government the kind of regulatory powers it confers.

I am thus drawn toward a two-tier view: one that gives an important

Reprinted by permission of the author and D. Reidel Publ. Co., from *Erkenntnis*, Vol. II, No. 1, May 1977, pp. 81–94, copyright © 1977 by D. Reidel Publishing Company, Dordrecht, Holland.

* The original version of this paper was presented at the Reisensberg Conference on Decision Theory and Social Ethics. I am indebted to a number of people for critical comments and helpful discussion, particularly to Ronald Dworkin, Derek Parfit, Gilbert Harman, Samuel Scheffler, and Milton Wachsberg. Work on this paper was supported in part by a fellowship from the National Endowment for the Humanities.

role to consequences in the justification and interpretation of rights but which takes rights seriously as placing limits on consequentialist reasoning at the level of casuistry. Such a view looks like what has been called rule-utilitarianism, a theory subject to a number of very serious objections. First, rule-utilitarians are hard pressed to explain why, if at base they are convinced utilitarians, they are not thoroughgoing ones. How can they square their utilitarianism with the acceptance of individual actions that are not in accord with the utilitarian formula? Second, rule-utilitarianism seems to be open to some of the same objections levelled against utilitarianism in its pure form; in particular it seems no more able than act-utilitarianism is to give a satisfactory place to considerations of distributive justice. Third, in attempting to specify which rules it is that are to be applied in the appraisal of acts and policies rule utilitarians of the usual sort are faced with an acute dilemma. If it is some set of ideal rules that are to be applied—those rules general conformity to which would have the best consequences—then the utilitarian case for a concern with rules, rather than merely with the consequences of isolated acts, appears lost. For this case must rest on benefits that flow from the general observance of rules but not from each individual act, and such benefits can be gained only if the rules are in fact generally observed. But if, on the other hand, the rules that are to be applied must be ones that are generally observed, the critical force of the theory seems to be greatly weakened.

The problem, then, is to explain how a theory can have, at least in part, a two-tier structure; how it can retain the basic appeal of utilitarianism, at least as it applies to the foundation of rights, and yet avoid the problems that have plagued traditional rule-utilitarianism. As a start towards describing such a theory I will consider three questions. (1) What consequences are to be considered, and how is their value to be determined? (2) How do considerations of distributive justice enter the theory? (3) How does one justify taking rights (or various moral rules) as constraints on the production of valued consequences?

I. CONSEQUENCES AND THEIR VALUES

Here I have two remarks, one of foundation, the other of content. First, as I have argued elsewhere[1] but can only here assert, I depart from the classical utilitarians and many of their modern followers in rejecting subjective preferences as the basis for the valuation of outcomes. This role is to be played instead by an ethically significant, objective notion of the relative importance of various benefits and burdens.

[1] In 'Preference and Urgency', *The Journal of Philosophy* 72 (1975), pp. 655–70.

Second, as to content, the benefits and burdens with which the theory is concerned must include not only the things that may happen to people but also factors affecting the ability of individuals to determine what will happen. Some of these factors are the concern of what are generally called rights, commonly[2] distinguished into (claim-) rights to command particular things, where others have a correlative duty to comply; liberties to do or refrain from certain things, where others have no such correlative duties; powers to change people's rights or status; and immunities from powers exercised by others. I take it to be the case that the familiar civil rights as well as such things as rights of privacy and 'the right to life', are complexes of such elements. The *de facto* ability effectively to choose among certain options and the *de facto* absence of interference by others with one's choices are not the same thing as rights, although if it is generally believed that a person has a particular right, say a claim-right, this may contribute to his having such *de facto* ability or lack of interference. But, however they are created, such abilities and protections are important goods with which any moral theory must be concerned, and the allocation of rights is one way in which this importance receives theoretical recognition.

Any theory of right, since it deals with what agents should and may do, is in a broad sense concerned with the assignment of rights and liberties. It is relevant to ask, concerning such a theory, how much latitude it gives a person in satisfying moral requirements and how much protection it gives a person through the constraints it places on the actions of others. Traditional utilitarianism has been seen as extreme on both these counts. It is maximally specific in the requirements it imposes on an agent, and, since there are no limits to what it may require to be done, it provides a minimum of reliable protection from interference by others. Objections to utilitarianism have often focused on its demanding and intrusive character,[3] and other theories of right may grant individuals both greater discretion and better protection. But these are goods with costs. When one individual is given a claim-right or liberty with respect to a certain option, the control

[2] Following Hohfeld and others. See W. N. Hohfeld, *Fundamental Legal Conceptions* (New Haven, 1923), and also Stig Kanger, 'New Foundations for Ethical Theory', in Risto Hilpinen, ed., *Deontic Logic: Introductory and Systematic Readings* (Dordrecht, 1971), pp. 36–58. On the distinction between concern with outcomes and concern with the allocation of competences to determine outcomes see Charles Fried, 'Two Concepts of Interests: Some Reflections of the Supreme Court's Balancing Test', *The Harvard Law Review*, 76 (1963), pp. 755–78.

[3] See Bernard Williams, 'A Critique of Utilitarianism', in J. J. C. Smart and B. Williams, *Utilitarianism: For and Against* (Cambridge, 1973).

that others are able to exercise over their own options is to some degree diminished. Further, if we take the assignment of rights to various individuals as, in at least some cases, an end-point of justification, then we must be prepared to accept the situation resulting from their exercise of these rights even if, considered in itself, it may be unattractive, or at least not optimal. Both these points have been urged by Robert Nozick,[4] the latter especially in his attack on 'end-state' and 'patterned' theories. What follows from these observations, however, is not Nozick's particular theory of entitlements but rather a general moral about the kind of comparison and balancing that a justification of rights requires: the abilities and protections that rights confer must be assigned values that are comparable not only with competing values of the same kind but also with the values attached to the production of particular end-results.

The same moral is to be drawn from some of Bernard Williams's objections to utilitarianism.[5] Williams objects that utilitarianism, in demanding total devotion to the inclusive goal of maximum happiness, fails to give adequate recognition to the importance, for each individual, of the particular projects which give his life content. The problem with such an objection is that taken alone it may be made to sound like pure self-indulgence. Simply to demand freedom from moral requirements in the name of freedom to pursue one's individual projects is unconvincing. It neglects the fact that these requirements may protect interests of others that are at least as important as one's own. To rise clearly above the level of special pleading these objections must be made general. They must base themselves on a general claim about how important the interests they seek to protect are for any person as compared with the interests served by conflicting claims.

The two preceding remarks—of foundation and of content—are related in the following way. Since the ability to influence outcomes and protection from interference or control by others are things people care about, they will be taken into account in any subjective utilitarian theory. I will later raise doubts as to whether such a theory can take account of them in the right way, but my present concern is with the question what value is to be assigned to these concerns. On a subjective theory these values will be determined by the existing individual preferences in the society in question. I would maintain, however, that prevailing preferences are not an adequate basis for the justification of rights. It is not relevant, for example, to the determination of rights of

[4] In *Anarchy, State and Utopia* (New York, 1974), esp. pp. 32–5 and ch. 7.
[5] In Sect. 5 of 'A Critique of Utilitarianism'.

religious freedom that the majority group in a society is feverishly committed to the goal of making its practices universal while the minority is quite tepid about all matters of religion. This is of course just an instance of the general objection to subjective theories stated above. The equally general response is that one has no basis on which to 'impose' values that run contrary to individual preferences. This objection draws its force from the idea that individual autonomy ought to be respected and that it is offensive to frustrate an individual's considered preferences in the name of serving his 'true interests'. This idea does not itself rest on preferences. Rather, it functions as the objective moral basis for giving preferences a fundamental role as the ground of ethically relevant valuations. But one may question whether this theoretical move is an adequate response to the intuitive idea from which it springs. To be concerned with individual autonomy is to be concerned with the rights, liberties, and other conditions necessary for individuals to develop their own aims and interests and to make their preferences effective in shaping their own lives and contributing to the formation of social policy. Among these will be rights protecting people against various forms of paternalistic intervention. A theory that respects autonomy will be one that assigns all these factors their proper weight. There is no reason to think that this will be accomplished merely by allowing these weights, and all others, to be determined by the existing configuration of preferences.

II. FAIRNESS AND EQUALITY

Rather than speaking generally of 'distributive justice', which can encompass a great variety of considerations, I will speak instead of fairness, as a property of processes (e.g. of competitions), and equality, as a property of resultant distributions. The question is how these considerations enter a theory of the kind I am describing. One way in which a notion of equality can be built into a consequentialist theory is through the requirement that, in evaluating states of affairs to be promoted, we give equal consideration to the interests of every person. This principle of equal consideration of interests has minimal egalitarian content. As stated, it is compatible with classical utilitarianism which, after all, 'counts each for one and none for more than one'. Yet many have felt, with justification, that utilitarianism gives insufficient weight to distributive considerations. How might this weight be increased? Let me distinguish two ways. The first would be to strengthen the principle of equal consideration of interests in such a way as to make it incompatible with pure utilitarianism. 'Equal consideration' could, for example, be held to mean that in any justification by appeal to consequences we must give priority to those individual interests that are 'most urgent'. To neglect such interests in order to serve instead less urgent interests even of a greater number of people would, on this interpretation, violate 'equality of consideration'. Adoption of this interpretation would ward off some objections to utilitarianism based on its insensitivity to distributive considerations but would at the same time preserve other characteristic features of the doctrine, e.g. some of its radically redistributive implications. Such a 'lexical interpretation' has, of course, its own problems. Its strength (and plausibility) is obviously dependent on the ranking we choose for determining the urgency of various interests.

The nature of such a ranking is an important problem, but one I cannot pursue here. Whatever the degree of distributive content that is built into the way individual interests are reckoned in moral argument, however, there is a second way in which distributive considerations enter a theory of the kind I wish to propose: equality of distributions and fairness of processes are among the properties that make states of affairs worth promoting. Equality in the distribution of particular classes of goods is at least sometimes of value as a means to the attainment of other valued ends, and in other cases fairness and equality are valuable in their own right.

Classical utilitarianism, of course, already counts equality as a means, namely as a means to maximum aggregate utility. Taken alone, this seems inadequate—too instrumental to account for the moral importance equality has for us. Yet I do think that in many of the cases in which we are most concerned with the promotion of equality we desire greater equality as a means to the attainment of some further end. In many cases, for example, the desire to eliminate great inequalities is motivated primarily by humanitarian concern for the plight of those who have least. Redistribution is desirable in large part because it is a means of alleviating their suffering (without giving rise to comparable suffering elsewhere). A second source of moral concern with redistribution in the contemporary world lies in the fact that great inequalities in wealth give to those who have more an unacceptable degree of control over the lives of others. Here again the case for greater equality is instrumental. Were these two grounds for redistribution to be eliminated (by, say, greatly increasing the standard of living of all concerned and preventing the gap between rich and poor, which remains unchanged, from allowing the rich to dominate) the moral case for equality would not be eliminated, but I believe that it would seem less pressing.

Beyond these and other instrumental arguments, fairness and equality often figure in moral argument as independently valuable states of affairs. So considered, they differ from the ends promoted in standard utilitarian theories in that their value does not rest on their being good things *for* particular individuals: fairness and equality do not represent ways in which individuals may be *better off*.[6] They are, rather, special morally desirable features of states of affairs or of social institutions. In admitting such moral features into the evaluation of consequences, the theory I am describing departs from standard consequentialist theories, which generally resist the introduction of explicitly moral considerations into the maximand. It diverges also from recent deontological theories, which bring in fairness and equality as specific moral requirements rather than as moral goals. I am inclined to pursue this 'third way' for several reasons.

First, it is not easy to come up with a moral argument for substantive equality (as distinct from mere formal equality or equal consideration of interests) which makes it look like an absolute moral requirement. Second, considerations of fairness and equality are multiple. There are many different processes that may be more or less fair, and we are concerned with equality in the distribution of many different and separable benefits and burdens. These are not all of equal importance; the strength of claims of equality and fairness depends on the goods whose distribution is at issue. Third, these claims do not seem to be absolute. Attempts to achieve equality or fairness in one area may conflict with the pursuit of these goals in other areas. In order to achieve greater equality we may, for example, change our processes in ways that involve unfairness in the handling of some individual cases. Perhaps the various forms of fairness and equality can be brought together under one all-encompassing notion of distributive justice which is always to be increased, but it is not obvious that this is so. In any event, it would remain the case that attempts to increase fairness and equality can have costs in other terms; they may interfere with processes whose efficiency is important to us, or involve unwelcome intrusions into individuals' lives. In such cases of conflict it does not seem that considerations of fairness and equality, as such, are always dominant. An increase of equality may in some cases not be worth its cost; whether it is will depend in part on what it is equality *of*.

Economists often speak of 'trade-offs' between equality and other

[6] Here I am indebted to Kurt Baier. Defending the claim that fairness and equality are intrinsically valuable is of course a further difficult task. Perhaps all convincing appeals to these notions can be reduced to instrumental arguments, but I do not at present see how. Such a reduction would move my theory even closer to traditional utilitarianism.

concerns (usually efficiency). I have in the past been inclined, perhaps intolerantly, to regard this as crassness, but I am no longer certain that it is in principle mistaken. The suggestion that equality can be 'traded-off' against other goods arouses suspicion because it seems to pave the way for defences of the status quo. Measures designed to decrease inequality in present societies are often opposed on the ground that they involve too great a sacrifice in efficiency or in individual liberty, and one way to head off such objections is to hold that equality is to be pursued whatever the cost. But one can hold that appeals to liberty and efficiency do not justify maintaining the status quo—and in fact that considerations of individual liberty provide some of the strongest arguments in favour of increased equality of income and wealth—without holding that considerations of equality are, as such, absolute and take priority over all other values.

III. RIGHTS

Why give rights a special place in a basically consequentialist theory? How can a two-tier theory be justified? One common view of the place of rights, and moral rules generally, within utilitarianism holds that they are useful as means to the co-ordination of action. The need for such aids does not depend on imperfect motivation; it might exist even in a society of perfect altruists. A standard example is a rule regulating water consumption during a drought. A restriction to one bucket a day per houshold might be a useful norm for a society of utilitarians even though their reasons for taking more water than this would be entirely altruistic. Its usefulness does not depend on self-interest. But the value of such a rule does depend on the fact that the agents are assumed to act independently of one another in partial ignorance of what the others have done or will do. If Dudley knows what others will do, and knows that this will leave some water in the well, then there is no utilitarian reason why he should not violate the rule and take more than his share for some suitable purpose—as the story goes, to water the flowers in the public garden.

I am of two minds about such examples. On the one hand, I can feel the force of the utilitarian's insistence that if the water is not going to be used how can we object to Dudley's taking it? On the other hand, I do not find this line of reply wholly satisfying. Why should *he* be entitled to do what others were not? Well, because he knows and they didn't; he alone has the opportunity. But just because he has it does that mean he can exercise it unilaterally? Perhaps, to be unbearably priggish, he should call the surplus to the attention of the others so that they can all decide how to use it. If this alternative is available is it all right for him to pass it up and act on his own? A utilitarian might respond here that he is not saying that Dudley is entitled to do whatever he wishes with the surplus water; he is entitled to do with it what the principle of utility requires and nothing else.

Here a difference of view is shown. Permission to act outside the rule is seen by the non-utilitarian as a kind of freedom for the agent, an exemption, but it is seen by a utilitarian as a specific moral requirement. Dudley is required to do something that is different from what the others do because his situation is different, but he has no greater latitude for the exercise of discretion or personal preference than anyone else does. This suggests that one can look at an assignment of rights in either of two ways: as a way of constraining individual decisions in order to promote some desired further effect (as in the case of a system of rules defining a division of labour between co-workers) or as a way of parcelling out valued forms of discretion over which individuals are in conflict. To be avoided, I think, is a narrow utilitarianism that construes all rights on the first model, e.g. as mechanisms of co-ordination or as hedges against individual errors in judgement. So construed, rights have no weight against deviant actions that can be shown to be the most effective way of advancing the shared goal.

If, however, the possibility of construing some rights on the second model is kept open, then rights can be given a more substantial role within a theory that is still broadly utilitarian. When, as seems plausible on one view of the water-shortage example, the purpose of an assignment of rights is to ensure an equitable distribution of a form of control over outcomes, then these rights are supported by considerations which persist even when contrary actions would promote optimum results. This could remain true for a society of conscientious (though perhaps not single-minded) consequentialists, provided that they are concerned with 'consequences' of the sort I have described above. But to say that a rule or a right is not in general subject to exceptions justified on act-utilitarian grounds is not to say that it is absolute. One can ask how important it is to preserve an equitable distribution of control of the kind in question, and there will undoubtedly be some things that outweigh this value. There is no point in observing the one-bucket restriction when the pump-house is on fire. Further, the intent of an assignment of rights on the second model is apt to be to forestall certain particularly tempting or likely patterns of behaviour. If this is so, there may be some acts which are literally contrary to the formula in which the right is usually stated but which do not strike us as actual violations of the right. We are inclined to allow them even though the purposes they serve may be less important than the values the right is intended to secure. Restrictions on speech which none the less are not violations of freedom of expression are a good example of such 'apparent exceptions'.

Reflections of this kind suggest to me that the view that there is a moral right of a certain sort is generally backed by something like the following:

(i) An empirical claim about how individuals would behave or how institutions would work in the absence of this particular assignment of rights (claim-rights, liberties, etc.).

(ii) A claim that this result would be unacceptable. This claim will be based on valuation of consequences of the sort described in Section I above, taking into account also considerations of fairness and equality.

(iii) A further empirical claim about how the envisaged assignment of rights will produce a different outcome.

The empirical parts of this schema play a larger or at least more conspicuous role in some rights than in others. In the case of the right to freedom of expression this role is a large one and fairly well recognized. Neglecting this empirical element leads rights to degenerate into implausible rigid formulae. The impossibility of taking such a formula literally, as defining an absolute moral bar, lends plausibility to a 'balancing' view, according to which such a right merely represents one important value among others, and decisions must be reached by striking the proper balance between them. Keeping in mind the empirical basis of a right counters this tendency and provides a ground (1) for seeing that 'apparent exceptions' of the kind mentioned above are not justified simply by balancing one right against another; (2) for seeing where genuine balancing of interests is called for and what its proper terms are; and (3) for seeing how the content of a right must change as conditions change. These remarks hold, I think, not only for freedom of expression but also for other rights, for example, rights of due process and rights of privacy. In each of these cases a fairly complex set of institutional arrangements and assumptions about how these arrangements operate stands, so to speak, between the formula through which the right is identified and the goals to which it is addressed. This dependence on empirical considerations is less evident in the case of rights, like the right to life, that lie more in the domain of individual morality. I will argue below, however, that this right too can profitably be seen as a system of authorizations and limitations of discretion justified on the basis of an argument of the form just described.

This view of rights is in a broad sense consequentialist in that it holds rights to be justified by appeal to the states of affairs they promote. It seems to differ from the usual form of rule-utilitarianism, however, in that it does not appear to be a maximizing doctrine. The case for most familiar rights—freedom of expression, due process, religious toleration—seems to be more concerned with the avoidance of particular bad consequences than with promoting maximum benefit. But this difference is in part only apparent. The dangers that these rights are supposed to ward off are major ones, not likely to be overshadowed by everyday considerations. Where they are overshadowed, the theory I have described allows for the rights in question to be set aside. Further, the justification for the particular form that such a right takes allows for the consideration of costs. If a revised form of some right would do the job as well as the standard form at clearly reduced costs to peripheral interests, then this form would obviously be preferred. It should be noted, however, that if something is being maximized here it cannot, in view of the role that the goals of fairness and equality play in the theory, be simply the sum of individual benefits. Moreover, this recognition of an element of maximization does not mean that just any possible improvement in the way people generally behave will become the subject of a right. Rights concern the alleviation of certain major problems, and incremental gains in other goods become relevant to rights in the way just mentioned only when they flow from improvements in our ways of dealing with such problems.

I have suggested that the case for rights derives in large part from the goal of promoting an acceptable distribution of control over important factors in our lives. This general goal is one that would be of importance to people in a wide range of societies. But the particular rights it calls for may vary from society to society. Thus, in particular, the rights we have on the view I have proposed are probably not identical with the rights that would be recognized under the system of rules, general conformity to which in our society would have the best consequences. The problems to which our rights are addressed are ones that arise given the distribution of power and the prevailing patterns of motivation in the societies in which we live. These problems may not be ones that would arise were an ideal code of behaviour to prevail.[7] (And they might not be the same either as those we would

[7] How much this separates my view of rights from an ideal rule-utilitarian theory will depend on how that theory construes the notion of an ideal system of rules being 'in force' in a society. In Brandt's sophisticated version, for example, what is required is that it be true, and known in the society, that a high proportion of adults subscribe to these rules, that is, chiefly, that they are to some extent motivated to avoid violating the rules and feel guilty when they believe they have done so. ('Some Merits of One Form of Rule Utilitarianism' in Gorovitz, ed., *Mill: Utilitarianism, with Critical Essays* (Indianapolis, Ind., 1971.) This may

face in a 'state of nature'.) Concern with rights does not involve accepting these background conditions as desirable or as morally unimpeachable; it only involves seeing them as relatively fixed features of the environment with which we must deal.

Which features of one's society are to be held fixed in this way for purposes of moral argument about rights? This can be a controversial moral question and presents a difficult theoretical issue for anyone holding a view like rule-utilitarianism. As more and more is held fixed, including more about what other agents are in fact doing, the view converges toward act-utilitarianism. If, on the other hand, very little is held fixed then the problems of ideal forms of rule-utilitarianism seem to loom larger: we seem to risk demanding individual observance of rights when this is pointless given the lack of general conformity.

This dilemma is most acute to the degree that the case for rights (or moral rules) is seen to rest on their role in promoting maximum utility through the co-ordination of individual action. Where this is actually the case—as it is with many rules and perhaps some rights—it is of undoubted importance what others are in fact doing—to what degree these rights and rules are generally observed and how individual action will affect general observance. I suggest, however, that this is not the case with most rights. On the view I propose, a central concern of most rights is the promotion and maintenance of an acceptable distribution of control over important factors in our lives. Where a certain curtailment of individual discretion or official authority is clearly required for this purpose, the fact that this right is not generally observed does not undermine the case for its observance in a given instance. The case against allowing some to dictate the private religious observances of others, for example, does not depend on the existence of a general practice of religious toleration. Some of the benefits at which rights of religious freedom are aimed—the benefits of a general climate of religious toleration—are secured only when there is general compliance with these rights. But the case for enforcing these rights does not depend in every instance on these benefits.

not ensure that the level of conformity with these rules is much greater than the level of moral behaviour in societies we are familiar with. If it does not, then Brandt's theory may not be much more 'ideal' than the theory of rights offered here. The two theories appear to differ, however, on the issues discussed in sects. 1 and 2 above. These issues also divide my view from R. M. Hare's version of rule-utilitarianism, with which I am otherwise in much agreement. See his 'Ethical Theory and Utilitarianism', in H. D. Lewis, ed., *Contemporary British Philosophy, Fourth Series* (London, 1976). Like these more general theories, the account of rights offered here has a great deal in common with the view put forward by Mill in the final chapter of *Utilitarianism* (particularly if Mill's remarks about 'justice' are set aside).

For these reasons, the view of rights I have proposed is not prey to objections often raised against ideal rule-utilitarian theories. A further question is whether it is genuinely distinct from an act-consequentialist doctrine. It may seem that, for reasons given above, it cannot be: if an act in violation of a given right yields some consequence that is of greater value than those with which the right is concerned, then on my view the right is to be set aside. If the act does not have such consequences then, in virtue of its conflict with the right and the values that right protects, it seems that the act would not be justifiable on act-consequentialist grounds anyway. But this rests on a mistake. The values supporting a particular right need not all stand to be lost in every case in which the right is violated. In defending the claim that there is a right of a certain sort, e.g. a particular right of privacy, we must be prepared to compare the advantages of having this right—the advantages, e.g. of being free to decline to be searched—against competing considerations—e.g. the security benefits derived from a more lenient policy of search and seizure. But what stands to be gained or lost in any given instance in which a policeman would like to search me need not coincide with either of these values. It may be that in that particular case I don't care.[8]

There is, then, no incoherence in distinguishing between the value of having a right and the cost of having it violated on a particular occasion. And it is just the values of the former sort that we must appeal to in justifying a two-tier view. What more can be said about these values? From an act-consequentialist point of view the value attached to the kind of control and protection that rights confer seems to rest on mistrust of others. If everyone could be relied upon to do the correct thing from an act-consequentialist standpoint would we still be so concerned with rights? This way of putting the matter obscures several important elements. First, it supposes that we can all agree on the best thing to be done in each case. But concern with rights is based largely on the warranted supposition that we have significantly differing ideas of the good and that we are interested in the freedom to put our own conceptions into practice. Second, the objection assumes that we are concerned only with the correct choice being made and have no independent concern with who makes it. This also seems clearly false. The independent value we attach to being able to make our own choices should, however, be distinguished from the further value we may attach to having it recognized that we are *entitled* to

[8] On the importance of establishing the proper terms of balancing see Fried, 'Two Concepts of Interests', p. 758.

make them. This we may also value in itself as a sign of respect and personhood, but there is a question to what degree this value is an artifact of our moral beliefs and customs rather than a basis for them. Where a moral framework of rights is established and recognized, it will be important for a person to have his status as a right-holder generally acknowledged. But is there something analogous to this importance that is lost for everyone in a society of conscientious act-consequentialists where no one holds rights? It is not clear to me that there is, but, however this may be, my account emphasizes the value attached to rights for the sake of what they may bring rather than their value as signs of respect.

If the factors just enumerated were the whole basis for concern with rights then one would expect the case for them to weaken and the force of act-consequentialist considerations to grow relatively stronger as (1) the importance attached to outcomes becomes absolutely greater and hence, presumably, also relatively greater as compared with the independent value of making choices oneself, and as (2) the assignment of values to the relevant outcomes becomes less controversial. To some extent both these things happen in cases where life and death are at stake, and here mistrust emerges as the more plausible basis for concern with rights.

IV. CASES OF LIFE AND DEATH

From the point of view suggested in this paper, the right to life is to be seen as a complex of elements including particular liberties to act in one's own defence and to preserve one's life, claim-rights to aid and perhaps to the necessities of life, and restrictions on the liberty of others to kill or endanger. Let me focus here on elements in these last two categories, namely limits on the liberty to act in ways that lead to a person's death. An act-consequentialist standard could allow a person to take action leading to the death of another whenever this is necessary to avoid greater loss of life elsewhere. Many find this policy too permissive, and one explanation of this reaction is that it represents a kind of blind conservatism. We know that our lives are always in jeopardy in many ways. Tomorrow I may die of a heart attack or a blood clot. I may be hit by a falling tree or discover I have a failing liver or find myself stood up against a wall by a group of terrorists. But we are reluctant to open the door to a further form of deadly risk by allowing others to take our life should this be necessary to minimize loss of life overall. We are reluctant to do this even when the effect would be to increase our net chances of living a long life by decreasing the likelihood that we will actually die when one of the natural hazards of life befalls us. We adopt, as it were, the attitude of hoping against hope not to run foul of any of these hazards, and we place less stock on the prospect of escaping alive should we be so unlucky. It would not be irrational for a person to *decide* to increase his chances of survival by joining a transplant-insurance scheme, i.e. an arrangement guaranteeing one a heart or kidney should he need one provided he agrees to sacrifice himself to become a donor if he is chosen to do so. But such a decision is sufficiently controversial and the stakes so high that it is not a decision that can be taken to have been made for us as part of a unanimously acceptable basis for the assignment of rights. What I have here called conservatism is, however, uncomfortably close to a bias of the lucky against the unlucky in so far as it rests on a conscious turning of attention away from the prospect of our being one of the unlucky ones.

A substitute for conservatism is mistrust. We are reluctant to place our life in *anyone's* hands. We are even more reluctant to place our lives in *everyone's* hands as the act-consequentialist standard would have us do. Such mistrust is the main factor supporting the observed difference between the rationality of joining a voluntary transplant-insurance scheme and the permissibility of having a compulsory one (let alone the universally administered one that unrestricted act-consequentialism could amount to). A person who joins a voluntary scheme has the chance to see who will be making the decisions and to examine the safeguards on the process. In assessing the force of these considerations one should also bear in mind that what they are to be weighed against is not 'the value of life itself' but only a small increase in the probability of living a somewhat longer life.

These appeals to 'conservatism' and mistrust, if accepted, would support something like the distinction between killing and letting die: we are willing to grant to others the liberty not to save us from threat of death when this is necessary to save others, but we are unwilling to allow them to put us under threat of death when we have otherwise escaped it. As is well known, however, the killing/letting die distinction appears to permit some actions leading to a person's death that are not intuitively permissible. These are actions in which an agent refrains from aiding someone already under threat of death and does so because that person's death has results he considers advantageous. (I will assume that they are thought advantageous to someone other than the person who is about to die.) The intuition that such actions are not permitted would be served by a restriction on the liberty to fail to save, specifying that this course of action cannot be undertaken on the basis of conceived advantages of having the person out of the way. Opponents of the law of double-effect have sometimes objected that it is strange to make the permissibility of an action depend on quite subtle features of its rationale. In the context of the present theory, however, the distinction just proposed is not formally anomalous. Conferrals of authority and limitations on it often take the form not simply of allowing certain actions or barring them but rather of restricting the grounds on which actions can be undertaken. Freedom of expression embodies restrictions of this kind, for example, and this is one factor responsible for the distinction between real and apparent violations mentioned above.[9]

Reasons for such a restriction in the present case are easy to come by. People have such powerful and tempting reasons for wanting others removed from the scene that it is obviously a serious step to open the door to calculations taking these reasons into account. Obviously, what would be proposed would be a qualified restriction, allowing consideration of the utilitarian, but not the purely self-interested, advantages to be gained from a person's death. But a potential agent's perception of this distinction does not seem to be a factor worth depending on.

The restriction proposed here may appear odd when compared to our apparent policy regarding mutual aid. If, as seems to be the case, we are prepared to allow a person to fail to save another when doing so would involve a moderately heavy sacrifice, why not allow him to do the same for the sake of a much greater benefit, to be gained from that person's death? The answer seems to be that, while a principle of mutual aid giving less consideration to the donor's sacrifice strikes us as too demanding, it is not nearly as threatening as a policy allowing one to consider the benefits to be gained from a person's death.

These appeals to 'conservatism' and mistrust do not seem to me to provide adequate justification for the distinctions in question. They may explain, however, why these distinctions have some appeal for us and yet remain matters of considerable controversy.

[9] For a view of freedom of expression embodying this feature, see Scanlon, 'A Theory of Freedom of Expression', *Philosophy and Public Affairs*, 1 (1972), pp. 204–26.

VII

RIGHTS AS TRUMPS

RONALD DWORKIN

I. RIGHTS AND UTILITY

RIGHTS are best understood as trumps over some background justification for political decisions that states a goal for the community as a whole.[1] If someone has a right to publish pornography, this means that it is for some reason wrong for officials to act in violation of that right, even if they (correctly) believe that the community as a whole would be better off if they did. Of course, there are many different theories in the field about what makes a community better off on the whole; many different theories, that is, about what the goal of political action should be. One prominent theory (or rather group of theories) is utilitarianism in its familiar forms, which suppose that the community is better off if its members are on average happier or have more of their preferences satisfied. There are, of course, many other theories about the true goal of politics. To some extent, the argument in favour of a political right must depend on which of these theories about desirable goals has been accepted; it must depend, that is, on what general background justification for political decisions the right in question proposes to trump. In the following discussion I shall assume that the background justification with which we are concerned is some form of utilitarianism which takes, as the goal of politics, the fulfilment of as many of people's goals for their own lives as possible. This remains, I think, the most influential background justification, at least in the informal way in which it presently figures in politics in the Western democracies.

Suppose we accept then that, at least in general, a political decision is justified if it promises to make citizens happier, or to fulfil more of their preferences, on average, than any other decision could. Suppose

Adapted by the author from Ronald Dworkin, 'Is There a Right to Pornography?', *Oxford Journal of Legal Studies*, 1 (1981), pp. 177–212.

[1] See Ronald Dworkin, *Taking Rights Seriously* (London, 1978).

we assume that the decision to prohibit pornography altogether does in fact, meet that test, because the desires and preferences of publishers and consumers are outweighed by the desires and preferences of the majority, including their preferences about how others should lead their lives. How could any contrary decision, permitting even the private use of pornography, then be justified?

Two modes of argument might be thought capable of supplying such a justification. First, we might argue that, though the utilitarian goal states one important political ideal, it is not the only important ideal, and pornography must be permitted in order to protect some other ideal that is, in the circumstances, more important. Second, we might argue that further analysis of the grounds that we have for accepting utilitarianism as a background justification in the first place—further reflection of why we wish to pursue that goal—shows that utility must yield to some right of moral independence here. The first form of argument is pluralistic: it argues for a trump over utility on the ground that though utility is always important, it is not the only thing that matters, and other goals or ideals are sometimes more important. The second supposes that proper understanding of what utilitarianism is, and why it is important, will itself justify the right in question.

I do not believe that the first, or pluralistic, mode of argument has much prospect of success, at least as applied to the problem of pornography. But I shall not develop the arguments now that would be necessary to support that opinion. I want instead to offer an argument in the second mode, which is, in summary, this. Utilitarianism owes whatever appeal it has to what we might call its egalitarian cast. (Or, if that is too strong, would lose whatever appeal it has but for that cast.) Suppose some version of utilitarianism provided that the preferences of some people were to count for less than those of others in the calculation how best to fulfil most preferences overall either because these people were in themselves less worthy or less attractive or less well-loved people, or because the preferences in question combined to form a contemptible way of life. This would strike us as flatly unacceptable, and in any case much less appealing than standard forms of utilitarianism. In any of its standard versions, utilitarianism can claim to provide a conception of how government treats people as equals, or, in any case, how government respects the fundamental requirement that it must treat people as equals. Utilitarianism claims that people are treated as equals when the preferences of each, weighted only for intensity, are balanced in the same scales, with no distinctions for persons or merit. The corrupt version of utilitarianism just described, which gives less weight to some persons than to others, or discounts some preferences because these are ignoble, forfeits that claim. But if utilitarianism in practice is not checked by something like the right of moral independence (and by other allied rights) it will disintegrate, for all practical purposes, into exactly that version.

Suppose a community of many people including Sarah. If the constitution sets out a version of utilitarianism which provides in terms that Sarah's preferences are to count for twice as much as those of others, then this would be the unacceptable, non-egalitarian version of utilitarianism. But now suppose that the constitutional provision is the standard form of utilitarianism, that is, that it is neutral towards all people and preferences, but that a surprising number of people love Sarah very much, and therefore strongly prefer that her preferences count for twice as much in the day-to-day political decisions made in the utilitarian calculus. When Sarah does not receive what she would have if her preferences counted for twice as much as those of others, then these people are unhappy, because their special Sarah-loving preferences are unfulfilled. If these special preferences are themselves allowed to count, therefore, Sarah will receive much more in the distribution of goods and opportunities than she otherwise would. I argue that this defeats the egalitarian cast of the apparently neutral utilitarian constitution as much as if the neutral provision were replaced by the rejected version. Indeed, the apparently neutral provision is then self-undermining because it gives a critical weight, in deciding which distribution best promotes utility, to the views of those who hold the profoundly un-neutral (some would say anti-utilitarian) theory that the preferences of some should count for more than those of others.

The reply that a utilitarian anxious to resist the right to moral independence would give to this argument is obvious: utilitarianism does not give weight to the truth of that theory, but just to the fact that many people (wrongly) hold that theory and so are disappointed when the distribution the government achieves is not the distribution they believe is right. It is the fact of their disappointment, not the truth of their views, that counts, and there is no inconsistency, logical or pragmatic, in that. But this reply is too quick. For there is in fact a particularly deep kind of contradiction here. Utilitarianism must claim (as I said earlier any political theory must claim) truth for itself, and therefore must claim the falsity of any theory that contradicts it. It must itself occupy, that is, all the logical space that its content requires. But neutral utilitarianism claims (or in any case presupposes) that no one is, in principle, any more entitled to have any of his preferences fufilled than anyone else is. It argues that the only reason for denying the fulfilment of one person's desires, whatever these are, is that more or more intense desire must be satisfied instead. It insists that justice and political morality can supply no other reason. This is, we might say, the neutral utilitarian's *case* for trying to achieve a political structure in which the average fulfilment of preferences is as high as possible. The question is not whether a government can achieve that political structure if it counts political preferences like the preferences of the Sarah-lovers[2] or whether the government will in fact then have counted any particular preference twice and so contradicted utilitarianism in that direct way. It is rather whether the government can achieve all this without implicitly contradicting that case.

Suppose the community contains a Nazi, for example, whose set of preferences includes the preference that Aryans have more and Jews less of their preferences fulfilled just because of who they are. A neutral utilitarian cannot say that there is no reason in political morality, for rejecting or dishonouring that preference, for not dismissing it as simply wrong, for not striving to fulfil it with all the dedication that officials devote to fulfilling any other sort of preference. For utilitarianism itself supplies such a reason: its most fundamental tenet is that people's preferences should be weighed on an equal basis in the same scales, that the Nazi theory of justice is profoundly wrong, and that officials should oppose the Nazi theory and strive to defeat rather than fulfil it. A neutral utilitarian is in fact barred, for reasons of consistency, from taking the same politically neutral attitude to the Nazi's political preference that he takes to other sorts of preferences. But then he cannot make the case just described in favour of highest average utility computed taking that preference into account.

I do not mean to suggest, of course, that endorsing someone's right to have his preference satisfied automatically endorses his preference as good or noble. The good utilitarian, who says that the push-pin player is equally entitled to satisfaction of that taste as the poet is entitled to the satisfaction of his, is not for that reason committed to the proposition that a life of push-pin is as good as a life of poetry. Only vulgar critics of utilitarianism would insist on that inference. The utilitarian says only that nothing in the theory of justice provides any reason why the political and economic arrangements and decisions of society should be any closer to those the poet would prefer than those the push-pin player would like. It is just a matter, from the standpoint of political justice, of how many people prefer the one to the other and how strongly. But he cannot say that about the conflict between the

[2] Though there are obvious dangers of a circle here. See Dworkin, 'What is Equality? Part I: Equality of Welfare', *Philosophy and Public Affairs* (1981).

Nazi and the neutral utilitarian opponent of Nazism, because the correct political theory, his political theory, the very political theory to which he appeals in attending to the fact of the Nazi's claim, does speak to the conflict. It says that what the neutral utilitarian prefers is just and accurately describes what people are, as a matter of political morality, entitled to have, but that what the Nazi prefers is deeply unjust and describes what no one is entitled, as a matter of political morality, to have. But then it is contradictory to say, again as a matter of political morality, that the Nazi is as much entitled to the political system he prefers as is the utilitarian.

The point might be put this way. Political preferences, like the Nazi's preference, are on the same level—purport to occupy the same space—as the utilitarian theory itself. Therefore, though the utilitarian theory must be neutral between personal preferences like the preferences for push-pin and poetry, as a matter of the theory of justice, it cannot, without contradiction, be neutral between itself and Nazism. It cannot accept at once a duty to defeat the false theory that some people's preferences should count for more than other people's and a duty to strive to fulfil the political preferences of those who passionately accept that false theory, as energetically as it strives for any other preferences. The distinction on which the reply to my argument rests, the distinction between the truth and the fact of the Nazi's political preferences, collapses, because if utilitarianism counts the fact of these preferences it has denied what it cannot deny, which is that justice requires it to oppose them.

We could escape this point, of course, by distinguishing two different forms or levels of utilitarianism. The first would be presented simply as a thin theory about how a political constitution should be selected in a community whose members prefer different kinds of political theories. The second would be a candidate for the constitution to be so chosen; it might argue for a distribution that maximized aggregate satisfaction of personal preferences in the actual distribution of goods and opportunities, for example. In that case the first theory would argue only that the preferences of the Nazi should be given equal weight with the preferences of the second sort of utilitarian in the choice of a constitution, because each is equally entitled to the constitution he prefers, and there would be no contradiction in that proposition. But of course the neutral utilitarian theory we are now considering is not simply a thin theory of that sort. It proposes a theory of justice as a full political constitution, not simply a theory about how to choose one, and so it cannot escape contradiction through modesty.

Now the same argument holds (though perhaps less evidently) when the political preferences are not familiar and despicable, like the Nazi theory, but more informal and cheerful, like the preferences of the Sarah-lovers who think that her preferences should be counted twice. The latter might, indeed, be Sarahocrats who believe that she is entitled to the treatment they recommend by virtue of birth or other characteristics unique to her. But even if their preferences rise from special affection rather than from political theory, these preferences nevertheless invade the space claimed by neutral utilitarianism and so cannot be counted without defeating the case utilitarianism provides. My argument, therefore, comes to this. If utilitarianism is to figure as part of an attractive working political theory, then it must be qualified so as to restrict the preferences that count by excluding political preferences of both the formal and informal sort. One very practical way to achieve this restriction is provided by the idea of rights as trumps over unrestricted utilitarianism. A society committed to utilitarianism as a general background justification which does not in terms disqualify any preferences might achieve that disqualification by adopting a right to political independence: the right that no one suffer disadvantage in the distribution of goods or opportunities on the ground that others think he should have less because of who he is or is not, or that others care less for him than they do for other people. The right of political independence would have the effect of insulating Jews from the preferences of Nazis, and those who are not Sarah from the preferences of those who adore her.

The right of moral independence can be defended in a parallel way. Neutral utilitarianism rejects the idea that some ambitions that people might have for their own lives should have less command over social resources and opportunities than others, except as this is the consequence of weighing all preferences on an equal basis in the same scales. It rejects the argument, for example, that some people's conception of what sexual experience should be like, and of what part fantasy should play in that experience, and of what the character of that fantasy should be, are inherently degrading or unwholesome. But then it cannot (for the reasons just canvassed) count the moral preferences of those who do hold such opinions in the calculation whether individuals who form some sexual minority, including homosexuals and pornographers, should be prohibited from the sexual experiences they want to have. The right of moral independence is part of the same collection of rights as the right of political independence, and it is to be justified as a trump over an unrestricted utilitarian defence of prohibitory laws against pornography, in a community of those who find offence just in the idea that their neighbours are reading dirty books, in much the same way as the latter right is justified as a trump over a utilitarian justification of giving Jews less or Sarah more in a society of Nazis or Sarah-lovers.

It remains to consider whether the abstract right to moral independence, defended in this way, would nevertheless permit restriction of public display of pornography in a society whose preferences against that display were backed by the mixed motives we reviewed in the last part. This is a situation in which the egalitarian cast of utilitarianism is threatened from not one but two directions. To the extent to which the motives in question are moral preferences about how others should behave, and these motives are counted, then the neutrality of utilitarianism is compromised. But to the extent to which these are the rather different sort of motives we reviewed, which emphasize not how others should lead their lives, but rather the character of the sexual experience people want for themselves, and these motives are disregarded, the neutrality of utilitarianism is compromised in the other direction, for it becomes unnecessarily inhospitable to the special and important ambitions of those who then lose control of a crucial aspect of their own self-development. The situation is therefore not an appropriate case for a prophylactic refusal to count any motive whenever we cannot be sure that the motive is unmixed with moralism, because the danger of unfairness lies on both sides rather than only on one. The alternative I described in the last part is at least better than that. This argues that restriction may be justified even though we cannot be sure that the preferences people have for restriction are untinged by the kind of preferences we should exclude, provided that the damage done to those who are affected adversely is not serious damage, even in their own eyes. Allowing restrictions on public display is in one sense a compromise; but it is a compromise recommended by the right of moral independence, once the case for that right is set out, not a compromise of that right.

II. HART'S OBJECTIONS

There are, then, good grounds for those who accept utilitarianism as a general background justification for political decisions also to accept, as part of the same package, a right of moral independence. I shall end this essay by considering certain objections that Professor H. L. A. Hart has made, in a recent article,[3] to a similar argument that I made some years ago about the connection between utilitarianism and these rights.[4]

[3] Hart, 'Between Utility and Rights', *Col. L. Rev.*, 79 (1980), pp. 828, 836 ff.

[4] See Dworkin, *Taking Rights Seriously*, Introduction, ch. 12, and Appendix,

Hart's objections show what I think is a comprehensive misunderstanding of this argument, which my earlier statement, as I now see, encouraged, and it might therefore be helpful, as insurance against a similar misunderstanding now, to report these objections and my reasons for thinking that they misconceive my argument.

I suggested, in my earlier formulation of the present argument, that if a utilitarian counts preferences like the preferences of the Sarah-lovers, then this is a 'form' of double-counting because, in effect, Sarah's preferences are counted twice, once on her own account, and once through the second-order preferences of others that incorporate her preferences by reference. Hart says that this is a mistake, because in fact no one's preferences are counted twice. and it would *under*-count the Sarah-lovers' preferences, and so fail to treat them as equals, if their preferences in her favour were discarded. There would be something in this last point if votes rather than preferences were in issue, because if someone wished to vote for Sarah's success rather than his own, his role in the calculation would be exhausted by this gift, and if his vote was then discarded he might well complain that he had been cheated of his equal power over political decision. But preferences (as these figure in utilitarian calculations) are not like votes in that way. Someone who reports more preferences to the utilitarian computer does not (except trivially) diminish the impact of other preferences he also reports; he rather increases the role of his preferences overall, compared with the role of other people's preferences, in the giant calculation. So someone who prefers Sarah's success to the success of people generally, and through the contribution of that preference to an unrestricted utilitarian calculation secures more for her, does not have any less for himself—for the fulfilment of his more personal preferences—than someone else who is indifferent to Sarah's fortunes.

I do not think that my description, that counting his preferences in favour of Sarah is a form of double-counting, is misleading or unfair. But this description was meant to summarize the argument, not to make it, and I will not press that particular characterization. (Indeed, as Hart notices, I made it only about some of the examples I gave in which unrestricted utilitarianism produced obviously inegalitarian results.) Hart makes more substantial points about a different example I used, which raised the question of whether homosexuals have the right to practice their sexual tastes in private. He thinks I want to say 'that if, as a result of [preferences that express moral disapproval of

pp. 357–8. See also Dworkin, 'Liberalism', in Hampshire (ed.), *Public and Private Morality*, (Cambridge, 1978); and Dworkin, 'Social Science and Constitutional Rights: the Consequences of Uncertainty', *J of L & Educ*, 6 (1977), p. 3.

homosexuals] tipping the balance, persons are denied some liberty, say to form some sexual relations, those so deprived suffer because by this result their concept of a proper or desirable form of life is despised by others, and this is tantamount to treating them as inferior to or of less worth than others, or not deserving of equal concern, and respect'.[5]

But this misstates my point. It is not the result (or, as Hart later describes it, the 'upshot') of the utilitarian calculation that causes or achieves the fact that homosexuals are despised by others. It is rather the other way round: if someone is denied liberty of sexual practice by virtue of a utilitarian justification that depends critically on other people's moralistic preferences, then he suffers disadvantage in virtue of the fact that his concept of a proper life is already despised by others. Hart says that the 'main weakness' in my argument—the feature that makes it 'fundamentally wrong'—is that I assume that if someone's liberty is restricted this must be interpreted as a denial of his treatment as an equal. But my argument is that this is not inevitably or even usually so, but only when the constraint is justified in some way that depends on the fact that others condemn his convictions or values. Hart says that the interpretation of denial of liberty as a denial of equal concern is 'least credible' in exactly the case I discuss, that is, when the denial is justified through a utilitarian argument, because (he says) the message of that justification is not that the defeated minority or their moral convictions are inferior, but only that they are too few to outweigh the preferences of the majority, which can only be achieved if the minority is in fact denied the liberty it wishes. But once again this ignores the distinction I want to make. If the utilitarian justification for denying liberty of sexual practice to homosexuals can succeed without counting the moralistic preferences of the majority in the balance (as it might if there was good reason to believe what is in fact incredible, that the spread of homosexuality fosters violent crime) then the message of prohibition would, indeed, be only the message Hart finds, which might be put this way: 'It is impossible that everyone be protected in all his interests, and the interests of the minority must yield, regrettably, to the concern of the majority for its safety' There is (at least in my present argument) no denial of treatment as an equal in that message. But if the utilitarian justification cannot succeed without relying on the majority's moralistic preferences about how the minority should live, and the government nevertheless urges that justification, then the message is very different, and, in my view, nastier. It is exactly that the minority must suffer

[5] Hart, *supra*, p. 842.

because others find the lives they propose to lead disgusting, which seems no more justifiable, in a society committed to treating people as equals, than the proposition we earlier considered and rejected, as incompatible with equality, that some people must suffer disadvantage under the law because others do not like them.

Hart makes further points. He suggests, for example, that it was the 'disinterested' political preferences of liberals that tipped the balance in favour of repealing laws against homosexual relationships in 1967 in England, and asks how anyone could object that counting *those* preferences at that time offended anyone's rights to be treated as an equal. But this question misunderstands my point in a fundamental way. I do not argue—how could anyone argue?—that citizens in a democracy should not campaign and vote for what they think is just. The question is not whether people should work for justice, but rather what test we and they should apply to determine what is just. Utilitarianism holds that we should apply this test: we should work to achieve maximum possible satisfaction of the preferences we find distributed in our community. If we accepted this test in an unrestricted way, then we would count the attractive political convictions of the liberals of the nineteen-sixties simply as data, to be balanced against the less attractive convictions of others, to see which carried the day in the contest of number and intensity. Conceivably the liberal position would have won this contest. Probably it would not have.

But I have been arguing that this is a false test, which in fact undermines the case of utilitarianism, if political preferences of either the liberals or their opponents are counted and balanced to determine what justice requires. That is why I recommend, as part of any overall political theory in which utilitarianism figures as a background justification, rights to political and moral independence. But the liberals who campaigned in the interests of homosexuals in England in the nineteen-sixties most certainly did not embrace the test I reject. They of course *expressed* their own political preferences in their votes and arguments, but they did not *appeal* to the popularity of these preferences as providing an argument in itself for what they wanted, as the unrestricted utilitarian argument I oppose would have encouraged them to do. Perhaps they appealed instead to something like the right of moral independence. In any case they did not rely on any argument inconsistent with that right. Nor is it necessary for us to rely on any such argument to say that what they did was right, and treated people as equals. The proof is this: the case for reform would have been just as strong in political theory even if there had been very few or no heterosexuals who wanted reform, though of course reform would not then have been practically possible. If so, then we cannot condemn the procedure that in fact produced reform on the ground that that procedure offended anyone's rights to independence.

Hart's misunderstanding here was no doubt encouraged by my own description of how rights like the right to moral independence function in a constitutional system, like that of the United States, which uses rights as a test of the legality of legislation. I said that a constitutional system of this sort is valuable when the community as a whole harbours prejudices against some minority or convictions that the way of life of that minority is offensive to people of good character. In that situation, the ordinary political process is antecedently likely to reach decisions that would fail the test we have constructed, because these decisions would limit the freedom of the minority and yet could not be justified, in political theory, except by assuming that some ways of living are inherently wrong or degrading, or by counting the fact that the majority thinks them so as itself part of the justification. Since these *repressive* decisions would then be wrong, for the reasons I offer, the constitutional right forbids them in advance.

Of course, the decision for reform that Hart describes would not—could not—be a decision justified only on these offending grounds. Even if the benign liberal preferences figured as data rather than argument, as I think they should not, no one would be in a position to claim the right to moral or political independence as a shield against the decision that was in fact reached. But someone might have been led to suppose, by my discussion, that what I condemn is any political process that would allow any decision to be taken if people's reasons for supporting one decision rather than another are likely to lie beyond their own personal interests. I hope it is now plain why this is wrong. *That* position would not allow a democracy to vote for social welfare programmes, or foreign aid, or conservation for later generations. Indeed, in the absence of an adequate constitutional system, the only hope for justice is precisely that people will vote with a disinterested sense of fairness. I condemn a political process that assumes that the fact that people have such reasons is itself part of the case in political morality for what they favour. Hart's heterosexual liberals may have been making the following argument to their fellow citizens. 'We know that many of you find the idea of homosexual relationships troubling and even offensive. Some of us do as well. But you must recognize that it would deny equality, in the form of moral independence, to count the fact that we have these feelings as a justification for penal legislation. Since that is so, we in fact have no justification for the present law, and we ought, in all justice, to reform it.' Nothing in this argument counts the fact that either the liberals or those they address happen to have any particular political preferences or convictions as itself an argument: the argument is made by appeal to justice, not to the fact that many people want justice. There is nothing in that argument that fails to treat homosexuals as equals. Quite the contrary. But that is just my point.

I shall consider certain of the remaining objections Hart makes together. He notices my claim, that the rights people have depend on the background justification and political institutions that are also in play, because the argument for any particular right must recognize that right as part of a complex package of other assumptions and practices that it trumps. But he finds this odd. It may make sense to say, he remarks, that people *need* rights less under some forms of government than others. But does it make sense to say that they *have* less rights in one situation rather than another? He also objects to my suggestion (which is of course at the centre of the argument I made in the last section) that rights that have long been thought to be rights to liberty, like the rights of homosexuals to freedom of sexual practice or the right of pornographers to look at what they like in private, are in fact (at least in the circumstances of modern democracies) rights to treatment as an equal. That proposition, which Hart calls 'fantastic', would have the consequence, he says, that a tyrant who had forbidden one form of sexual activity or the practice of one religion would actually eliminate the evil rather than increase it if he broadened his ban to include all sex and all religions, and in this way removed the inequality of treatment. The vice in prohibitions of sexual or religious activity, he says, is in fact that these diminish liberty, not equal liberty; adding a violation of equality to the charge makes equality an empty and idle idea with no work to do.

These different objections are plainly connected, because they suppose that whatever rights people have are at least in large part timeless rights necessary to protect enduring and important interests fixed by human nature and fundamental to human development, like interests in the choice of sexual partners and acts and choice of religious conviction. That is a familiar theory of what rights are and what they are for, and I said that I would not give my reasons, in this essay, for thinking that it is in the end an inadequate theory of rights. I did say that this theory is unlikely to produce a defence of the right I have been considering, which is the right of moral independence as applied to the use of pornography, because it seems implausible that any important human interests are damaged by denying dirty books or films. But that is not much of an argument against the general fundamental-interests theory of rights, because those who accept that theory might be ready to concede (or perhaps even to insist) that the appeal to rights in favour of pornographers is an error that cheapens the idea of rights, and that there is nothing in political morality that condemns the prohibition of pornography altogether if that is what will best fulfil the preferences of the community as a whole.

My aim is to develop a theory of rights that is relative to the other elements of a political theory, and to explore how far that theory might be constructed from the exceedingly abstract (but far from empty) idea that government must treat people as equals. Of course that theory makes rights relative in only one way. I am anxious to show how rights fit into different packages, so that I want to see, for example, which rights should be accepted as trumps over utility if utility is accepted, as many people think it should be accepted, as the proper background justification. That is an important question because, as I said, at least an informal kind of utilitarianism has for some time been accepted in practical politics. It has supplied, for example, the working justification of most of the constraints on our liberty through law that we accept as proper. But it does not follow from this investigation that I must endorse (as I am sometimes said to endorse)[6] the package of utilitarianism together with the rights that utilitarianism requires as the best package that can be constructed. In fact I do not. Though rights are relative to packages, one package might still be chosen over others as better, and I doubt that in the end any package based on any familiar form of utilitarianism will turn out to be best. Nor does it follow from my argument that there are no rights that any defensible package must contain—no rights that are in this sense natural rights—though the argument that there are such rights, and the explanation of what these are, must obviously proceed in a rather different way from the route I followed in arguing for the right to moral independence as a trump over utilitarian justifications.

But if rights figure in complex packages of political theory, it is both unnecessary and too crude to look to rights for the only defence against either stupid or wicked political decisions. No doubt Hitler and Nero violated whatever rights any plausible political theory would provide; but it is also true that the evil these monsters caused could find no support even in the background justification of any such theory. Suppose some tyrant (an Angelo gone even more mad) did forbid sex altogether on penalty of death, or banned all religious practice in a community whose members were all devout. We should say that what

[6] See, e.g, Hart, *supra*, p. 845 n.43.

he did (or tried to do) was insane or wicked or that he was wholly lacking in the concern for his subjects which is the most basic requirement that political morality imposes on those who govern. Perhaps we do not need the idea of equality to explain that last requirement. (I am deliberately cautious here.) But neither do we need the idea of rights.

We need rights, as a distinct element in political theory, only when some decision that injures some people nevertheless finds prima-facie support in the claim that it will make the community as a whole better off on some plausible account of where the community's general welfare lies. But the most natural source of any objection we might have to such a decision is that, in its concern with the welfare or prosperity or flourishing of people on the whole, or in the fulfilment of some interest, widespread within the community, the decision pays insufficient attention to its impact on the minority; and some appeal to equality seems a natural expression of an objection from that source. We want to say that the decision is wrong, in spite of its apparent merit, because it does not take the damage it causes to some into account in the right way and therefore does not treat these people as equals entitled to the same concern as others.

Of course, that charge is never self-validating. It must be developed through some theory about what equal concern requires, or, as in the case of the argument I offered, about what the background justification itself supposes that equal concern requires. Others will inevitably reject any such theory. Someone may claim, for example, that equal concern requires only that people be given what they are entitled to have when their preferences are weighed in the scales with the preferences, including the political and moral preferences, of others. In that case (if I am correct that the right to sexual freedom is based in equality) he would no longer support that right. But how could he? Suppose the decision to ban homosexuality even in private is the decision that is reached by the balance of preferences that he thinks respects equality. He could not say that, though the decision treats homosexuals as equals, by giving them all that equal concern for their situation requires, the decision is nevertheless wrong because it invades their liberty. If some constraints on liberty can be justified by the balance of preferences, why not this one?[7] Suppose he falls back on the idea that sexual freedom is a fundamental interest. But does it treat people as equals to invade their fundamental interests for the sake of minor gains to a very large number of other citizens? Perhaps he will say that it does, because

[7] See Dworkin, *Taking Rights Seriously*, pp. 266–72.

the fundamental character of the interests invaded have been taken into account in the balancing process, so that if these are outweighed the gains to others, at least in the aggregate, were shown to be too large in all fairness to be ignored. But if this is so, then deferring to the interests of the outweighed minority would be giving the minority more attention than equality allows, which is favouritism. How can he then object to the decision the balancing process reached? So if anyone really does think that banning homosexual relationships treats homosexuals as equals, when this is the decision reached by an unrestricted utilitarian balance, he seems to have no very persuasive grounds left to say that that decision nevertheless invades their rights. My hypothesis, that the rights which have traditionally been described as consequences of a general right to liberty are in fact the consequences of equality instead, may in the end prove to be wrong. But it is not, as Hart says it is, 'fantastic'.

VIII

CAN THERE BE A RIGHT-BASED MORAL THEORY?

J. L. MACKIE

IN THE course of a discussion of Rawls's theory of justice, Ronald Dworkin suggests a 'tentative initial classification' of political theories into goal-based, right-based, and duty-based theories.[1] Though he describes this, too modestly, as superficial and trivial ideological sociology, it in fact raises interesting questions. In particular, does some such classification hold for moral as well as for political theories? We are familiar with goal-based or consequentialist moral views and with duty-based or deontological ones; but it is not easy to find right-based examples, and in discussions of consequentialism and deontology this third possibility is commonly ignored. Dworkin's own example of a right-based theory is Tom Paine's theory of revolution; another, recent, example might be Robert Nozick's theory of the minimal state.[2] But each of these is a political theory; the scope of each is restricted to the criticism of some political structures and policies and the support of others; neither is a fully developed general moral theory. If Rawls's view is, as Dworkin argues, fundamentally right-based, it may be the only member of this class. Moreover, it is only for Rawls's 'deep theory' that Dworkin can propose this identification: as explicitly formulated, Rawls's moral philosophy is not right-based. The lack of any convincing and decisive example leaves us free to ask the abstract question, 'Could there be a right-based general moral theory, and, if there were one, what would it be like?'

Reprinted by permission of the University of Minnesota Press and Mrs J. Mackie, from *Studies in Ethical Theory* (Midwest Studies in Philosophy, Vol. 3), edd. Peter A. French, Theodore E. Uehling, Jr., and Howard K. Wettstein, University of Minnesota Press, copyright © 1978 by the University of Minnesota.

[1] R. Dworkin, *Taking Rights Seriously* (London, 1977), ch. 6, 'Justice and Rights', esp. pp. 171–2. This chapter appeared first as an article, 'The Original Position', *University of Chicago Law Review*, 40 (1973), reprinted as ch. 2 in N. Daniels (ed.), *Reading Rawls* (Oxford, 1975).

[2] R. Nozick, *Anarchy, State, and Utopia* (New York and Oxford, 1974).

It is obvious that most ordinary moral theories include theses about items of all three kinds, goals, duties, and rights, or, equivalently, about what is good as an end, about what is obligatory, or about what ought or ought not to be done or must or must not be done, and about what people are entitled to have or receive or do. But it is also obvious that moral theories commonly try to derive items of some of these sorts from items of another of them. It is easy to see how a consequentialist, say a utilitarian, may derive duties and rights from his basic goal. There are certain things that people must or must not do if the general happiness is to be maximized. Equally, the securing for people of certain entitlements and protections, and therefore of areas of freedom in which they can act as they choose, is, as Mill says, something which concerns the essentials of human well-being more nearly, and is therefore of more absolute obligation, than any other rules for the guidance of life.[3]

Again, it is possible to derive both goals and rights from duties. Trivially, there could just be a duty to pursue a certain end or to respect and defend a certain right. More interestingly, though more obscurely, it is conceivable that sets of goals and rights should follow from a single fundamental duty. Kant, for example, attempts to derive the principle of treating humanity as an end from the categorical imperative, 'Act only on that maxim through which you can at the same time will that it should become a universal law.'[4] Taken as literally as it can be taken, the principle of treating humanity—that is, persons, or more generally rational beings—as an end would seem to set up a goal. But it could well be interpreted as assigning rights to persons. Alternatively it could be argued that some general assignment of rights would follow directly from the choice of maxims which one could will to be universal. In either of these ways rights might be derived from duties.

But is it possible similarly to derive goals and duties from rights? And, if we are seeking a systematic moral theory, is it possible to derive a multiplicity of rights from a single fundamental one or from some small number of basic rights?

A right, in the most important sense, is the conjunction of a freedom and a claim-right. That is, if someone, A, has the moral right to do X, not only is he entitled to do X if he chooses—he is not morally required not to do X—but he is also protected in his doing of X—others are morally required not to interfere or prevent him. This way of putting

[3] J. S. Mill, *Utilitarianism*, ch. 5.

[4] I. Kant, *Groundwork of the Metaphysic of Morals*, sect. 2.

it suggests that duties are at least logically prior to rights: this sort of right is built up out of two facts about duties, that A does not have a duty not to do X and that others have a duty not to interfere with A's doing of X. But we could look at it the other way round: what is primary is A's having this right in a sense indicated by the prescription 'Let A be able to do X if he chooses', and the duty of others not to interfere follows from this (as does the absence of a duty for A not to do X). Here we have one way, at least, in which duties (and negations of duties) may be derived from rights.

I cannot see any way in which the mere fact of someone's having a certain right would in itself entail that anyone should take something as a goal. Nor does someone's having a right in itself require the achievement or realization of any goal. But the achievement of certain things as goals, or of things that may be taken as goals, may well be a necessary condition for the exercise of a right. Things must be thus and so if A is really to be able to do X, his merely having the right is not in itself sufficient. In this way a goal may be derived from a right, as a necessary condition of its exercise.

Rights can be derived from other rights in fairly obvious logical ways. For example, if I have a right to walk from my home to my place of work by the most direct route, and the most direct route is across Farmer Jones's potato field, then I have a right to walk across Farmer Jones's potato field. Again, there may be a right to create rights—in Hohfeld's terminology, a power. If someone has a certain power, and exercises it appropriately, then it follows that there will be the rights he has thus created. But what may be of more interest is a causal derivation of rights from rights. Suppose that A has a right to do X, but it is causally impossible for him to do X unless he does Y. It does not follow from this alone that he has a right to do Y. But at least a prima-facie case for his having the right to do Y could be based on the fact that doing Y is causally necessary for doing X, which he already has the right to do.

It seems, then, to be at least formally possible to have a system of moral ideas in which some rights are fundamental and other rights, and also goals and duties, are derived from these. But is it substantially possible? Are rights really the sort of thing that could be fundamental?

It is true that rights are not plausible candidates for objective existence. But neither are goods or intrinsic goals, conceived as things whose nature in itself requires that they should be pursued, or duties taken as intrinsic requirements, as constituting something like commands for which there need be, and is, no commander, which issue from no source. A belief in objective prescriptivity has flourished within the tradition of moral thinking, but it cannot in the end be defended.[5] So we are not looking for objective truth or reality in a moral system. Moral entities—values or standards or whatever they may be—belong within human thinking and practice: they are either explicitly or implicitly posited, adopted, or laid down. And the positing of rights is no more obscure or questionable than the positing of goals or obligations.

We might, then, go on to consider what rights to posit as fundamental. But it will be better, before we do this, to consider the comparative merits of right-based, goal-based, and duty-based theories. When we know what advantages a right-based theory might secure, we shall be better able to specify the rights that would secure them.

Rights have obvious advantages over duties as the basis and ground of morality. Rights are something that we may well want to have; duties are irksome. We may be glad that duties are imposed on others, but only (unless we are thoroughly bloody-minded) for the sake of the freedom, protection, or other advantages that other people's duties secure for us and our friends. The point of there being duties must lie elsewhere. Duty for duty's sake is absurd, but rights for their own sake are not. Duty is, as Wordsworth says, the stern daughter of the voice of God, and if we deny that there is a god, her parentage becomes highly dubious. Even if we accepted a god, we should expect his commands to have some further point, though possibly one not known to us; pointless commands, even from a god, would be gratuitous tyranny. Morality so far as we understand it might conceivably be thus based on divine commands, and therefore have, for us, a duty-based form; but if we reject this mythology and see morality as a human product we cannot intelligibly take duties as its starting-point. Despite Kant, giving laws to oneself is not in itself a rational procedure. For a group to give laws to its members may be, but not for the sake of the restrictions they impose, or even for the sake of the similarity of those restrictions, but only for the sake of the correlative rights they create or the products of the co-operation they maintain.

However, such points as these can be and commonly are made against duty-based theories on behalf of goal-based ones. When duties have been eliminated from the contest, is there anything to be said for rights as against goals?

A central embarrassment for the best-known goal-based theories, the various forms of utilitarianism, is that they not merely allow but positively require, in certain circumstances, that the well-being of one

[5] This is argued at length in ch. 1 of my *Ethics, Inventing Right and Wrong* (Harmondsworth, 1977).

individual should be sacrificed, without limits, for the well-being of others. It is not that these theories are collectivist in principle; it is not that the claims of individual welfare are overridden by those of some unitary communal welfare. They can and usually do take utility to be purely a resultant of individual satisfactions and frustrations. It is, quite literally, to other individuals that they allow one individual to be sacrificed. If some procedure produces a greater sum of happiness made up of the enjoyments experienced separately by B and C and D and so on than the happiness that this procedure takes away from A —or a sum greater than that needed to balance the misery that this procedure imposes on A—then, at least on a simple utilitarian view, that procedure is to be followed. And of course this holds whether the quantity to be maximized is total or average utility.

I have called this an embarrassment for utilitarianism, and it is no more than this. There are at least three well-known possible reactions to it. The tough-minded act-utilitarian simply accepts this consequence of his principles, and is prepared to dismiss any contrary 'intuitions'. Indirect utilitarianism, of which rule-utilitarianism is only one variety, distinguishes two levels of moral thinking.[6] At the level of ordinary practical day-to-day thinking, actions and choices are to be guided by rules, principles, dispositions (virtues), and so on, which will indeed protect the welfare of each individual against the claims of the greater happiness of others: rights, in fact, will be recognized at this level. But at a higher level of critical or philosophical thinking these various provisions are to be called in question, tested, explained, justified, amended, or rejected by considering how well practical thinking that is guided by them is likely to promote the general happiness. Such intermediate devices, interposed between practical choices and the utilitarian goal, may for various reasons do more for that goal than the direct application of utility calculations to everyday choices. But in this goal itself, the general happiness which constitutes the ultimate moral aim and the final test in critical moral thought, the well-being of all individuals is simply aggregated, and the happiness of some can indeed compensate for the misery (even the undeserved misery) of others. This, then, is the second possible reaction. The third says that the difficulty or embarrassment results, not because utilitarianism is a goal-based theory, but because it is a purely aggregative one, and that what is required is the addition to it of a distributive principle that prescribes

[6] For example, R. M. Hare, 'Ethical Theory and Utilitarianism', in *Contemporary British Philosophy—Personal Statements* Fourth Series, ed. H. D. Lewis (London, 1976).

fairness in the distribution of happiness. It is not fair to sacrifice one individual to others.

Of these three reactions, the first would be attractive only if there were some strong *prima facie* case for adopting a simple utilitarian morality; but there is not.[7] The indirect view also has to assume that there are good general grounds for taking a sheer aggregate of happiness as the ultimate moral aim. But its great difficulty lies in maintaining the two levels of thinking while keeping them insulated from one another. There is, I admit, no difficulty in distinguishing them. The problem is rather the practical difficulty, for someone who is for part of the time a critical moral philosopher in this utilitarian style, to keep this from infecting his everyday moral thought and conduct. It cannot be easy for him to retain practical dispositions of honesty, justice, and loyalty if in his heart of hearts he feels that these don't really matter, and sees them merely as devices to compensate for the inability of everyone, himself included, to calculate reliably and without bias in terms of aggregate utility. And a thinker who does achieve this is still exposed to the converse danger that his practical morality may weaken his critical thinking. He will be tempted to believe that the virtues built into his own character, the principles to which he automatically appeals in practice, are the very ones that will best promote the general happiness, not because he has reached this conclusion by cogent reasoning, but just because his belief reconciles his theory with his practice. He may come to cultivate a quite artificial distrust of his own ability to work out the consequences of actions for the general happiness. And what happens if the two levels cannot be kept apart? If the critical thinkers let their higher level thinking modify their own day-to-day conduct, the division will cease to be between two levels of thinking for at least some people, and become a division between two classes of people, those who follow a practical morality devised for them by others, and those who devise this but themselves follow a different, more directly utilitarian, morality. If, alternatively, the critical thinkers let their practical morality dominate their criticism, there can indeed be the same moral system for everyone, but it will have ceased to be a goal-based one. The derivation of the working principles from utility will have become a mere rationalization. Altogether, then, indirect utilitarianism is a rather unhappy compromise. And it is inadequately motivated. Why should it not be a *fundamental* moral principle that the well-being of one person cannot be simply replaced by that of another?

[7] I have tried to show this in ch. 6 of *Ethics, Inventing Right and Wrong*, appealing to radical weaknesses in anything like Mill's proof of utility.

There is no cogent proof of purely aggregative consequentialism at any level.[8]

Is the remedy, then, to add a distributive principle? This is still not quite what we need. If one individual is sacrificed for advantages accruing to others, what is deplorable is the ill-treatment of this individual, the invasion of his rights, rather than the relational matter of the unfairness of his treatment in comparison with others. Again, how are we to understand fairness itself? Within a purely goal-based theory it would have to be taken as an end or good, presumably a collective good, a feature of multi-person distributions which it is good to have in a group, or perhaps good for the group, though not good for any one member. And this would be rather mysterious. Further, within a goal-based theory it would be natural to take fairness, if it were recognized, as one additional constituent of utility, and then, unless it were given an infinite utility value, it in turn could be outweighed by a sufficient aggregate of individual satisfactions. There could still be a moral case for sacrificing not only A's welfare but also fairness along with it to the greater utility summed up in the welfare of B and C and so on.

Fairness as a distributive principle, added to an otherwise aggregative theory, would prescribe some distribution of utility. But what distribution? Presumably an equal one would be the ideal, to which distributions in practice would be expected to approximate as closely as was reasonably possible. But though extreme inequalities of satisfaction are deplorable, it is not clear that simple equality of satisfaction is the ideal. We surely want to leave it open to people to make what they can of their lives. But then it is inevitable that some will do better for themselves than others. This same point can be made about groups rather than individuals. Consider a society containing two groups, A and B, where the members of each group are in contact mainly with co-members of their own group. Suppose that the members of A are more co-operative, less quarrelsome, and so more successful in co-ordinating various activities than the members of B. Then the members of A are likely to do better, achieve more satisfaction, than the members of B. And why shouldn't they? Would there be any good reason for requiring an equal distribution of welfare in such circumstances? There is, of course, no need to adopt the extravagances and the myths of sturdy individualism, above all no ground for supposing that all actual inequalities of satisfaction result from some kind of merit and are therefore justified. All I am suggesting is that inequalities

[8] The discussion referred to in n. 7 applies here also.

may be justified, and in particular that we should think of protecting each individual in an opportunity to do things rather than of distributing satisfactions.

Perhaps when fairness is added to an otherwise goal-based theory it should be thought of as a duty-based element. But then the arguments against duty-based systems apply to this element. What merit has even the duty to be fair for its own sake? It would be easier to endorse something like fairness as a right-based element, giving us a partly goal-based and partly right-based system.

But even this is not enough. A plausible goal, or good for man, would have to be something like Aristotle's *eudaimonia*: it would be in the category of activity. It could not be just an end, a possession, a termination of pursuit. The absurdity of taking satisfaction in the sense in which it is such a termination as the moral goal is brought out by the science-fictional pleasure machine described by Smart.[9] But Aristotle went wrong in thinking that moral philosophy could determine that a particular sort of activity constitutes the good for man in general, and is objectively and intrinsically the best way of life. People differ radically about the kinds of life that they choose to pursue. Even this way of putting it is misleading: in general people do not and cannot make an overall choice of a total plan of life. They choose successively to pursue various activities from time to time, not once and for all. And while there is room for other sorts of evaluation of human activities, morality as a source of constraints on conduct cannot be based on such comparative evaluations.[10] I suggest that if we set out to formulate a goal-based moral theory, but in identifying the goal try to take adequate account of these three factors, namely that the 'goal' must belong to the category of activity, that there is not one goal but indefinitely many diverse goals, and that there are the objects of progressive (not once-for-all or conclusive) choices, then our theory will change insensibly into a right-based one. We shall have to take as central the right of persons progressively to choose how they shall live.

This suggestion is dramatically illustrated by some of the writings of the best known of utilitarian moralists, John Stuart Mill. When he reiterates, in *On Liberty*, that he regards utility 'as the ultimate appeal on all ethical questions', he hastens to add that 'it must be utility in the largest sense, grounded on the permanent interests of a man as a progressive being'. Not, as it is sometimes misquoted, 'of man as a

[9] J. J. C. Smart and B. Williams, *Utilitarianism, For and Against* (Cambridge, 1973), pp. 18–21.

[10] I am speaking here of what I call morality in the narrow sense in *Ethics, Inventing Right and Wrong*, ch. 5.

progressive being': that would imply a collectivist view, but here the stress is on the claims of each individual. 'These interests, I contend, authorize the subjection of individual spontaneity to external control, only in respect to those actions of each, which concern the interest of other people.' And the next few lines make it clear that he is thinking not of any interests of other people, but particularly of their rights and the defence of their rights. It is at least as plausible to say that the deep theory of *On Liberty* is right-based as that this holds of Rawls's *A Theory of Justice*.[11] The same point emerges from a close examination of the last chapter of *Utilitarianism*, 'On the Connection between Justice and Utility.' There Mill argues that what is morally required or obligatory is included in but not co-extensive with what is expedient or worthy, and that what is just (or rather, what is required for justice) is similarly a proper sub-class of what is obligatory. By 'justice' he makes it clear that he means the body of rules which protect rights which 'reside in persons.' They are 'The moral rules which forbid mankind to hurt one another (in which we must never forget to include wrongful interference with each other's freedom)' and 'are more vital to human well-being than any maxims, however important, which only point out the best way of managing some department of human affairs'. And though he still says that general utility is the reason why society ought to defend me in the possession of these rights, he explains that it is an 'extraordinarily important and impressive kind of utility which is concerned'. 'Our notion, therefore, of the claim we have on our fellow-creatures to join in making safe for us the very groundwork of our existence, gathers feelings around it so much more intense than those concerned in any of the more common cases of utility, that the difference in degree . . . becomes a real difference in kind.' In such passages as these we can see Mill, while still working within the framework of a goal-based theory, moving towards a right-based treatment of at least the central part of morality.

When we think it out, therefore, we see that not only can there be a right-based moral theory, there cannot be an acceptable moral theory that is not right-based. Also, in learning why this approach is superior to those based either on duties or on goals, we have at least roughly identified what we may take as the fundamental right. If we assume that, from the point of view of the morality we are constructing, what matters in human life is activity, but diverse activities determined by successive choices, we shall, as I have said, take as central the right of persons progressively to choose how they shall live. But this is only a

[11] Dworkin makes this point, at least implicitly, in ch. 11., 'Liberty and Liberalism', of *Taking Rights Seriously*.

rough specification, and at once raises problems. Who is to have this right? Let us make what is admittedly a further decision and say that all persons are to have it, and all equally. It is true that this leaves in a twilight zone sentient and even human beings that are not and never will be persons; let us simply admit that there are problems here, but postpone them to another occasion.[12] Other problems are more pressing. The rights we have assigned to all persons will in practice come into conflict with one another. One person's choice of how to live will constantly be interfering with the choices of others. We have come close to Jefferson's formulation of fundamental rights to life, liberty and the pursuit of happiness. But one person's pursuit of happiness will obstruct another's, and diverse liberties, and even the similar liberties of different people, are notoriously incompatible. Liberty is an all-purpose slogan: in all wars and all revolutions both sides have been fighting for freedom. This means that the rights we have called fundamental can be no more than *prima facie* rights: the rights that in the end people have, their final rights, must result from compromises between their initially conflicting rights. These compromises will have to be worked out in practice, but will be morally defensible only in so far as they reflect the equality of the *prima facie* rights. This will not allow the vital interests of any to be sacrificed for the advantage of others, to be outweighed by an aggregate of less vital interests. Rather we might think in terms of a model in which each person is represented by a point-centre of force, and the forces (representing *prima facie* rights) obey an inverse square law, so that a right decreases in weight with the remoteness of the matter on which it bears from the person whose right it is. There will be some matters so close to each person that, with respect to them, his rights will nearly always outweigh any aggregate of other rights, though admittedly it will sometimes happen that issues arise in which the equally vital interests of two or more people clash.

In discussing what rights we have, Dworkin has argued against any general right to liberty and in favour of a fundamental right to equal concern and respect.[13] The latter has, indeed, the advantage that it could be a final, not merely a *prima facie* right: one person's possession or enjoyment of it does not conflict with another's. But it will not serve as the foundation of a right-based moral theory. Dworkin is, indeed, putting it forward as a fundamental *political* right: it is governments that must treat those whom they govern with equal concern and

[12] I have touched on it in ch. 8, sec. 8, of *Ethics, Inventing Right and Wrong*.

[13] *Taking Rights Seriously*, ch. 12, 'What Rights Do We Have?'

respect, or, more generally, social and economic arrangements that must represent these in a concrete form. But this cannot be what is morally fundamental. The right to be treated in a certain way rests on a prior, even if somewhat indeterminate, right to certain opportunities of living. Dworkin's main reason for rejecting a general right to liberty is that it cannot explain or justify the discriminations we want between legitimate and illegitimate restrictions of freedom, or the special stress liberals place on freedom of speech and political activity. But we can discriminate in terms of how closely a certain freedom is bound up with a person's vital central interests—but, of course, it may tell against a freedom which is fairly vital in this sense to someone if his exercise of it tends to affect adversely at least equally central interests of some others. The specifically political liberties may not be thus vital to many people, but they are important, far more widely, in an indirect way, as providing means for the defence of more central freedoms. That their importance is, morally speaking, thus derivative, and therefore contingent and relative to circumstances, is a conclusion which we should accept.

Dworkin is unwilling to recognize a general right to liberty also because this supposed right is commonly used to support a right to the free use of property. However, on the view I am putting forward such a right would be qualified and restricted by the consideration of how the ways in which this or that kind of property was acquired and used affect the central interests not only of the owner but of other people as well. I believe that a right to some sorts of property and some uses of it would be supported by such considerations; but by no means all the kinds and uses of property that are current in 'bourgeois' society.

Any right-based moral or political theory has to face the issue whether the rights it endorses are 'natural' or 'human' rights, universally valid and determinable *a priori* by some kind of reason, or are historically determined in and by the concrete institutions of a particular society, to be found out by analysis of its actual laws and practices. However, the view I am suggesting straddles this division. The fundamental right is put forward as universal. On the other hand I am not claiming that it is objectively valid, or that its validity can be found out by reason: I am merely adopting it and recommending it for general adoption as a moral principle. Also, I have argued that this fundamental right has to be formulated only as a *prima facie* right. Derived specific rights (which can be final, not merely *prima facie*) will be historically determined and contingent upon concrete circumstances and upon the interplay of the actual interests and preferences that people have. But the fact that something is an institutional right, recognized and defended by the laws and practices of a particular society, does not necessarily establish it as a moral right. It can be criticized from the moral point of view by considering how far the social interactions which have generated and maintain this institutional right express the fundamental right of persons progressively to choose how they shall live, interpreted along the lines of our model of centres of force, and to what extent they violate it. Our theory could have conservative implications in some contexts, but equally it could have reforming or revolutionary implications in others.

It may be asked whether this theory is individualist, perhaps too individualist. It is indeed individualist in that individual persons are the primary bearers of rights, and the sole bearers of fundamental rights, and one of its chief merits is that, unlike aggregate goal-based theories, it offers a persistent defence of some interests of each individual. It is, however, in no way committed to seeing individuals as spontaneous originators of their thoughts and desires. It can recognize that the inheritance of cultural traditions and being caught up in movements help to make each individual what he is, and that even the most independent individuals constitute their distinctive characters not by isolating themselves or making 'existential' choices but by working with and through inherited traditions. Nor need it be opposed to co-operation or collective action. I believe that Rousseau's description of a community with a general will, general 'both in its object and in its essence', that is, bearing in its expression upon all members alike and located in every member of the community, provides a model of a conceivable form of association, and there is nothing in our theory that would be hostile to such genuine co-operation. But I do not believe that there could actually be a community with a genuine, not fictitious, general will of this sort of the size of an independent political unit, a sovereign state. The fundamental individual rights could, however, be expressed in joint activity or communal life on a smaller scale, and organizations of all sorts can have derived, though not fundamental, moral rights. Our theory, therefore, is not anti-collectivist; but it will discriminate among collectivities, between those which express and realize the rights of their members and those which sacrifice some of even most of their members to a supposed collective interest, or to the real interest of some members, or even to some maximized aggregate of interests.

I hope I have not given the impression that I think it an easy matter to resolve conflicts of rights and to determine, in concrete cases, what the implications of our theory will be. What I have offered is not an algorithm or decision procedure, but only, as I said, a model, an indication of a framework of ideas within which the discussion of actual specific issues might go on. And in general this paper is no more than a tentative initial sketch of a right-based moral theory. I hope that others will think it worth further investigation.

POSTSCRIPT

This paper has been read at a number of universities in the United States and Canada, and has met with some acute and forceful criticisms. I do not know how to cope with all of them, but at least some further clarifications are needed.

It has been asked whether this right-based theory is extensionally equivalent to some form of utilitarianism, yielding exactly the same output of practical prescriptions, and whether it is even just a notational variant of some form of utilitarianism. This question has, as yet, no determinate answer, because the right-based theory has not yet been made sufficiently precise. I hope that it will not turn out to be an extensional equivalent, let alone a mere notational variant, of any form of utilitarianism. But even if it does, there may be some merit in the formulation in terms of rights. It may be easier to keep this distinct from other forms of utilitarianism. And there would be no reason for preferring to formulate it in a utilitarian style unless there were some general presumption that *some* version of utilitarianism must be correct, that moral thinking ought somehow to be cast in a utilitarian mould; and I would argue that there is no ground for such a presumption.

It may also be asked just what is it to *base* a moral theory on goals or duties or rights. One possible view is that an X-based theory is one which takes 'X' as its only undefined term, and defines other moral terms in relation to 'X'. In this sense G. E. Moore's moral system is good-based. Since I have allowed that statements about rights can be analysed into conjunctions of affirmative and negative statements about duties, my account seems not to be right-based in this sense, but rather duty-based. However, this is not what I find most important. Another interpretation is that a moral theory is X-based if it forms a system in which some statements about Xs are taken as basic and the other statements in the theory are derived from them, perhaps with the help of the non-moral, purely factual, premisses. But what would make a theory X-based in the most important sense is that it should be such a system not merely formally but in its purpose, that the basic statements about Xs should be seen as capturing what gives point to the whole moral theory. The possibility into which I am inquiring is that of a theory which is right-based in this most important sense.

The greatest difficulties concern the suggestions about how to deal with conflicts of *prima facie* rights. One question is whether each agent can say, authoritatively, how vital some matter is to him. If we were working out a detailed theory, we would want to give considerable weight to sincere claims of this sort, but not complete authority: we may have to tell a busybody that something is not as vital to him, from the point of view of this moral theory, as he thinks it is. Another problem is that a model of point-centres of force seems to offer no solution at all to conflicts of equally vital interests. This difficulty is partly met by the reflection that the proposed theory calls for compromises worked out in practice, for the historical development of institutional rights as derivatives from and realizations of the prima-facie rights, rather than for direct solution of conflicts as they arise at any moment by reference to the general theory alone. Institutional rights may resolve what would be insoluble conflicts of claims. The suggested theory is only right-*based*; it does not make rights, let alone fundamental *prima facie* rights, the only moral elements; it provides for the derivation of goals and duties from those fundamental rights. But this reply leads to a further difficulty: will not an indirect right-based theory be open to objections similar to those pressed against indirect utilitarianism? I think it will be less open to such objections, because the protection of rights can be seen throughout as what gives force to the derived moral judgements: there is less need to detach them from this source than there is to detach the working principles of an indirect utilitarianism from a purely aggregative basic theory. Whatever problems there are about adjusting conflicts of rights, this theory is not saddled with the embarrassing presumption that one person's well-being can be simply replaced by that of another.

Finally, it does not seem to me to be a reasonable requirement for a moral theory that it should, even when fully developed, be able to resolve all conflicts. But my main thesis is that this right-based approach is worth some further study, similar to that which has been lavished on various forms of utilitarianism.

IX

RIGHT-BASED MORALITIES

J. RAZ

ANY MORAL theory allows for the existence of rights if it regards the interests of some individuals to be sufficient for holding others to be subject to duties. Some writers on morality and politics have in recent years revived the Lockian tradition of regarding rights as the foundation of political morality or even of morality generally. R. M. Dworkin has suggested that 'political theories differ from one another . . . not simply in the particular goals, rights, and duties each sets out, but also in the way each connects the goals, rights, and duties it employs. . . . It seems reasonable to suppose that any particular theory will give ultimate pride of place to just one of these concepts; it will take some overriding goal, or some set of fundamental rights, or some set of transcendent duties, as fundamental, and show other goals, rights, and duties as subordinate and derivative.'[1] Dworkin expressed the view that political morality is right-based. J. L. Mackie, adopting this classification, applied it to moral theories generally and claimed that morality is right-based (or rather that we should invent one which is).[2]

My purpose in this article is to suggest that morality is not right-based. I do not propose to urge the view that it is either duty-based or goal-based. My suggestion will be that among its fundamental precepts are to be found values, rights, and duties. I shall present considerations which tend to undermine the rights view of morality and, in combination, to support a pluralistic understanding of the foundation of morality. These considerations do not amount to proof. Some of them need not apply to all right-based moralities and they all presuppose certain moral views for which I shall not argue here.

We are to envisage a moral theory the fundamental principles of

This paper is published for the first time in this collection, by permission of the author.

[1] R. M. Dworkin, *Taking Rights Seriously* (London, 1978), p. 171.

[2] J. L. Mackie, 'Can There be a Right-Based Moral Theory', *Midwest Studies in Philosophy*, 3 (1978), p. 350. (Reprinted here.)

which state that certain individuals have certain rights. They are its fundamental principles for, first, their justification does not presuppose any other moral principles, and, secondly, all valid moral views derive from them (with the addition of premisses which do not by themselves yield any moral conclusions). Is any moral theory of this kind valid? Or, if you prefer, does a correct or sound morality have this structure? To simplify the discussion I will endorse right away the humanistic principle which claims that the explanation and justification of the goodness or badness of anything derives ultimately from its contribution, actual or possible, to human life and its quality.

Humanism, thus conceived, is not a moral theory. It merely sets a necessary condition to the acceptability of moral theories, a condition which can be satisfied by many different moral theories. Nor are all humanists committed to the view that all human life is of ultimate moral value. Their only commitment is that if some human life has no value or if some lives have more intrinsic value than others, this is in virtue of the quality of those lives. Our goal is, therefore, to examine the plausibility of the view that morality is based on fundamental principles assigning rights to some or all human beings.

I. SOME PRELIMINARY DOUBTS

'x has a right' means that, other things being equal, an aspect of x's well-being (his interest) is a sufficient reason for holding some other person(s) to be under a duty. I have argued at some length for this conception of rights elsewhere.[3] Though the definition differs from others in various respects, it is firmly placed within one major tradition of understanding rights which is often called the beneficiary view of rights. As such it seems congenial to a humanistic rights-based approach to morality. It would fit well with a view which regards the interests of people as the only ultimate value. The protection and promotion of such human interests through the rights of people could be said to be what morality is all about.

But is it? The following sections will suggest that right-based moralities are impoverished moral theories and are unlikely to provide adequate foundation for an acceptable humanistic morality. The purpose of the present section is to introduce those critical reflections by explaining the respects in which right-based moralities could be considered to be impoverished. They all stem from the fact that rights are the grounds of duties and nothing more. A right-based morality is a morality of rights and duties. Many moral views presuppose that there

[3] See 'The Nature of Rights', *Mind*, 93 (1984), p. 194.

is more to morality than rights and duties and precepts which can be derived from them. Consider the following three examples in order to illustrate the ways in which right-based moralities can be thought to be impoverished.

(1) Though several moral philosophers use 'ought' and 'duty' interchangeably, many moral views presuppose a distinction between what one ought to do and what it is one's duty to do. The common view is that one ought to do that which one has a duty to do but that one does not always have a duty to do that which one ought. Thus, while I ought to allow my neighbour who locked himself out of his house to use my phone, I have no duty to do so. On the other hand, since I have promised my neighbour to saw off this week a branch overhanging a corner in his garden, I have a duty, and therefore I ought, to do so. It is sometimes supposed that the difference is simply that there is greater reason to do that which one has a duty to do than to do that which one ought but has no duty to do. If this were so, then the difference between ought and duty presents no difficulty to the rights-theorists, for they may claim that they merely use 'duty' as equivalent to 'ought', and can use 'strong duty' as equivalent to the normal 'duty'. The two examples above refute the suggestion that the difference between one's duties and what one simply ought to do is in the weight of the supporting reason since there probably is more reason to let my locked-out neighbour use my phone than to saw off the branch this week rather than next week. This is so even if one takes account of the harm my breaking my promise does to the reliability and credibility of promises between neighbours and in general. Duties are not reasons for action of a great weight. They are a special kind of requirements for action.[4] Right-based moralities consist of rights and those special requirements which we call duties.

They do not allow for the moral significance of ordinary reasons for action. It is easy to see that this point is deeply embedded in our understanding of rights and is not an arbitrary result of my definition of rights. Most people will agree, e.g. that I ought to give other people information which it is in their interest to have. It is, however, generally thought that they have no right that I should do so and therefore that I have no duty to give them the information. Rights are tied to duties. Reasons for action which do not amount to duties escape the notice of a right-based morality.

(2) A second respect in which right-based moralities are impoverished is in not allowing for the moral significance of supererogation. Acts are

[4] This argument is developed in greater detail in my 'Promises and Obligations' in P. Hacker and J. Raz (edd.), *Law, Morality and Society* (Oxford, 1977).

supererogatory if their performance is praiseworthy and yet it is not morally wrong to omit them. There is no obligation to act in a supererogatory way. Indeed supererogation is identified with action beyond the call of duty.[5] Right-based moralities cannot account for the nature of supererogation and its role in moral life.

(3) Finally, right-based moralities cannot allow intrinsic moral value to virtue and the pursuit of excellence. Again the reason is much the same as before. None of the commonly recognized virtues and morally significant forms of excellence consists in discharging one's duties or being disposed to do so. Honesty is a virtue which is particularly closely tied to the duty not to deceive, and yet even it is not exhausted by compliance with the duty. The exemplary honest man is one who does more than his duty to make sure that his behaviour does not mislead others. He acts honestly out of certain motives and he holds certain appropriate beliefs regarding interpersonal communications and these display themselves in appropriate attitudes which he possesses.

Rights-theorists may reply to all three examples that their views do not bar them from accommodating, in a derivative role, ordinary moral reasons for action, supererogation, and moral excellence in their moral theories. This is true, but is no reply to the objections, which are not that right-based theories cannot make room for these notions at all, but rather that they cannot allow them their true moral significance. Let me explain.

Any moral theory which allows for the existence of duties must allow for the existence of reasons which are not duties. This is a result of the fact that rights and duties are not transitive regarding the means which they require. Reasons for action transfer their force to the means by which their realization is facilitated. If I have a reason to bring you a glass of water then I have a reason to go to the kitchen to fetch a glass and fill it with water. But even if I have a duty to be in London at noon, it does not follow that I have a duty to take the 10 a.m. train, even though it will bring me to London by noon.[6] Rights are like duties in this respect. The fact that you have a right that I be in London at noon does not entail that you have a right that I shall take the 10 a.m. train. Needless to say, one has reason to take steps to discharge one's duties. Therefore, any moral theory which allows for the existence of

[5] Action beyond the call of duty is naturally not just any action one ought to do but has no duty to.

[6] I leave it open whether or not one has a duty to do that which is both necessary and sufficient to comply with a duty. My claim is merely that one has no duty to do something because it is sufficient to comply with a duty. I do have reason to do that which is sufficient to follow a reason.

duties must allow for the existence of ordinary reasons for duty-holders, to take action to discharge their duties. Right-based theories allow for ordinary moral reasons of a derivative kind. This does not however avoid the objections which are that ordinary reasons are no less important and central to moral thinking than duties.

Similarly with virtue. Right-based theories can regard the cultivation of certain dispositions as instrumentally valuable if they predispose individuals to do their duty. They may even approve of individuals cultivating such dispositions for what they erroneously believe is their intrinsic value. But right-based theories (like utilitarian theories) cannot allow personal characteristics which are virtuous or morally praiseworthy to be judged intrinsically desirable and cultivated for their own sake. It is less clear to me what room there might be for supererogation within right-based theories. They can allow for a near relation, i.e. a special category of duties performance of which requires exceptional personal qualities such that their performance deserves praise and failure to discharge them, though wrong, is excusable. Despite this palliative, the objection remains that supererogation in its proper sense which involves action beyond the call of duty is not recognized in right-based theories.

The preceding discussion was meant to illustrate and explain the ways in which right-based theories are impoverished. It has not established that the impoverishment involves any real moral loss. To show that is the aim of the rest of this article.

II. RIGHTS AND INDIVIDUALISM

Right-based moral theories are usually individualistic moral theories. There is as little agreement about the sense in which a moral outlook is or is not a form of individualism as there is on the sense of any other '–ism'. My explanation of moral individualism is therefore necessarily stipulative in part. My hope is that it captures an important element traditionally associated with individualism and a most important difference between humanistic moralities.[7] A moral theory will be said to be individualistic if it is a humanistic morality which does not recognize any intrinsic value in any collective good. In other words, individualistic moralities are humanistic moralities which hold that collective goods have instrumental value only.

Before we explore the connection between right-based theories and individualism a few further remarks on the nature of moral individualism

[7] For a survey of different notions of individualism see S. Lukes, *Individualism*, (Oxford, 1973).

will be in order. A good is a public good in a certain society if and only if the distribution of its benefits in that society is not subject to voluntary control by anyone other than each potential beneficiary controlling his share of the benefits. I shall distinguish between contingent and inherent public goods.[8] Water supply in a certain town may be a public good if the water pipe network does not allow for the switching-off of individual households. But it is only contingently a public good, as it is possible to change the supply system to enable control over distribution. Clean air is similarly a contingent public good. In this case we do not have the technology to control air distribution. But the limitation of our technological ability in this respect is only a contingent one.

General beneficial features of a society are inherently public goods. It is a public good, and inherently so, that this society is a tolerant society, that it is an educated society, that it is infused with a sense of respect for human beings, etc. Living in a society with these characteristics is generally of benefit to individuals. These benefits are not to be confused with the benefit of having friends or acquaintances who are tolerant, educated, etc. One's friends can voluntarily control the distribution of the benefits of their friendship. The benefits I have in mind are the more diffuse ones deriving from the general character of the society to which one belongs. Different people benefit from the good qualities of the society to different degrees. But the degree to which they benefit depends on their character, interests, and dispositions, and cannot be directly controlled by others. (Usually they themselves have only partial and imperfect control over these factors.) Naturally one can exclude individuals from benefiting from such goods by excluding them from the society to which they pertain. But that does not affect the character of the goods as public goods which depends on non-exclusivity of enjoyment among members of the society in which they are public goods. I shall call inherent public goods 'collective goods'.

For obvious reasons economists have concerned themselves mostly with contingent public goods and those are mostly only of instrumental value: clean air is important for one's health, and so on. If any public goods are intrinsically valuable then some of the collective goods are the most likely candidates. Commitment to a humanistic morality, however, often inclines people to believe that even collective goods can only be instrumentally valuable. Living in a tolerant society, for example, is thought good because it spares one the pain of petty-minded

[8] I am grateful to L. Green for drawing my attention to this distinction.

social persecution and the fear of it, and enables one to have a happier life by enabling one to develop freely one's inclinations and tastes. To suggest otherwise, to suggest that living in a tolerant society is good independently of its consequences, that it is intrinsically good is, in their opinion, to reject humanism, for it amounts to asserting the intrinsic value of something which is not human life or its quality.

To understand why such misgivings are misplaced, and to explain why humanism is compatible with holding some collective goods to be intrinsically valuable, a brief sketch of a few more distinctions may prove helpful. Something is instrumentally good if its value derives from the value of its consequences or from the fact that it makes certain consequences more likely, or that it can contribute to producing certain consequences. Something is intrinsically good or valuable if it is valuable independently of the value of its actual or probable consequences, and not on account of any consequences it can be used to produce or to the production of which it can contribute. We need to distinguish among the intrinsically valuable things three different categories: those things that are valuable in themselves or valuable *per se* if their existence is valuable irrespective of what else exists. Things are constituent goods if they are elements of what is good in itself which contribute to its value, i.e. elements but for which a situation which is good in itself would be less valuable. Both goods in themselves and constituent goods are intrinsically good. So are ultimate goods or values. The aspects of a good in itself which are of ultimate value are those which explain and justify the judgement that it is good in itself, and which are such that their own value need not be explained or be justified by reference to other values. The relation of ultimate values to intrinsic values which are not ultimate is an explanatory or justificatory one. Ultimate values are referred to in explaining the value of non-ultimate goods.

I hope that consideration of the following example will help explain these distinctions and show that humanism is compatible with the view that collective goods have intrinsic value. Consider the value of works of art: I mean their value not to their creators, but to their public. No doubt their value is many-sided. Owning works of art could be a sound investment, studying them could be a way of acquiring prestige, or knowledge of human psychology, and so on almost indefinitely. Let us concentrate exclusively on their value to their public as works of art (rather than as a means of acquiring prestige or knowledge etc.). One view of their value holds it to be intrinsic. Watching and contemplating works of art are valuable activities and a life which includes them is enriched because of them. If the life thus enriched is intrinsically good, then the existence of works of art is equally an intrinsic good. It is a constituent of the good which is a life including the experiencing of works of art. Let me refer to such a life as a life with art. The point is of course that one cannot experience works of art unless they exist. The value of the experience is in its being an experience of art. The experience cannot be explained except by reference to a belief in the existence of its object and its value depends on the truth of that belief. On this view the existence of works of art is intrinsically valuable.

Such a view is compatible with humanism since the explanation of the intrinsic value of art is in its relation to the quality of life with art. A life with art is a good in itself, the existence of works of art is a constituent good and the quality of life with art which explains its value is the ultimate good. All three are intrinsic goods.

The value of art is interpreted differently by classical utilitarians who regard it as instrumentally valuable in as much as it may cause valuable sensations or emotions in an individual. The classical utilitarians interpret these sensations and emotions as capable of being caused in some other way and therefore as only contingently connected with the works of art which are therefore merely instrumentally valuable.

The existence of works of art is not a collective good. My aim so far has been to show that humanism is consistent with holding that not only life and its quality are intrinsically valuable. Hence regarding collective goods as intrinsically valuable is compatible with a commitment to humanism. It is in principle also compatible with the view that morality is right-based. Nevertheless right-based moral theories tend to be individualistic and to deny the intrinsic value of collective goods. The reason is not far to seek. Consider collective goods such as living in a beautiful town, which is economically prosperous, and in a society tolerant and cultured. Living in such an environment is in the interest of each of the inhabitants: it is more agreeable to live in such a society, whatever one's personal circumstances, than to live in one which lacks these attributes. But the fact that it is in my interest to live in such a society is not normally considered sufficient to establish that I have a right to live in such a society. The common view is that my interest that my society shall be of this character is a reason to develop it in such a direction, but that the existence of such a reason is not enough to show that I have a right that my society shall have this character. This is explicable on the definition of rights offered above, according to which a right is a sufficient ground for holding another to have a duty. It is the common view that my interest in living in a prosperous, cultured, and tolerant society and in a beautiful environment is not enough to impose a duty on anyone to make my society and environment so. It does not follow that no one has such duties. I am inclined to say that the government has a duty to achieve all those goals or at least to try to do so. But its duty is not grounded in my interest alone. It is based on my interest and on the interests of everyone else, together with the fact that governments are special institutions whose proper functions and (normative) powers are limited.

Nothing in this section shows that right-based moralities must be individualistic. But its argument explains that it is not accidental that right-based theories have been and are likely to be individualistic. Given some widely accepted views of the kinds of consideration which establish one person's duty to another, it is unlikely that individuals have basic rights to collective goods. If, for example, others' duty to me is confined to not violating my integrity as a person and providing me with basic needs, then I have no right to collective goods as my interest in them is not among my basic needs for survival. Generally, since the maintenance of a collective good affects the life and imposes constraints on the activities of the bulk of the population it is difficult to imagine a successful argument imposing a duty to provide a collective good which is based on the interest of one individual.

III. AUTONOMY AND RIGHTS

Is there anything wrong with moral individualism? Are any collective goods intrinsically desirable? I will suggest that some collective goods are intrinsically desirable if personal autonomy is intrinsically desirable. If this is so then right-based theories cannot account for the desirability of autonomy. This conclusion is of great interest to the contemporary debate, since some rights-theories tend to emphasize the importance and value of personal autonomy. J. L. Mackie, for example, suggests that the fundamental right is, roughly speaking, a right to liberty: 'If we assume that, from the point of view of the morality we are constructing, what matters in human life is activity, but diverse activities determined by successive choices, we shall . . . take as central the right of persons progressively to choose how they shall live.'[9] Though he does not explicitly refer to autonomy, he seems to regard his invented morality as right-based because he maintains that only a right-based morality can express the fundamental value of autonomy. D. A. J. Richards, though not committed to the view that morality is right-based, seems to think that our concern for personal autonomy requires

[9] J. L. Mackie, op. cit., p. 355.

a commitment to at least some fundamental rights.[10] Exploring the relations between the ideal of personal autonomy and the rights protecting personal autonomy is of interest for all those who care about personal autonomy, whether or not they are inclined to endorse the view that morality is right-based.

For the purpose of the present argument only one aspect of the ideal of personal autonomy need concern us.[11] An autonomous person is one who is the author of his own life. His life is his own making. The autonomous person's life is marked not only by what it is but also by what it might have been and by the way it became what it is. A person is autonomous only if he has a variety of acceptable options available for him to choose from and his life became as it is through his choice of some of these options. A person who has never had any significant choice, or was not aware of it, or never exercised choice in significant matters but simply drifted through life is not an autonomous person.

It should be clear from these observations that autonomy is here construed as a kind of achievement. To this sense of autonomy corresponds another, according to which it is the capacity to achieve the autonomous life. In this sense a person is autonomous if he can become the author of his own life, i.e. if he can be autonomous in the first or primary sense. By the second sense of autonomy, a person is autonomous if the conditions of autonomous life obtain. Those are partly to do with the state of the individual concerned (that he is of sound mind, capable of rational thought and action, etc.) and partly to do with the circumstances of his life (especially that he has a sufficient number of significant options available to him at different stages of his life).

This distinction between an autonomous life as an achievement and a capacity for autonomy which is its precondition would not look quite the same to a supporter of a rights view of autonomy. He cannot claim that rights are justified because they protect autonomy. This would be to justify them instrumentally. He has to maintain that autonomy is constituted by rights and nothing else: the autonomous life is a life within unviolated rights. Unviolated rights create or protect opportunities. What one makes of them is left undetermined by the sheer existence of the rights. Therefore in terms of my distinction this would

[10] D. A. J. Richards, 'Human Rights and Human Ideals', *Social Theory and Practice*, 5 (1979), p. 461; 'Rights and Autonomy', *Ethics*, 92 (1981), p. 3.

[11] I have said a little more on the nature of personal autonomy in 'Liberalism, Autonomy and the Politics of Neutral Concern', *Midwest Studies in Philosophy*, 7 (1982).

be to maintain that a capacity for autonomy guarantees that one's life is autonomous, e.g. that no use or neglect of that capacity can make the life of those who have it more or less autonomous. There are serious objections to this view. But none of my arguments here depends on maintaining that autonomy is more than the life of a person with a certain capacity.

If having an autonomous life is an ultimate value, then having a sufficient number of acceptable alternative options is of intrinsic value, for it is constitutive of an autonomous life that it is lived in circumstances where acceptable alternatives are present. The alternatives must be acceptable if the life is autonomous. A person whose every major decision was coerced, extracted from him by threats to his life or that of his children, has not led an autonomous life. Similar considerations apply to a person who has spent his whole life fighting starvation and disease, and has had no opportunity to accomplish anything other than to stay alive (imagine a person abandoned defenceless on an uninhabited island infested with deadly insects, where food is very scarce and who just managed to stay alive). I shall not try to analyse what choices are acceptable.[12] All that concerns us is that the ideal of personal autonomy (whose realization is clearly a matter of degree) requires not merely the presence of options but of acceptable ones.

The existence of many options consists in part in the existence of certain social conditions. One cannot have an option to be a barrister, a surgeon, or a psychiatrist in a society where those professions and the institutions their existence presupposes, do not exist. While this will be readily acknowledged, it is sometimes overlooked that the same is true of options of being an architect or of getting married. It is true that one need not live in a society at all to design buildings regularly, or to cohabit with another person. But doing so is not the same as being an architect or being married. An architect is one who belongs to a socially recognized profession. In many countries a homosexual can cohabit with, but cannot be married to his homosexual partner, since to be married is to partake of a socially (and legally) recognized and regulated type of relationship. Homosexuals cannot do that if their society does not recognize and regulate a pattern of relationship which could apply to them. They can imitate some other recognized relationships. But essentially they have to develop their relations as they go along, and do not have the option of benefiting from existing social frameworks.

[12] See the article cited in n. 11 above.

At least some of the social conditions which constitute such options are collective goods. The existence of a society with a legal profession or with recognized homosexual marriages is a collective good, for the distribution of its benefits is not voluntarily controlled by anyone other than the potential beneficiary. In a society where such opportunities exist and make it possible for individuals to have autonomous life, their existence is intrinsically valuable. The ideal of personal autonomy entails, therefore, that collective goods are at least sometimes intrinsically valuable. I think that it entails much more than that. Commonly accepted views about humans as essentially social animals, and equally common views about which options are worthwhile in life (for it is a condition of a life being autonomous that the available options include an adequate range of worthy opportunities) yield the conclusion that many collective goods are intrinsically good. At the very least, living in a society, which is a collective good, is on this view intrinsically good.

What conclusions is one to draw from these reflections (assuming they are sound) concerning the relation between rights and autonomy? In a way the most important one is that the ideal of personal autonomy is incompatible with moral individualism. Some may proceed to claim that morality is nevertheless right-based, but that since one of the fundamental rights is a right to autonomy it follows that there are rights to collective goods. Others may resist the idea that I have a right that my society shall continue to exist and a right that it shall have architects and surgeons and monogamous marriages. My interest in being autonomous shows that it is in my interest to live in a society where all those and many other options are available. But it is not enough by itself to justify holding others to be duty-bound to make sure that my society shall offer all these options. Given that the existence of these options is intrinsically valuable, they would conclude that morality includes fundamental values or ideals as well as fundamental rights.

It is inevitable that the existence or absence of collective goods affects the life of many individuals. This makes it unlikely that a successful argument can be found to establish an individual's right to a collective good. It also helps explain why writers who belong to the rights tradition regard fundamental human rights as including rights to individuated goods only. Yassir Arafat, being a Palestinian, has an interest in Palestinian self-determination. Furthermore, it is his interest, in combination with that of other Palestinians, which justifies the claim that there is a right to self-determination of the Palestinian people. But because the right rests on the interests of many, and because Arafat's interest by itself does not justify it, it is not his right, but the right of the Palestinian people as a group. It is important to realize that there need not be an actual conflict of interests to establish the insufficiency of an individual's interest as a foundation of an individual right to a collective good. Palestinian self-determination may be against the interests of some Israelis and Jordanians. The preservation of the historical and aesthetic character of Oxford may happen not to conflict with anyone's interest. Even if that is so I do not have a right to this result, despite my undoubted strong interest in it. The reason is plain. A right is a ground for a duty of another. And a duty exists only if it would defeat certain conflicting considerations were they to exist. The absence of actual conflict is not enough to justify a claim of a right. For this reason one may indeed be doubtful of the possibility of a justification for a fundamental individual right to a collective good.[13] Given the intrinsic desirability of some collective goods it is reasonable to conclude that morality is not right-based.

More important is the conclusion that if autonomy is an ultimate value, then it affects wide-ranging aspects of social practices and

[13] I will not consider the possibility that there are fundamental collective or group rights. A collective right exists when the following three conditions are met: first, it exists because the interests of human beings justify holding some person(s) to be subject to a duty. Secondly, the interests in question are the interests of individuals as members of a group in a public good and the right is a right to that public good because it serves their interest as members of the group. Thirdly, the interest of no single member of that group in that public good is sufficient by itself to justify holding another person to be subject to a duty.

The first condition is required for collective rights to be consistent with humanism. The other two conditions distinguish a collective right from a set of individual rights. The most frequently invoked collective right, the right to self-determination, exemplifies the three features. It is valued because of the contribution of self-determination to the well-being of individual members of the oppressed group. Self-determination is not merely a public good but a collective one. Finally, though many individual members of the group have an interest in the self-determination of their group the interest of any one of them is an inadequate ground for holding others to be duty-bound to satisfy that interest. The right rests on the cumulative interests of many individuals. (This explains why though the existence of the right does not depend on the size of the group, its weight or strength does.)

The same features are displayed by other collective rights. Consider, e.g. the right of the British public to know how Britain was led into the Falkland war. It is a right for information to be made public, and therefore for a public good. It is held to be a collective right by those who think that it cannot be justified just on the basis of the interests of a single member of the public, but that it can be justified on the ground that the interests of many are at stake.

If this is so then though a right-based morality including fundamental collective rights is richer than one which does not include them, it is still open to all the objections made in the text.

institutions. It would be wrong to postulate a right against coercion, for example, as a right to autonomy and to claim that it defeats, because of its importance, all, or almost all, other considerations. Many rights contribute to making autonomy possible, but no short list of concrete rights is sufficient for this purpose. Almost all major social decisions and many of the considerations both for and against each one of them bear on the possibility of personal autonomy, either instrumentally or inherently. If there is a right to autonomy then its effect on political action and institutions is very different from what we are often led to believe.

IV. RIGHTS AND DUTIES

The considerations advanced above are intended to suggest that apart from some rights one finds other values at the foundations of morality. In passing I have referred to the possibility that governments have duties which do not derive from the rights of individual human beings. The possibility that there are duties which do not correspond to any rights is allowed for by the definition of rights and is generally acknowledged by legal and political theorists. Yet the view that such duties must ultimately derive from fundamental rights or at least be based on the interests of people other than those subject to the duty has become sufficiently widespread that it is important to explain why it is rational to expect that there are fundamental moral duties which do not derive solely from the rights and interests of their potential beneficiaries, or which have no potential beneficiaries at all. I shall briefly discuss two cases purporting to show that some duties require non-instrumental justification, i.e. that their existence is of intrinsic, even if not necessarily of ultimate, value. They will also show that there are duties which do not derive from anyone's rights.

Both cases are designed to show how one particularly troublesome objection to the possibility of non-instrumental duties can be met. Let me, therefore, begin by stating the objection. Suppose it were said that people have a duty to behave in a certain way because failing to do so is wicked or just plain morally wrong. The claim may then be made that that can be so only if there is some independent reason for objecting to that action. Otherwise there is no way of explaining why there is a duty to behave in this way rather than in any other. It would seem to follow that if an action is wrong because it is a breach of duty then there must be a reason (other than the fact that the action is wrong) to justify the existence of the duty. That reason is bound to be that the duty is necessary to avoid infringing someone's rights or to prevent harm or to refrain from jeopardizing some value. If so, then the duty is instrumentally justified. But how else can it be justified? In what way can the order of justification be reversed, justifying the duty not to act in a certain way by the wrongfulness of the action without proceeding to explain the wrongfulness of this action, rather than any other, by reference to the fact that it harms values or violates rights?

A first step towards meeting the objection is to suggest that there might be an instrumental reason to act in that way but one which does not establish a duty so to act. The instrumental reason explains why it is a duty to act in this way rather than some other way. But as the instrumental reason does not establish a duty, the existence of the duty is intrinsically valuable. The flaw with this argument, if that is what it is, is that its premisses are compatible with another possibility as well, namely that the duty is not justified. One has still to find some non-instrumental justification which, added to the instrumental one, establishes the duty. Still the first step is helpful since I believe that often the justification of intrinsic duties includes an instrumental component.[14] Let me now turn to my two cases of intrinsic duties.

For the purposes of the first example I shall assume that there is a duty among friends which obliges a person to compensate his friend if his action harmed the friend even though the harm was not caused through any fault of his. Normally our responsibility to make good harm we cause to others depends on fault or on special responsibility. Friends have a no-fault obligation to each other though normally they do not have to provide full compensation. Evidently the fact that compensating someone is likely to benefit him is an instrumental reason for doing so. That reason is not enough to establish an obligation to compensate or else everyone will have an obligation to compensate everyone for any loss or harm they cause. Yet this instrumental reason provides an essential component in the non-instrumental justification of the duty to compensate friends for harm done to them. The other elements in the justification turn on the nature of friendship. Friendships entail a special concern for the welfare of the friend, concern for his welfare over and above the concern required of us towards other human beings generally. That concern manifests itself in many ways. But its expression is particularly urgent when we are the cause of harm to our friends. The urgency is not because then their need is greatest—it may not be. Nor is it because their need is our fault—for it need not be. The duty to friends we are considering results from the natural cultural convention to regard unsolicited acts

[14] There are intrinsic duties which do not presuppose any instrumental reason for the duty act. These are ceremonial or symbolic duties. But I shall not consider those here.

of compensation for harm one causes, even without fault, as particularly expressive of one's concern for the welfare of the compensated person (if he is one's friend or not). Because such action expresses concern and because friendship is in part the expression of concern one has a duty to compensate one's friend for harm caused. Since friendship consists in part in such duties the existence of the duty is intrinsically justified if the desirability of friendship itself is, as I shall assume without argument, intrinsically justified. By recognizing and respecting such duties towards another, as well as in other ways, one develops a friendship with another and by denying them one undermines or ends friendships.[15]

For my second example imagine that I own a Van Gogh painting. I therefore have the right to destroy it. I have an instrumental reason not to do so. I can sell it for a large sum. Furthermore many would derive great pleasure and enrichment if they could watch it. But no one has a right that I shall not destroy the painting. Nevertheless, while I owe no one a duty to preserve the painting I am under such a duty. The reason is that to destroy it and deny the duty is to do violence to art and to show oneself blind to one of the values which give life a meaning. The duty exists regardless of whether I profess to be a lover of art. If I do so profess then to deny the duty is to compromise my integrity.[16] But everyone has a duty of respect towards the values which give meaning to human life, even to those on which one's life does not depend for its meaning. The moral conception I am relying on here is similar to the one underlying the previous example. One's respect for values does to a degree consist in action expressing it. Where such action is particularly apt and urgent there may be a duty which is then an intrinsic duty.

One common objection to such a line of argument is that while it is true that one ought to compensate one's friends and to preserve works of art there is no duty to do so. One ought to do so because of one's concern for one's friends and one's respect for art and not out of duty. But the objection is based on the wrong presupposition that if one has a duty one should comply with it because it is a duty. One may well have a duty to do something because of one's concern for a friend or one's respect for art.

V. RIGHTS AND NARROW MORALITY

The examples I used to argue for the existence of intrinsic duties are unlikely to convince anyone who does not at least half wish to be

[15] On the non-instrumental relation between friendship and its normative constituents see further J. Raz, *The Authority of Law*, (Oxford, 1979), pp. 253–8.

[16] See on integrity Gabriele Taylor, 'Integrity', *Aristotelian Society*, Supp. Vol. 55 (1981), p. 143.

persuaded anyway. They presuppose not only controversial views which I did nothing to defend but also a way of analysing them which is not without rivals. Even if my examples do not convince I hope they make the view that there are intrinsic duties more plausible and less absurd or irrational. Sometimes a moral theory gains conviction because it seems to be the only one which is coherently statable. Whichever views we accept we always gain by being able to see them as just one of several alternative moral outlooks of various degrees of acceptability.

One objection which might be raised against the general way in which the argument about right-based moralities was conducted is that it misinterprets the general nature of morality, or at least that it overlooks the fact that rights are supposed by their proponents to be the foundation of morality in the narrow sense.[17]

Morality in the narrow sense is meant to include only all those principles which restrict the individual's pursuit of his personal goals and his advancement of his self-interest. It is not 'the art of life', i.e. the precepts instructing people how to live and what makes for a successful, meaningful, and worthwhile life. It is clear that right-based moralities can only be moralities in the narrow sense. An individual's rights do not provide him with reasons for action (though if he can expect his rights to be respected they inform him of some of his opportunities). It is implausible to assume that an individual can conduct his whole life on the basis of the sole motivation of respecting other people's rights. Nor is there any reason to commend such a mode of existence. It would be a life of total servitude to others. On the other hand, morality in the narrow sense may be right-based. Rights do exactly what narrow morality is supposed to do. They set limits to the individual's pursuit of his own goals and interests. On the plausible assumption that the only valid grounds on which the free pursuit by people of their own lives can be restricted are the needs, interests, and preferences of other people it becomes plausible to regard (narrow) morality as right-based.

We have reached here one of the fundamental divides between the right-based views and the outlook which informs all the preceding objections to the thought that morality is right-based. There is a fundamental objection to the very notion of morality in the narrow sense. Of course one may for convenience of exposition or other superficial purposes hive off any aspect of morality and discuss some of its problems separately. There can be no objection to that. The objection

[17] On morality in the narrow sense see, e.g., G. J. Warnock, *The Object of Morality* (London, 1971), esp. chs. 2 and 5, and J. L. Mackie, *Ethics: Inventing Right and Wrong* (Harmondsworth, 1977), pp. 134–6.

is to the notion that there is such a division at a fundamental level, that one can divide one's principles of action into those concerned with one's own personal goals and those concerned with others, in such a way that the principles are independent of each other. The mistake is to think that one can identify, say, the rights of others, while being completely ignorant of what values make a life meaningful and satisfying and what personal goals one has in life. Conversely, it is also a mistake to think that one can understand the values which can give a meaning to life and have personal goals and ideals while remaining ignorant of one's duties to others. There is no doubt a mutual independence at the superficial level. I need not decide whether to become a middle-distance runner or a professional chess player before I understand my obligation to others. But by the time that is the main remaining problem about the kind of life I would like to have, all fundamental problems have already been settled.

It may be best to approach my objection to the conception of a narrow morality from the examples discussed earlier in this article. My duty not to destroy the Van Gogh is appropriate for inclusion in narrow morality for it is not based on my interests nor does it depend on the preservation of the painting being part of my personal goals. It can be seen as a potential limitation on my freedom to pursue self-interest or personal desires. And yet I have suggested earlier that the duty is not exclusively based on the interests of others. Those would establish a reason not to destroy the painting, but not an obligation not to do so. There is no way of analysing the respect due to art into two components, one representing a person's obligations to others concerning art, the other expressing the importance art has for his own personal tastes and interests. Consider a person who has no interest in the arts. Even he should respect them. Some will say that that requirement of respect is derived from the requirement to respect other persons, some of whom have an interest in art. But this is a partial and limited view. The general requirement of respecting art is one which people should regard not as a restriction on the pursuit of their personal goals, but as part of their general outlook on life. It is no mere internalization of a requirement based on the interests of others. It is part of the necessary process through which a person learns of the worthwhile options in life and through which he develops his own tastes and goals. It is also part of the process through which he relates to other people. It is crucial for the development of normal personal relations that each person understands his own tastes and goals in ways which relate them to other people's goals and tastes. He must regard his own goals and tastes as valuable because they exemplify universal values or values which form part of a mosaic which in its entirety makes for valuable social life. He must, if he is to be capable of personal relations, find room for other people's values within that scheme. If I recognize an obligation to preserve the Van Gogh this is because I express thereby my recognition of the value of art and through doing so I have come to recognize some of the worthwhile options, on which, even though I did not pursue them, my autonomy depends. By recognizing that very same value I also create the possibility of creating personal relations with other people, for those depend at the deepest level on a sharing of values.

Personal relations, on which we have just touched, are another area in which the boundary between morality in the narrow and wide sense is invisible. Personal friendships, marital relations, one's loyalty and sense of pride in one's workplace or one's country are among the most valuable and rewarding aspects of many people's lives. Such relations are culturally determined forms of human interaction and it is through learning their value that one acquires a sense both of the possibilities of one's own life and of one's obligations to others. The two are aspects of one and the same conception of value. Consider one's sense of belonging to a certain country as a factor determining one's sense of identity and of the very same factor as requiring sacrifices in the interests of others. I do not deny that at times the two elements are separate. At times the obligation to one's country clearly conflicts with one's interests. In normal circumstances however one's relations to one's country help to shape one's interests, tastes, and goals. At all times one's obligations to one's country come from the same source. Whether they are perceived as restrictions on one's freedom or as determining one's identity and interests they defy the division of morality into wide and narrow components.

We have come full circle to a consideration of the intrinsic value of some collective goods. If collective goods such as membership in a society are intrinsically valuable then it is to be expected that they provide the source both of personal goals and of obligations to others. The confrontational view of morality which pitches a person's own interests and goals as not only occasionally in conflict with his obligations to others but as deriving from independent and fundamentally different sources is essentially an individualistic conception. My objections to the view that morality is right-based derives from a sense of the inadequacy of the conception of morality in the narrow sense which itself is a reflection of the rejection of moral individualism.

NOTES ON CONTRIBUTORS

RONALD DWORKIN is a Fellow of University College and Professor of Jurisprudence at Oxford. He is the author of *Taking Rights Seriously* (1977) and editor of *The Philosophy of Law* (1977) in this series.

ALAN GEWIRTH is Edward Carson Waller Distinguished Service Professor at the University of Chicago. He was Professor of Philosophy at Columbia 1947–75. His books include *Reason and Morality* (1978) and *Human Rights* (1982).

H. L. A. HART is a Fellow of University College, and was Professor of Jurisprudence 1952–68 and Principal of Brasenose College 1972–8, at Oxford. His books include *The Concept of Law* (1961), *Law, Liberty, and Morality* (1963), and *Essays on Bentham* (1982).

DAVID LYONS is Professor of Law and Philosophy at Cornell. He is the author of *The Forms and Limits of Utilitarianism* (1965) and *In the Interest of the Governed* (1973).

MARGARET MACDONALD was Lecturer (and subsequently Reader) in Philosophy at Bedford College, London from 1945 till her death in 1956. She was the editor of *Philosophy and Analysis* (1954).

J. L. MACKIE was Fellow of University College and Praelector in Philosophy at Oxford at the time of his death in 1981. He was formerly Professor of Philosophy at Otago (1955–9) and Sydney (1959–63). His many books include *The Cement of the Universe* (1974), *Ethics: Inventing Right and Wrong* (1977), and, posthumously, *The Miracle of Theism* (1982).

JOSEPH RAZ is Fellow and Tutor in Jurisprudence at Balliol College, Oxford. He is the author of *The Concept of a Legal System* (1970), *Practical Reason and Norms* (1975), and *The Authority of Law* (1979), and editor of *Practical Reasoning* (1978) in this series.

T. M. SCANLON is Professor of Philosophy at Princeton. He is the editor (with Marshall Cohen and Thomas Nagel) of the collection *Marx, Justice and History* (1980).

GREGORY VLASTOS was Professor of Philosophy at Cornell 1948–55 and Princeton 1955–76, and Visiting Professor at the University of California, Berkeley 1977–82. He is the author of *Platonic Studies* (1973) and *Plato's Universe* (1975).

BIBLIOGRAPHY

I. GENERAL AND INTRODUCTORY

BENN, S. and PETERS, R. S., *Social Principles and the Democratic State* (George Allen & Unwin, 1959), ch. 4.

BRANDT, R., *Ethical Theory* (Prentice-Hall), 1959), ch. 17.

FEINBERG, J., *Social Philosophy* (Prentice-Hall, 1973), chs. 4–6.

KAMENKA, E. and TAY, A. E. S. (edd.), *Human Rights* (Edward Arnold, 1978) (cited hereafter as *Kamenka and Tay*).

MARTIN, R. and NICKEL, J. W., 'Recent Work on the Concept of Rights', *American Phil. Quar.*, 17 (1980), 165.

PENNOCK, J. R. and CHAPMAN, J. W. (edd.), *Human Rights*: NOMOS XXIII (New York University Press, 1981) (cited hereafter as *Pennock and Chapman*).

RAPHAEL, D. D. (ed.), *Political Theory and the Rights of Man* (Macmillan, 1967) (cited hereafter as *Raphael*).

II. HISTORY

The best recent discussion of the early history of the idea of rights is:

TUCK, R., *Natural Rights Theories: Their Origin and Development* (Cambridge University Press, 1979).

See also:

HOBBES, T., *Leviathan* (1651), esp. chs. 13–14, 21, and 29.

LOCKE, J., *Two Treatises of Government* (1689), esp. II, chs. 2, 5, 11, and 18–19.

ROUSSEAU, J-J., *The Social Contract* (1762), Bks. I and II.

BURKE, E., *Reflections on the Revolution in France* (1790).

PAINE, T., *The Rights of Man* (1791).

BENTHAM, J., 'Anarchical Fallacies' (1824), in *Works*, ed. J. Bowring, Vol. II.

MARX, K., 'On the Jewish Question' (1843), in any collection of Marx's early writings.

MILL, J. S., *On Liberty* (1859).

GREEN, T. H., *The Principles of Political Obligation* (1882), esp. Lectures H–I.

RITCHIE, D. G., *Natural Rights* (1894).

III. ANALYTICAL ISSUES

FEINBERG, J., 'Duties, Rights and Claims', *American Phil. Quar.*, 3 (1966), 137.

— 'The Nature and Value of Rights', *Journal of Value Inquiry*, 4 (1970), 243.

HART, H. L. A., 'The Ascription of Responsibility and Rights', *Proc. Arist. Soc.*, 49 (1948–9), 171.

— 'Bentham on Legal Rights', in *Oxford Essays in Jurisprudence*, Second Series, ed. A. W. B. Simpson (Oxford University Press, 1973).

HOHFELD, W. N., *Fundamental Legal Conceptions* (Yale University Press, 1923).

LYONS, D., 'Rights, Claimants and Beneficiaries', *American Phil. Quar.*, 6 (1969), 173.

— 'Correlativity of Rights and Duties', *Noûs*, 4 (1970), 45.

MACCORMICK, N., 'Rights in Legislation', in *Law, Morality, and Society—Essays in Honour of H. L. A. Hart*, edd. P. M. S. Hacker and J. Raz (Oxford University Press, 1977).

MCCLOSKEY, H. J., 'Rights', *Phil. Quar.*, 15 (1965), 115.

— 'Rights—Some Conceptual Issues', *Australian Journ. of Phil.*, 54 (1976), 99.

MARSHALL, G., 'Rights, Options and Entitlements', in *Oxford Essays in Jurisprudence*, Second Series, ed. A. W. B. Simpson (Oxford University Press, 1973).

MAYO, B., 'What are Human Rights?', in *Raphael*.

MILLER, D., *Social Justice* (Clarendon Press, 1976), ch. 2.

PERRY, R., 'A Paradigm of Philosophy: Hohfeld on Legal Rights', *American Phil. Quar.*, 14 (1977), 41.

SEN, A., 'Rights and Agency', *Phil. and Public Affairs*, 11 (1981), 3.

WALDRON, J., 'A Right to do Wrong', *Ethics*, 92 (1981), 21.

IV. MODERN THEORIES OF RIGHTS

ANSCOMBE, G. E. M., 'On the Source of the Authority of the State', *Ratio*, 20 (1978), 1.

BENN, S. I., 'Human Rights—For Whom and What?', in *Kamenka and Tay*.

CRANSTON, M., *What are Human Rights*? (Bodley Head, 1973).

DWORKIN, R. M., *Taking Rights Seriously*, Revised Edition (Duckworth, 1978).

FINNIS, J., *Natural Law and Natural Rights* (Clarendon Press, 1980).

FRIED, C., *Right and Wrong* (Harvard University Press, 1978).

FRIEDRICH, C., 'Rights, Liberties and Freedoms—a Reappraisal', *American Pol. Sci. Rev.*, 57 (1963), 841.

GEWIRTH, A., 'The Basis and Content of Human Rights', in *Pennock and Chapman*.

GOLDING, M. P., 'Towards a Theory of Human Rights', *Monist*, 52 (1968), 521.

KAUFMAN, A. S., 'Sketch of a Liberal Theory of Fundamental Rights, *Monist*, 52 (1968), 595.

MCCLOSKEY, H. J., 'Human Needs, Rights, and Political Values' *American Phil. Quar.*, 13 (1976), 1.

MELDEN, A. I., *Rights and Persons* (Basil Blackwell, 1977).

NOZICK, R., *Anarchy, State and Utopia* (Basil Blackwell, 1974).

RAWLS, J., *A Theory of Justice* (Oxford University Press, 1971).

RICHARDS, D. A. J., 'Human Rights and Moral Ideals', *Social Theory and Practice*, 5 (1980), 461.

STEINER, H., 'The Natural Right to Equal Freedom', *Mind*, 83 (1974), 194.

WASSERSTROM, R., 'Rights, Human Rights and Racial Discrimination', *Journ. of Phil.*, 61 (1964), 628.

WELLMAN, C., 'A New Conception of Human Rights', in *Kamenka and Tay*.

V. MISGIVINGS ABOUT RIGHTS

CAMPBELL, T., *The Left and Rights*, (Routledge and Kegan Paul, 1983).

CHARVET, J., 'A Critique of Human Rights', in *Pennock and Chapman*.

MARCUSE, H., 'Repressive Tolerance', in R. P. Wolff, B. Moore, and H. Marcuse, *A Critique of Pure Tolerance* (Jonathan Cape, 1971).

NELSON, W., 'On the Alleged Importance of Moral Rights', *Ratio*, 18 (1976), 145.

NIELSEN, K., 'Scepticism and Human Rights', *Monist*, 52 (1968), 573.

RAZ, J., 'Professor Dworkin's Theory of Rights', *Polit. Studies*, 26 (1978), 123.

TAYLOR, C., 'Atomism', in *Powers, Possessions and Freedom: Essays in Honour of C. B. Macpherson*, ed. A. Kontos (University of Toronto Press, 1979).

YOUNG, R. 'Dispensing with Moral Rights', *Polit. Theory*, 6 (1978), 63.

VI. RIGHTS AND MORAL PROBLEMS

(a) *Life and Death*

FEINBERG, J., 'Voluntary Euthanasia and the Inalienable Right to Life', *Phil. and Public Affairs*, 7 (1978), 92.

FINNIS, J., 'The Rights and Wrongs of Abortion: A Reply to Judith Thomson', *Phil. and Public Affairs*, 2 (1973), 117.

GEWIRTH, A., 'Human Rights and the Prevention of Cancer', *American Phil. Quar.*, 17 (1980), 117.

MCCLOSKEY, H. J., 'The Right to Life', *Phil. Quar.*, 15 (1965), 115.

THOMSON, J. J., 'A Defense of Abortion', *Phil. and Public Affairs*, 1 (1971), 47.

(b) *Civil Liberties*

GEWIRTH, A., 'Civil Liberties as Effective Powers', in his collection *Human Rights: Essays on Justification and Applications* (University of Chicago Press, 1983).

MCCLOSKEY, H. J., 'Liberty of Expression, its Grounds and Limits', *Inquiry*, 13 (1970), 219.

SCANLON, T., 'A Theory of Freedom of Expression', *Phil. and Public Affairs*, 1 (1972), 204.

SHAPIRO, M., *Freedom of Speech: The Supreme Court and Judicial Review* (Prentice-Hall, 1966).

(c) *Punishment*

DWORKIN, R. M., 'Principle, Policy, Procedure', in *Crime, Proof and Punishment: Essays in Memory of Sir Rupert Cross* (Butterworths, 1981).

MORRIS, H., 'Persons and Punishment', *Monist*, 52 (1968), 475.

(d) *Property*

BECKER, L. C., *Property Rights: Philosophic Foundations* (Routledge and Kegan Paul, 1977).

GIBBARD, A., 'Natural Property Rights', *Noûs*, 10 (1976), 77.

HELD, V., 'Property Rights and Interests', *Social Research*, 46 (1979), 550.

NOZICK, R., *Anarchy, State and Utopia* (Basil Blackwell, 1974), ch. 7.

STEINER, H., 'The Structure of a Set of Compossible Rights', *Journ. of Phil.*, 74 (1977), 767.

(e) *Welfare Rights*

CRANSTON, M., 'Human Rights: Real and Supposed', in *Raphael.*

GEWIRTH, A., 'Starvation and Human Rights', in his collection, *Human Rights: Essays on Justification and Applications* (University of Chicago Press, 1983).

MICHELMAN, F. I., 'Constitutional Welfare Rights and *A Theory of Justice*', in *Reading Rawls: Critical Studies of A Theory of Justice*, ed. N. Daniels (Basil Blackwell, 1975).

RAPHAEL, D. D., 'Human Rights: Old and New', in *Raphael.*

(f) *Status of Animals*

FEINBERG, J., 'The Rights of Animals and Unborn Generations', in *Philosophy and Environmental Crisis*, ed. W. T. Blackstone (University of Georgia Press, 1974).

FREY, R., *Interests and Rights: The Case Against Animals* (Clarendon Press, 1980).

MCCLOSKEY, H. J., 'Moral Rights and Animals', *Inquiry*, 22 (1979), 23.

NARVESON, J., 'Animal Rights', *Canadian Journ. of Phil.*, 7 (1977), 161.

REGAN, T., 'The Moral Basis of Vegetarianism', *Canadian Journ. of Phil.*, 5 (1975), 193.

INDEX OF NAMES